Mainstreaming the Environment

JAN POST

Developing countries are rejecting the old-fashioned development-versus-the-environment paradigm in favor of a new environmentalism, which recognizes that economic development and environmental sustainability are partners. In the water sector, one example of this partnership is the support for a comprehensive view of water management issues that includes the participation of all water users, such as these Tanzanian fisherwomen.

Mainstreaming the Environment

THE WORLD BANK GROUP
AND THE ENVIRONMENT
SINCE THE RIO EARTH SUMMIT

FISCAL 1995

THE WORLD BANK
WASHINGTON, D.C.

© 1995 The International Bank for Reconstruction
and Development/The World Bank
1818 H Street, N.W.
Washington, D.C. 20433, U.S.A.

All rights reserved
Manufactured in the United States of America
First printing September 1995

This report is a study by the World Bank's staff, and the judgments made herein do not necessarily reflect the views of the Board of Executive Directors or of the countries they represent. The boundaries, colors, denominations, and other information shown on any map in this volume do not imply on the part of the World Bank any judgment on the legal status of any territory or the endorsement or acceptance of such boundaries.

The text is printed on recycled paper that exceeds the requirements of the 1988 guidelines of the U.S. Environmental Protection Agency, section 6002 of the Resource Conservation Recovery Act. The paper stock contains at least 50 percent recovered waste paper material as calculated by fiber content, of which at least 10 percent of the total fiber is postconsumer waste, and 20 to 50 percent of the fiber has been deinked.

Printed on Recycled Paper

ISBN 0-8213-3290-2
ISSN 1014-8132

Acknowledgments

This report was prepared by the Environment Department of the World Bank in close collaboration with regional environment divisions and country operations departments. The principal author was Jocelyn Mason. John Redwood III and John Dixon contributed to chapters 1 and 3, respectively; Lars Vidaeus and Stephen Lintner wrote chapter 2; chapter 5 drew on a background paper written by William Magrath of the Agriculture and Natural Resource Department; and chapter 6 drew on three background papers written by Alison Cave and Jerry Lebo (urban and transport, respectively) of the Transport, Water and Urban Development Department, and Rachel English (energy) of the Industry and Energy Department. Letitia Oliveira of the International Finance Corporation (IFC) wrote chapter 7. The Environment Department team included Kerstin Canby, John Kellenberg, Marian Mabel, and Mary McNeil. Clare Fleming provided advice for the illustrations and cover design. Andrew Steer provided guidance.

Contents

Foreword *xiii*

Abbreviations and Acronyms *xiv*

Overview *1*
    Targeted Programs for the Environment *4*
        The Portfolio of Environmental Projects *4*
        Regional and Global Programs *7*
        The Intellectual Journey *9*
    Greening the Entire Portfolio *12*
        Making a Difference with Environmental Assessments *13*
        Agriculture, Forestry, and Natural Resources *14*
        Making Infrastructure Environmentally Sustainable *16*
        Strengthening the Private Sector Role: The IFC and MIGA *19*
    Notes *20*

PART 1 *21*

1. Investing in Environmental Stewardship *22*
    The Changing Portfolio of Environment Projects *23*
        New Environmental Lending *25*
    Pollution and the Urban Environment: The Brown Agenda *28*
    Natural Resource Management: The Green Agenda *32*
    Institution Building *38*
    Managing the Environmental Portfolio *44*
    Creating Partnerships *47*
        Conference on Environmentally Sustainable Development *48*
        Interagency Activities *48*
        Bilateral Collaboration *49*
        Nongovernmental Organizations *49*
    Notes *52*

2. The Regional and Global Environment *54*
    Regional Freshwater, Coastal, and Marine Programs *55*
        Mediterranean Sea *56*
        Baltic Sea *56*
        Danube River Basin *56*
        Black Sea *58*

        Aral Sea   58
        Red Sea and Gulf of Aden   59
        Caspian Sea   60
        Lake Victoria   60
        New Global Marine Initiatives   60
   The Global Environment   62
        Bank Funding for the Global Environment   63
        Administering Global Environment Funds   66
        Channeling GEF Resources   67
        Evaluating and Improving GEF Performance   70
        Supporting the Montreal Protocol   70
        The Bank's Assistance Strategy   71
   Notes   80

3. The Intellectual Journey   81
   Country and Regional Environmental Strategies   82
        National Environmental Action Plans: A Key Tool
           for Project Design   82
        Developing Regional Strategies   84
        Integrating the Environment into Country Assistance Strategies
           and Economic Studies   87
        Enhancing Country-Focused Economic and Sector Work   88
   Identifying Best Practice and Defining Bank Policies   93
        Urban and Industrial Pollution Management   94
        Natural Resource Management   95
        Participation   98
        Social Assessment   99
        Beneficiary Assessment   102
        Resettlement   102
   Improving Methodologies and Indicators   104
        New Methodologies and Diagnostic Tools   104
        Developing Environmental Data and Indicators   108
   Providing Training and Outreach   111

PART 2   117

4. Making a Difference with Environmental Assessments   118
   A Brief History of World Bank Environmental Policy   119

Using Environmental Assessments to Direct Environmental
  Lending 122
Assessing the EA Portfolio 123
Making EA Effective 124
  The Quality Dimension 125
  Analysis of Alternatives 127
  Mitigation, Monitoring, and Management Plans 128
  Using Public Consultation 129
Improving EAs 131
  Integrate EAs into Project Preparation 132
  Convert EA Recommendations into Specific Deliverables 132
  Learn from Project Implementation 132
Emerging Challenges 133
  Sectoral and Regional EAs 133
  EA and Private Sector Development 135
Notes 137

5. Seeking New Directions: Agriculture and the Environment 138
Facing the Challenges Ahead 139
  Resource Conversion 139
  Intensification 140
Implementing a New Approach to Agricultural Lending 141
A New Emphasis in Agricultural Subsectors 141
  Land 142
  Irrigation, Drainage, and Water Resource Management 145
  Forestry 147
  Agricultural Research and Extension 150

6. Making Infrastructure Environmentally Sustainable 153
Energy 154
  Promoting Demand-Side and Supply-Side Efficiency 156
  Supporting Cleaner Energy Sources and Technologies 164
  Rural and Household Energy 169
Transport 170
  Developing New Policy and Training 171
  Integrating Transport and Environmental Approaches
    in Bank Lending 171
  Designing Better Projects 176
Urban Infrastructure 179

PART 3   189

7. The Private Sector: IFC and MIGA   190
Proactive Programs   194
   Environmental Business Development   195
   Global Environmental Initiatives   196
   Capital Markets   197
   Assistance for Project Sponsors   198
   Organization and Procedures   199
Lessons Learned and Future Directions   204
Notes   206

Annexes
A. Environment- and Social-Related Operational Policies and Bank Procedures   207
B. Guidance on Identification of World Bank Environmental Projects and Components   215
C. Projects with Primarily Environmental Objectives Approved in Fiscal 1995   218
D. Projects with Major Environmental Components Approved in Fiscal 1995   226
E. Active Environmental Projects under Implementation   237
F. Projects with Full Environmental Assessment Approved in Fiscal 1995, Category A Projects   255
G. Global Environment Facility (GEF) and Multilateral Fund for the Implementation of the Montreal Protocol (MFMP) Investments Approved in Fiscal 1995   276

Bibliography   289

Boxes
1. The Unfinished Agenda   3
2. Ten Hallmarks of the New Environmentalism   10
1.1. A New Approach for the Water Sector   26
1.2. From Pollution Control to Pollution Prevention in the Indian Industrial Sector   31
1.3. Mitigating the Komi Oil Spill: The Role of Public Participation   33
1.4. Lending for Environmental Improvement in the Baltic Countries   34
1.5. The Bank's Biodiversity Portfolio   37
1.6. Grants Approved by the Brazilian Rain Forest Pilot Program in Fiscal 1995   39

1.7. Strengthening Environmental Management in the Russian Federation *42*
1.8. Using the Institutional Development Fund to Improve Environmental Management *43*
1.9. Global Water Partnership *50*
1.10. Building Links with the IUCN *52*
2.1. Baltic Sea Environment Program *57*
2.2. Development of a Global Representative System of Marine Protected Areas *61*
2.3. The International Coral Reef Initiative: Protecting the "Forests of the Sea" *62*
2.4. Global Environmental Conventions—Recent Developments *64*
2.5. New Approaches to ODS Phaseout *72*
2.6. Biodiversity Strategies Leading to Action *74*
2.7. Tools and Early Applications in Global Environmental Analysis in Climate Change *76*
2.8. Multiplying GEF and MFMP Resources through Private Sector Leveraging *78*
3.1. Implementing National Strategies: The Case of Bulgaria *83*
3.2. Kyrgyz Republic National Environmental Action Plan *85*
3.3. Tunisia Country Economic Memorandum: Pricing Resource Use and Degradation *89*
3.4. Lessons from Successful Environmental Institutions in Latin America and East Asia *92*
3.5. Rapid Assessment of Biodiversity Priority Areas: Lessons from the Pilot Phase *96*
3.6. Integrated Coastal Zone Management in Africa *97*
3.7. How Participatory Approaches Improve Projects and Economic and Sector Work *98*
3.8. Social Assessment in Azerbaijan *101*
3.9. Where Is the Wealth of Nations? *109*
3.10. Conservation Assessment of the Terrestrial Ecoregions of Latin America and the Caribbean *112*
4.1. World Bank Environmental Policies *120*
4.2. A Policy for Cultural Heritage *121*
4.3. The Environmental Assessment Process *122*
4.4. Quantifying Impacts in China *126*
4.5. Economic Costs of Environmental Impacts *127*
4.6. Public Consultation and Project Design *130*
4.7. Public Consultation at EA Stages *131*
4.8. Translating EA Recommendations into Project, Contract, and Bidding Documents *133*

4.9. Lessons from EA Experience in Project Implementation   *134*
4.10. Credit Risk Management in the Russian Federation   *136*
5.1. Bangladesh: Environmental and Natural Resource Degradation from Intensive Agriculture   *142*
5.2. Revitalizing Land Reform in Colombia   *145*
5.3. A Win-Win Technology: Integrated Pest Management   *151*
6.1. Efficiency Improvements in District Heating in Estonia and Poland   *161*
6.2. Developing an Environmentally Sustainable Transport Policy   *172*
6.3. Promoting Bicycle Use in Ghana   *177*
6.4. Broadening the Range of Transport Options   *178*
6.5. Developing a Handbook on Roads and the Environment   *179*
6.6. Quality Water for Shanghai   *182*
6.7. Improving the Urban Environment in Colombia   *183*
6.8. Mexico's Northern Border Environment Project   *184*
7.1. Environmental Sector Projects   *194*
7.2. IFC Projects Endorsed by GEF/MFMP Executive Bodies   *197*
7.3. La Société d'Exploitation des Mines d'Or de Sadiola (Mali)   *201*
7.4. Liteksas Ir Calw A.B. (Lithuania) and SOCMA Americana (Argentina)   *202*
7.5. One Earth Diving Lodge (Tanzania)   *203*

Figures
1. The Active World Bank Environmental Portfolio   *5*
2. Countries with Environmental Projects   *6*
2.1. GEF Investment Portfolio Development, Overview   *68*
3.1. Investment and Savings: Nonfuel Primary Exporters, 1966–91   *110*
6.1. Areas for Reducing Environmental Impact in the Power Sector   *155*
6.2. Carbon Intensity of Electricity Production, Coal-Fired Plants   *156*
6.3. The Impact of Reform on Electricity Prices, Selected Countries   *159*
6.4. Sources of Reductions in Energy Intensity, China   *164*
7.1. Growth in IFC Operations   *191*
7.2. Project Approvals by Sector, Fiscal Years 1992 and 1995   *192*

Tables

1. Active Portfolio of Environmental Projects as of June 30, 1995 *4*
2. World Bank Lending since Rio—A Simple Accounting *13*
1.1. Projects for Urban Environmental Management and Pollution Control, Fiscal 1993–95 *29*
1.2. Projects for Natural Resources Management, Fiscal 1993–95 *35*
1.3. Projects for Environmental Institutions, Fiscal 1993–95 *40*
2.1. GEF and MFMP Projects Approved by World Bank Group Management, Fiscal 1995 *69*
3.1. Representative Environmental Economic and Sector Work, Fiscal 1993–95 *90*
3.2. Internal Training Courses for Bank Staff on Environmental Issues Offered in Fiscal 1993–95 *113*
3.3. EDI Environmental Training, Fiscal 1994 and 1995 and Projected Fiscal 1996 *114*
4.1. Projects with EA Category Screened since the Rio Earth Summit, Fiscal 1993–95 *124*
4.2. Distribution of Category A Projects, by Sector, Fiscal 1993–95 *125*
5.1. Agriculture Sector Projects Approved, Fiscal 1990–95, by Major Subsector *143*
5.2. Changing Patterns of Investment in Bank-Financed Forestry Projects, 1984–95 *148*
6.1. Approved Energy Projects with Sector Reform Components, Fiscal 1993–95 *157*
6.2. Approved Energy Projects with Pricing Components, Fiscal 1993–95 *160*
6.3. Approved Energy Projects with Stand-Alone Efficiency Components, Fiscal 1993–95 *163*
6.4. Approved Renewable Energy Projects, Fiscal 1990–94 *166*
6.5. Approved Oil and Gas Rehabilitation Projects, Fiscal 1993–95 *169*
7.1. Number of Approved Projects, by Environmental Review Category, Fiscal 1992–95 *200*

Foreword

It is now three years since almost all countries of the world endorsed the concept of environmentally sustainable development at the Earth Summit in Rio de Janeiro, Brazil. This report documents how the World Bank Group has sought to be an active partner in implementing the "Rio imperatives." It is divided into three parts. Part 1 explores progress in activities specifically targeted toward improving the environment. This includes an analysis of the Bank's growing loan portfolio of environmental projects—now $10 billion for 137 projects in 62 countries—and of the Bank's role as an implementing agency of the Global Environment Facility (GEF) and of the Montreal Protocol. Part 2 asks a broader question: How are environmental concerns being incorporated throughout *all* of the Bank's activities? It provides a preliminary "green accounting" of the $67 billion that the Bank has committed in the past three years. Part 3 documents the environmental programs of the International Finance Corporation (IFC) and the Multilateral Investment Guarantee Agency (MIGA).

While documenting the good progress that has been made to date, the report also tries to point to the areas where extra effort is now needed. In a sense, the Bank is now entering its "third generation" of environmental reforms. The first, in the 1987–92 period, was characterized by a major focus on reducing potential harm from Bank-financed projects and, specifically, the codification of environmental assessment (EA) procedures. The second might be termed the "post-Rio boom." It was characterized by a great expansion in the Bank's environmental capacity, and an aggressive effort to respond to the exploding demand for Bank assistance in environmental management.

The third generation is now under way. It is characterized by three main thrusts. The first is an overriding emphasis on on-the-ground implementation. The second is a major effort to move "upstream" from project-specific concerns in order to incorporate the environment into sectoral and national strategies. The third, undergirding all our activities, is a stronger focus on people and on social structures to find solutions and make development more sustainable.

Andrew Steer
Director
Environment Department
The World Bank

Abbreviations and Acronyms

AGETIP	Agence pour l'execution des travaux d'intérêt public
BA	beneficiary assessment
BAPEDAL	Indonesian Environment Agency
BCSD	Business Council for Sustainable Development
BP	Bank procedure
CARICOM	Caribbean Community
CAS	country assistance strategy
CBD	Convention on Biological Diversity
CEM	country economic memorandum
CFC	chlorofluorocarbon
CNPPA	Commission on National Parks and Protected Areas
DSS/IPC	Decision Support System for Industrial Pollution Control
EA	environmental assessment
EAP	environmental action programme
EDI	Economic Development Institute
EFP	Environmental Framework Program
ESMAP	Energy Sector Management Assistance Programme
ESW	economic and sector work
FCCC	U.N. Framework Convention for Climate Change
FIAHS	Fund for Innovative Approaches to Human and Social Development
GDP	gross domestic product
GEF	Global Environment Facility
GIS	geographic information system
GP	good practice
IBRD	International Bank for Reconstruction and Development
ICR	implementation completion report
ICRI	International Coral Reef Initiative
ICZM	integrated coastal zone management
IDA	International Development Association
IDF	Institutional Development Fund
IFC	International Finance Corporation
IPCP	Industrial Pollution Control Project

IPM	integrated pest management
IPPP	Industrial Pollution Prevention Project
IPPS	Industrial Pollution Projection System
IPTRID	International Program for Technology Research in Irrigation and Drainage
IUCN	World Conservation Union
MEDCITIES	Mediterranean Coastal Cities Network
METAP	Mediterranean Technical Assistance Program
MFMP	Multilateral Fund for the Montreal Protocol
MIGA	Multilateral Investment Guarantee Agency
MPA	marine protected areas
NEAP	national environmental assessment plan
NGO	nongovernmental organization
ODS	ozone-depleting substances
OECD	Organisation for Economic Co-operation and Development
OECS	Organization of Eastern Caribbean States
OED	Operations Evaluation Department
OMS	Operational manual statement
OP	operational policy
PERSGA	Program for the Environment of the Red Sea and the Gulf of Aden
PIC	Public Information Center
PID	project identification document
RAP	rapid assessment of biodiversity priorities
SA	social assessment
SAL	structural adjustment loan
SAR	staff appraisal report
TA	technical assistance
UNCED	United Nations Conference on Environment and Development
UNCHS	United Nations Centre for Human Settlements (Habitat)
UNDP	United Nations Development Programme
UNEP	United Nations Environment Programme
UNIDO	United Nations Industrial Development Organization
WBCSD	World Business Council for Sustainable Development

Overview

JAN POST

Ecuador is endowed with one of the highest concentrations of biological diversity per unit area in South America, of which the tree frog pictured above is only one example. To protect the country's biological heritage, the government of Ecuador has established a national system of protected areas with fifteen conservation units of global importance. Fourteen areas are located on the continental territory of Ecuador, and one, Galápagos National Park, is in the Galápagos Islands about 1,000 kilometers off the coast. A five-year GEF-funded project will support the management plans of eight of these sites, as well as outreach activities focusing on conflict resolution among key target groups and public awareness campaigns.

A quiet revolution has been under way during the first half of the 1990s, as environmental sustainability has become a theme of policymaking around the world. Environmental problems remain acute in most countries, and in many parts of the world continue to escalate. But there has been a quantum increase in awareness of the magnitude of the problem and of the need for action in the past few years, with the 1992 United Nations Conference on Environment and Development (UNCED) in Rio de Janeiro, known as the Rio Earth Summit, capturing the growing consensus and dramatically accelerating the momentum for change. More than 100 nations are trying to build environmental concerns into their planning processes, and in about half those nations substantial changes in policy and investment priorities are evident. Member countries have sought the World Bank Group's support in this endeavor—through financing, advisory services, and donor coordination.[1] This report attempts to document this growing partnership.

As the World Bank Group has assisted its member countries in making development sustainable, so has it undergone its own "greening." A series of operational policies addressing the environmental aspects of Bank activities has been put into place. Operational departments are strengthening their capacity for environmental analysis; the number of technical environmental staff has increased fivefold since the end of the 1980s; and a new Vice Presidency of Environmentally Sustainable Development has been created.

This report assesses this progress, giving special note to the acceleration of activities in the three years since the Rio Earth Summit, and paying particular attention to the most recent year, fiscal 1995. While capturing the substantial gains that have been made, it also shows that the journey is unfinished (see box 1). In the next three years, the World Bank Group will need to focus its attention in particular on the implementation of the investments and policies that have been designed over the recent past.

The report is divided into three parts. Part 1 addresses progress in those areas of financing and technical assistance that are targeted *specifically* toward the environment. This includes that portion of the Bank's active portfolio, currently $10 billion, directed primarily at helping borrowing countries improve their environmental management (chapter 1).[2] It also includes Bank-supported programs to address global environmental problems, often financed by the Global Environment Facility (GEF) and the Montreal Protocol (chapter 2). Finally, it covers the recent analytical, research, and policy work undertaken by the Bank on environmental issues (chapter 3).

However, while the specific environmental programs are important, of equal importance is the extent to which environmental concerns are

> **Box 1. The Unfinished Agenda**
>
> The report describes substantial progress in the way in which the World Bank assists its client countries in addressing environmental concerns, but it also notes that the agenda is unfinished. The following are among the challenges expected for the coming three to five years:
>
> - *Implementing the portfolio of environmental projects.* The majority of projects in the currently active portfolio of $10 billion in sixty-two countries are new, and $8 billion is scheduled to be disbursed over the next few years. Ensuring that these projects continue to perform well and that lessons from their innovative approaches are learned and disseminated will be major challenges.
> - *Moving beyond project-specific environmental assessment.* The past few years have seen a remarkable deepening in the effectiveness of the Bank's environmental assessment work. It is necessary now to broaden the focus to apply these techniques at the sectoral and regional levels. Such approaches are already being piloted to good effect.
> - *Improving the monitoring of on-the-ground impacts.* Information on environmental trends remains very weak. This undermines the ability of policymakers to set priorities and monitor the impact of programs. The Bank's new efforts to develop and implement indicators of progress will need to be deepened.
> - *Addressing the social dimensions of environmental management.* Ensuring that stakeholders are involved in the design and implementation of projects, that cultural issues are taken into account, and that the social costs and benefits of interventions are carefully discussed and addressed will need to receive greater attention in the future.
> - *Developing and applying global overlays.* There is a growing urgency for integrating global environmental objectives into national strategies and action plans for sustainable development (that is, global overlays). Extensions will be made to country economic and sector work with developing country partners.

incorporated into the *entire* portfolio of the Bank's activities. This is the focus of Part 2. It includes, for example, the extent to which potentially adverse environmental and social impacts of Bank-financed projects are assessed and mitigated (chapter 4) and the way in which the concept of environmental sustainability is reshaping the Bank's portfolio in major sectors of activity such as agriculture and forestry (chapter 5) and infrastructure (chapter 6).

Part 3 of the report examines how the International Finance Corporation (IFC) and the Multilateral Investment Guarantee Agency (MIGA) address environmental concerns in their private sector activities.

Targeted Programs for the Environment

The Bank's active portfolio of loans whose primary objective is to strengthen environmental management now stands at $10 billion for 137 projects in 62 countries (table 1). Of this amount, $5.6 billion has been committed in the three years since UNCED, and $1.1 billion for 21 projects was added in fiscal 1995 (see figure 1). New borrowers for the environment in fiscal 1995 included Honduras, Latvia, Lebanon, Lithuania, the Russian Federation, Thailand, Trinidad and Tobago, and the Organization of Eastern Caribbean States (see figure 2 for a map representing all countries with Bank-supported environment projects).

The Portfolio of Environmental Projects

Pollution management and urban environment projects account for about 61 percent of total lending for the environment, and 40 percent of the number of environmental projects in the active portfolio (table 1). Such projects typically include four types of components: capacity building for environmental management, including training, staffing, monitoring, and policy studies; resources for on-lending to enterprises and agencies for improved environmental management; direct investment

Table 1. Active Portfolio of Environmental Projects as of June 30, 1995

Focus of the project	Number of projects	Number of countries	World Bank contribution (loan or credit; billions of dollars)	Total project cost (billions of dollars)	Average size of loan or credit (millions of dollars)
Pollution management (brown agenda)	55	31	6.1	16.1	110.0
Natural resources (green agenda)	62	39	3.2	5.8	52.0
National institution building	20	19	0.7	1.2	33.0
Total	137	62[a]	10.0	23.1	73.0[b]

a. Total number of borrowing countries; some countries have more than one project.
b. Average size of loan for the whole portfolio.
Source: World Bank data.

Figure 1. The Active World Bank Environmental Portfolio

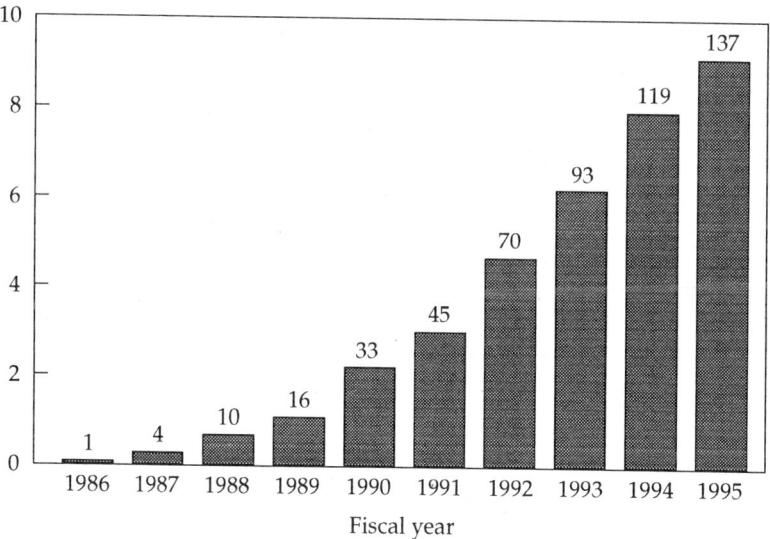

Note: Numbers at top of columns represent total number of active environmental projects, and include projects until the fiscal year in which they were closed or canceled.

in pollution prevention and treatment facilities; and support for research on new technologies and improved policy design. In fiscal 1995, fourteen new loans for environmental management and pollution control were made, with objectives varying from introducing clean fuel in Thailand to preventing industrial pollution in India and Poland; improved municipal water treatment and coastal zone management in the three Baltic countries; improved solid waste management and sanitation in Burkina Faso, Lebanon, and Sri Lanka; and emergency treatment of an oil spill in the Russian Federation.

Rural environmental projects, now under way in thirty-nine countries, cover a range of issues, including managing forests and conserving biodiversity; establishing or strengthening national parks and other protected areas; introducing integrated pest management; and investing in soil conservation, watershed rehabilitation, and integrated river basin management. New projects in fiscal 1995 in Venezuela (park protection), Pakistan (afforestation), India (forest management), and Brazil (Rain Forest Pilot Program) illustrate the new approaches in addressing rural environmental problems. Prepared in partnership with affected groups

Figure 2. Countries with Environmental Projects

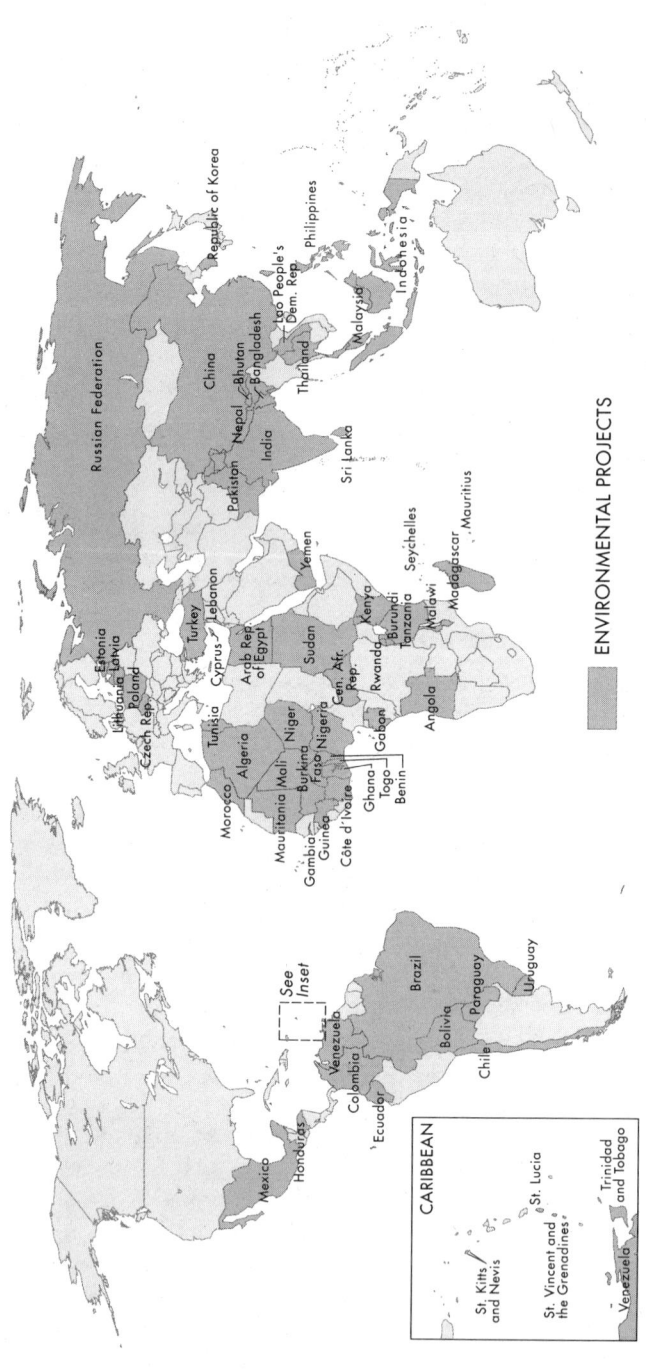

and nongovernmental organizations (NGOs), emphasizing the need for alternative livelihoods and changed incentive structures, and recognizing administrative capacity constraints, these projects will seek to ensure better livelihoods for local residents as a result of nondamaging activities.

Environmental institutions projects, directed toward strengthening national and local environmental management capacity (covering both pollution and rural issues), are under way in twenty countries. Two-thirds of these projects have been approved in the past three years, and in fiscal 1995 new borrowers included Benin, Honduras, Trinidad and Tobago, and the Russian Federation. The project in the Russian Federation, supported by a $110 million loan, is of particular note because it will help the Russian government to establish an Environmental Framework Program throughout the nation. Measures to strengthen public involvement in environmental decisionmaking have also increased in Bank-supported environmental institution-building projects.

Regional and Global Programs

The World Bank's work as coordinator or financier of regional or global activities that address transboundary environmental problems has grown markedly over the past few years.

COOPERATION AT THE REGIONAL LEVEL. Current examples at the regional level include the following:

- The Mediterranean Technical Assistance Program (METAP), which over the past four years has supported nearly 100 capacity-building and investment-preparation activities in the region. Its partners are currently preparing its third program cycle.
- The Baltic Seas Environment Program, for which the Bank has developed seven investment projects for financing by the end of calendar year 1995.
- The Danube River Basin Program, which this year completed, with assistance from the Bank, a strategic action plan for improving water quality and addressing hot spot problems. This plan will guide Bank and other coordinating agency activities in the Danube Basin.
- The Aral Sea Program, for which a priority action plan, prepared in collaboration with the GEF implementing agencies—the United Nations Environment Programme (UNEP), the United Nations Development Programme (UNDP), and the World Bank—has been agreed by the governments of Kazakhstan, the Kyrgyz Republic, Tajikistan, Turkmenistan, and Uzbekistan. Implementation is expected to begin in early 1996.

- The Lake Victoria Program, for which the governments of Kenya, Tanzania, and Uganda agreed in 1994 to prepare a joint investment program with support from the Bank and the GEF.

In addition to these activities, the past years have seen active engagement by the Bank in programs for the Caspian Sea, the Red Sea, and the International Coral Reef Initiative. In March 1995 the Bank issued, in collaboration with the World Conservation Union (IUCN) and the Great Barrier Reef Marine Park Authority, a major study identifying global priorities for marine protected areas (World Bank, IUCN, and the Great Barrier Reef Marine Park Authority 1995).

ADDRESSING GLOBAL PROBLEMS. The past year has seen the first meetings of the parties to the Convention on Biological Diversity and the Framework Convention for Climate Change, and rapid progress toward ratification of the Desertification Convention.[3] The Bank is actively supporting the implementation of each of these conventions and over the past year has presented strategy statements as to how, through its policy, advisory, and financing roles, and as implementing agency to the Global Environment Facility (GEF) and Montreal Protocol, it can make an active contribution.

The past year has seen the completion of the GEF pilot phase and the start of GEF 1, a program of $2 billion addressing global warming, biodiversity conservation, ozone depletion, and international waters. In the past twelve months, a new GEF project cycle has been introduced, and a comprehensive operational strategy setting priorities in the four focal areas has been drafted. In parallel, draft guidelines on social assessment in GEF and Montreal Protocol projects have been prepared to guide project designers.

As of July 1995 the GEF Council had endorsed World Bank Group financing (using GEF resources) of sixty-three projects, totaling $557 million, of which fifty-two projects ($454 million) were from the pilot phase, and eleven projects ($103 million) from GEF 1. The number of Bank-supported Montreal Protocol projects (for addressing ozone depletion) has risen this year to twenty-four in twenty different countries with a total funding of $145 million.

In helping to address global environmental problems, the Bank seeks to apply two principles: integration of these global concerns into national development policymaking and increased effectiveness of scarce grant resources through financial leverage and market-based approaches. The past year has witnessed some important innovations in Bank-supported projects, including introduction of sectoral approaches toward ozone-depleting investments emphasizing unit-cost reductions in China; experimentation with market-based approaches to resource allocation for phaseout of ozone-depleting substances in Chile; the development of rapid appraisal techniques for setting biodiversity priorities; partnership with the government of Norway on demonstration projects for market-based carbon emissions offsets in Poland and Mexico; market research on the feasibility of renewable energy and biodiversity venture capital funds; and initiation of a research program of "global overlays," assessing the opportunities, costs, and benefits of integrating global concerns into domestic policymaking.

The Intellectual Journey

The Bank's rapidly growing financing program has been supported by an active program of analytical and policy work. This work falls into three categories: preparation of country and regional strategies; cross-country analysis of best practice and policy; and the development and piloting of new methodologies.

COUNTRY AND REGIONAL STRATEGIES. The Bank has advocated and supported the preparation of National Environmental Action Plans (NEAPs) since 1992. These are prepared by national governments, although the Bank often provides analytical support and helps to mobilize resources. As of July 1995, sixty-three countries had completed NEAPs (forty-seven IDA borrowers and sixteen IBRD borrowers). NEAPs are also nearing completion for many of the new members of the Bank, such as the countries of the former Soviet Union, as well as for older but recently inactive borrowers, such as Algeria, Haiti, Lebanon, and Viet Nam. In March 1995 the Bank issued a review of experience to date with national environmental planning (World Bank 1995j). It concluded that these exercises were beginning to have a genuine and positive impact on policy, although the quality of the analysis and recommendations is variable. In identifying best practice to date, the review concluded that the most effective strategies explicitly address three questions:

- How to set priorities
- How to design cost effective interventions
- How to build capacity and remove obstacles to implementation.

The best strategies are those that effectively draw upon and weave together rigorous analysis and participatory consensus-building. Many exercises to date have emphasized one at the expense of the other—undermining either the quality of the recommendations or the likelihood of effective implementation.

The Bank has also sought to assist in defining strategies at the regional level. The Environmental Action Programme for Eastern and Central Europe, coordinated by the Bank and approved by governments in 1993, is now being implemented. This was followed in 1994 and 1995 by preparation of regional reports on East Asia, Sub-Saharan Africa, and North Africa and the Middle East.

DISTILLING BEST PRACTICE AND DEFINING BANK POLICIES. Accompanying these country and regional strategies has been a growing array of cross-country studies on special topics of concern to the Bank's clients. The Bank, like all others in the development community, remains on the steep part of the learning curve. While in many areas of policymaking the theory is clear, institutional constraints often call for adjustments to textbook solutions. Best-practice studies have been undertaken for most aspects of the environmental agenda—including pollution manage-

---

Box 2. Ten Hallmarks of the New Environmentalism

As developing countries struggle to forge development paths that provide both prosperity for their citizens *and* good stewardship of the environment, they are rejecting the old-fashioned development-versus-the-environment paradigm in favor of a new environmentalism that recognizes economic development and environmental sustainability as partners. Some of the principles underlying this new approach are listed below. These also underlie much of the Bank's environmental support to its member countries.

- *Set priorities carefully.* Not all problems can be addressed at once. Priorities need to be set using a combination of modern valuation techniques and participatory input from citizens and experts.
- *Go for win-win options first.* Although tradeoffs exist, there is often scope for improving the environment by adopting policies and investments that are justified for reasons other than the environment. These free lunches, however, need to be exploited carefully.
- *Promote cost-effectiveness.* As demonstrated by recent work in countries like Chile and Mexico and in regions such as Eastern Europe, huge opportunities exist for saving resources by carefully analyzing costs. This has rarely been the practice in industrial-country policymaking.
- *Use market incentives where feasible.* A growing body of evidence, some supported by Bank projects, points to the gains from market-based instruments. Chile, Hungary, Malaysia, Poland, and Thailand are examples.
- *Economize on administrative and regulatory capacity.* Administrative and enforcement capacity is often as scarce as money. In these cases, blunter instruments (with fewer points of intervention) and self-enforcing policies (for example, deposit-refund schemes) can help.

ment, sanitation, water management, natural habitat protection, forest policy, and so on. Chapter 3 of this report describes the lessons emerging from such studies and how they are being incorporated into the Bank's training, advisory, and project work. In certain key areas such findings are codified into Bank policy statements. In the recent past this has occurred for forest policy and water management. In addition, in fiscal 1995 an "Industrial Pollution Prevention and Abatement Handbook" (World Bank 1995g) was issued, and new insights into policies that work are disseminated widely through working papers and dissemination notes.

Although it is not possible to summarize the findings of all recent studies, some common themes are emerging. A new environmentalism is spreading throughout the Bank's member countries, supported in part

---

So can involving local communities and NGOs in enforcement and monitoring.
- *Set realistic standards and enforce them.* The old approach of adopting Western standards, failing to meet them, and thus undermining the credibility of the government's commitment is giving way to a new approach whereby realistic and phased targets are set and enforced.
- *Work with the private sector.* Much of the investment required to improve the environment will come from private businesses and farmers. A shift in attitude is required (and in many places is occurring), with an emphasis on incentives, consultation, good business citizenship, and public disclosure of good as well as bad corporate performance.
- *Recognize that public involvement is crucial.* Success or failure often depends more on the commitment of stakeholders, including local communities, than that of the central government. Protecting natural habitats, forests, and even river basins requires genuine community involvement in planning and implementation. Many successful examples are emerging.
- *Build constituencies for change.* Sustained improvements in environmental policymaking, which will usually involve losers as well as winners, are more likely with a well-informed public and active support from citizens. The most effective governments are building such constituencies for change—through education and awareness programs and through promotion of an active civil society.
- *Incorporate environmental concerns from the outset.* Prevention is usually much cheaper than cure. Environmental concerns need to be built not only into the beginning of each investment, but also into the fabric of economic policymaking, including tax and regulatory policy, and even into the national accounts.

by the active portfolio of Bank-supported projects. Some of the emerging hallmarks of this new environmentalism are presented in box 2. These principles, while seeming rather obvious today, certainly were not so even five to ten years ago, which in itself indicates how rapidly the new approach is spreading.

DEVELOPING NEW METHODOLOGIES AND INDICATORS. The analytical tool kit available to policymakers in many areas of the environment remains very weak, and the Bank is devoting substantial energy to developing new practical methodologies for identifying problems and designing efficient solutions. Examples during the past year are the refinement and piloting of new approaches for identifying and projecting pollution emissions; participatory decisionmaking for priority setting at the local level; the analysis of the impacts of road building on natural habitats; the identification of the impacts of economywide policy reforms on the environment; the enhancement of water resource management, and the assessment of the social impact of Bank-supported investments.

Finally, a major effort has been made over the past two years to improve the quality of environmental data and indicators. A major publication, *Monitoring Environmental Progress,* has just been published (World Bank 1995i). Given the poor quality of most environmental data, it proposes action to improve indicators in the coming years and computes a number of new indicators of progress. For example, it presents the first systematic adjustments of net national savings rates and national wealth calculations, taking into account natural as well as manmade capital. Follow-up work will be pursued jointly by the Bank's Environment and Development Economics departments.

Greening the Entire Portfolio

Part 2 of this report broadens the coverage to ask how the Bank's *entire* lending portfolio is being adjusted in the light of new knowledge and concern about the environment. In the three years since the Rio Earth Summit (fiscal years 1993–95), the Bank has committed $67 billion for investments around the world. How are the lessons of the new environmentalism being factored into these investments?

A simple—and rough—breakdown of Bank lending since Rio is presented in table 2. Part 2 of the report first looks at how environmental assessment procedures are increasingly affecting the design of those investments that could potentially harm the environment. It then explores two broad sectors of activity—agriculture and forestry, and infra-

Table 2. World Bank Lending since Rio—A Simple Accounting

Type of lending	Billions of dollars	Percentage
Total lending	67	100
Environment projects[a]	6	9
"Win-win" projects[b]	20	30
Investments with potentially significant harmful impacts on the environment[c]	13	19
All other lending	28	42

a. See annex C for a listing of environmental projects. Adjustments have been made elsewhere to avoid double counting. Dollar amounts have been rounded.
b. "Win-win" projects are those that promote both economic growth and improvements to the environment but are not classified in the table as specifically environmental. "Win-win" projects that are also categorized as A are not included.
c. Based on projects categorized as A by regional environment divisions.

structure—which, combined, account for 60 percent of the Bank's lending in the past three years.

Making a Difference with Environmental Assessments

All Bank projects must be screened for their potential environmental impacts. Those expected to have adverse impacts that may be sensitive and irreversible are considered to be in category A and are subject to a full environmental assessment. Category B projects are those whose impacts are expected to be less significant; they are subject to some environmental analysis. Category C projects are not expected to have any negative environmental impacts. Among the investment projects approved over the past year, 23 (10 percent) were classified as category A; 81 (36 percent) were classified as category B; and the remaining 124 (54 percent) were classified as category C.

In June 1995 the Bank completed its "Second Review of Environmental Assessment," covering the roughly 600 projects that have been screened in the three years since UNCED (World Bank forthcoming b). The review concluded that environmental assessments (EAs) are now firmly rooted as part of the Bank's normal business activity, and are continuing to improve in quality as Bank staff and borrowers learn from experience. EAs are now effecting changes in project design as a matter of course and are getting better at systematically considering investment alternatives, at including monitoring and management plans for mitigation measures, and at improving public consultation.

A number of areas for future work emerged from the review. One example is the use of sectoral EAs (SEAs), which move the EA upstream in the design process and enable EAs to affect project design more effectively early on.

Agriculture, Forestry, and Natural Resources

A growing recognition of the environmental challenges of both extensification and intensification and of the nonmarket values of forests, wetlands, and other natural habitats has had a major impact on lending in these sectors over recent years. Chapter 5 explores this evolution in terms of three broad issues:

IMPROVED LAND MANAGEMENT. In giving greater emphasis to ensuring that increases in yield are *sustained*, the Bank's support is shifting in three important ways:

- *Move to least-cost, quick-return methods of soil and moisture conservation* by supporting existing farmer practices, as in the Loess Plateau in China for example, and by developing easily implemented practices, such as water-harvesting techniques using rock bunds in Africa.
- *Encourage market-based land reform* by attacking the nexus of policies that favor large-scale farms at the expense of small family farms—policies that by restricting the poor's access to land lead to poverty, inefficient resource allocation, and natural resource degradation. Land reform, such as that under way with Bank support in Colombia, will become an important theme of Bank activity.
- *Shift toward decentralized rural development* to benefit the rural poor, take advantage of local knowledge, earn the support of populations affected by development, and benefit from the flexibility to adapt to local circumstances. Thus the Bank is encouraging community-based resource management, as in a number of projects for livestock management in Africa. In addition, providing finance to poor farmers, particularly women, has become an important way both of helping them break the cycle of poverty and of enabling them to invest in sustainable natural resource management.

IMPROVED WATER MANAGEMENT. In implementing the 1993 Bank policy for managing water resources (World Bank 1993c), Bank support is continuing to shift toward four imperatives:

- *Support a comprehensive view of water management issues*. The Bank is encouraging policies that are sustainable from economic, social, and environmental perspectives. This is particularly the case in fostering cooperation among riparian countries.

- *Emphasize improvement of the efficiency of existing irrigation systems before creating new ones.* Since issuing the new policy, the Bank has focused its irrigation portfolio on rehabilitating existing systems and their management. This has meant increasing user participation in the design of irrigation and drainage projects, as well as institutional strengthening for water management.
- *Encourage decentralization and local management of water resources.* In an effort to improve efficiency and accountability of public sector irrigation management agencies, more than half of Bank irrigation projects approved over the last two years included user participation in project management.
- *Impose charges for using water that reflect its value as a scarce resource.* More than one-third of irrigation water in developing countries is typically lost between farm gate and crops, leading to water scarcity, soil salinity, and groundwater pollution. A growing number of Bank projects support the implementation of equitable user charges for water.

IMPROVED FOREST MANAGEMENT. Since the adoption of its new forest policy in 1991 (World Bank 1991a), the Bank has significantly increased its lending to the sector and given special emphasis to four new principles. A progress report in fiscal 1995 (World Bank 1994i) highlighted action and continued room for progress in each of the principles above.

- *Rectify market and policy failures that encourage deforestation and inhibit sustainable land use,* by promoting sector policy and institutional reform and by seeking to bring a more realistic assessment of resource values into decisionmaking.
- *Give special emphasis to expanding public participation in forest resource planning and management and mobilizing private sector resources and skills,* by encouraging greater stakeholder participation in forest management and planning, and by increasing support for alternative livelihoods for the rural poor living within forest boundaries.
- *Expand and intensify the management of areas suitable for sustainable forest production, including establishing plantations to reduce pressures on the existing base of forest resources where the scope to do so is sound from a social, environmental, and economic perspective,* by low-cost technical improvements as well as farmer training.
- *Expand the designation of forest areas as parks and reserves by adopting and encouraging borrower governments to pursue a precautionary approach to forest use, particularly in tropical moist forests,* by increasing the share of lending for this purpose.

Making Infrastructure Environmentally Sustainable

Investments in energy, transport, and urban infrastructure pose the greatest threat to the environment, but also offer the greatest scope for improvement on past practice. Chapter 6 documents important shifts under way in each of these sectors.

ENERGY. Building on the principles laid out in 1993 in major policy papers on energy efficiency and electric power (World Bank 1993a, 1993e), the Bank continues to strengthen its support for a two-pronged strategy to make the energy sector more environmentally sound.

- *Improve demand and supply-side efficiency.* In the fiscal 1993–95 period, twenty loans have supported power sector reforms to improve efficiency in production and transmission and in demand and end use. Innovative approaches in a diverse range of countries—including Bulgaria, Colombia, Honduras, Pakistan, and Papua New Guinea—are being monitored closely. In addition, free-standing components to encourage energy efficiency have also increased substantially over the last three years. These include support for both the more traditional supply-side measures as well as innovative approaches to peak period use and other measures. The Bank's support for energy efficiency is having a demonstrable impact: projects to develop coal-fired electricity plants supported by the Bank, for example, are shown to be significantly more efficient, in terms of the quantity of carbon emitted for each unit of energy produced, than the developing-country average.
- *Encourage clean technologies.* However successful developing countries are in realizing efficiency gains in energy production, transmission, and use, these alone will not be enough to meet future demand in an environmentally acceptable way. The Bank is therefore increasingly supporting clean sources and technologies: shifting to natural gas and clean coal for power generation, improving the quality of automotive fuels, investing in emission control technologies, and supporting the development of renewable sources of energy. The growing portfolio of renewable energy projects includes three geothermal projects in the Philippines; a solar photovoltaic and wind-farm project in India; a biomass energy project in Mauritius; and (under final preparation) new renewable energy projects in India, Indonesia, and Sri Lanka. In 1995 the Bank inaugurated a Solar Initiative, whose objective is to accelerate the pace at which commercial and near-commercial

renewable energy applications reach the marketplace. The GEF is an important partner with the Bank in some of these new initiatives.

TRANSPORT. Since UNCED, Bank activities to balance transport activities and environmental concerns have focused on two critical issues.

- *Address transport-related pollution.* In many heavily polluted developing-country cities, transport already accounts for 95 percent of lead and carbon emission and 60 to 70 percent of nitrogen and hydrocarbons. In response, the Bank is sharply expanding its support for investments designed to reduce pollution—both through managing the demand for private road transport and through direct support for controlling vehicle emissions. The Mexico Transport Air Quality Management Project, which was designed on the basis of careful ranking of the cost-effectiveness of alternative measures and which began implementation this year, captures this new approach. The Bank has also actively advocated and supported the total phaseout of lead from gasoline. It is currently assisting countries in both the technical aspects of refinery conversion and the incentive and public education aspects of the transition.
- *Reduce urban congestion.* While the Bank has traditionally addressed this problem by investing in traffic management and support for transport planning, it is now increasingly promoting the use of demand management instruments such as pricing signals for congestion, fuel, and public transport. Parking charges in Tunis, Tunisia, and rationing of off-street parking in Pusan, Republic of Korea, are examples. The Bank is also exploring a wider range of options including, in some megacities, capital-intensive investments such as rapid rail systems, which until recently have not been economically viable. In São Paulo, Brazil, for example, the Integrated Transport Project will support the construction and operation of a rail connection between the suburban train systems and the subway.

A draft of a new paper (World Bank, TWU 1995) on sustainable transport was completed this year. The main thrust of this paper is to shift away from mitigating existing environmental problems toward preventing them in the first place. This paper will be followed by a program of training and research dissemination for Bank staff and borrower countries.

TOWARD SUSTAINABLE CITIES. The three years since UNCED have seen a major effort to implement the 1991 policy paper on urban development

(World Bank 1991b). The policy underscored the importance of sound urban environmental management both as a prerequisite for urban productivity and as essential to the health and well-being of the urban poor. Recent Bank work in urban areas has been guided by a number of principles, which include the following:

- *Promote integrated resource-based project design.* A new generation of projects, especially those dealing with water resources, recognize the need to coordinate interventions around a resource, rather than around a jurisdiction or sector. For instance, the Estonia Haapsalu and Matsalu Bays Environment Project includes both water supply and treatment and management plans to improve beaches for tourism and protect endangered wetland habitat. Similarly, the Organization of Eastern Caribbean States (OECS), partially supported by the GEF, will improve urban solid and liquid waste management with the objective of protecting sensitive coastal zones.
- *Encourage decentralization to municipalities and communities.* As urban centers grow and become more complicated to manage, it is increasingly clear that municipal governments are more likely than national governments to find effective solutions to urban management. Moreover, throughout Bank operations, and in the urban sector in particular, stakeholder participation is proving to be an essential component of successful project implementation. The Asunción Sewerage Project in Paraguay, for example, decentralizes activities to improve water and sewerage services. By doing so, Asunción will also enable and encourage private sector participation.
- *Incorporate cost recovery and demand management.* Subsidies for urban services not only are costly but rarely benefit the poor whose plight is used to justify their existence. Bank-financed projects continue to put an emphasis on applying appropriate tariffs and cost-recovery mechanisms for urban services. Recent examples include water supply projects in Brazil, China, Latvia, and Lebanon. In addition, in urban environmental management, as in environmentally sustainable development more generally, the participation of the private sector is of critical importance to mobilize private financial resources as well as its innovative capacities. Bank-supported urban infrastructure projects for privatization, or for the intermediary stage of corporatization, have been approved over the last three years throughout the developing world, including examples from the Baltic countries to Peru.

- *Build partnerships for the urban environment.* Finally, the Bank has increasingly reached out to join partners in addressing the issues of urban pollution. Notable among these efforts are the Metropolitan Environmental Improvement Program with the UNDP, the Urban Management Program with the United Nations Center for Human Settlements (UNCHS) (Habitat) and the UNDP, as well as such regional programs as the Mediterranean Technical Assistance Program with the Commission of the European Communities, the European Investment Bank, and the UNDP.

Strengthening the Private Sector Role: The IFC and MIGA

Developing countries have increasingly recognized the critical role the private sector must play in financing sustainable development. A rapid growth in IFC and MIGA activity since the Rio Earth Summit has reflected this. Concurrently, moreover, the nature of the Bank Group's support for the private sector has changed to reflect the fact that, in industrial and developing countries alike, businesses have become more aware of the environmental effects of their activities. As the IFC's emphasis on environmental issues has grown, the way in which it does business has changed in two key areas: it has become more proactive in using its strengths to encourage the private sector to address environmental issues, and its internal capability to address environmental matters has been strengthened.

PROACTIVE PROGRAMS. Taking an increasingly proactive approach to supporting the private sector in environmentally sustainable development, the IFC has focused on the development of primarily environmental projects. It has also improved guidance on environmental matters to small and medium-size firms, advised financial institutions on environmental risk management, and explored innovative financing mechanisms to address environmental issues, such as targeted investment funds.

Although expanding the portfolio of environmental projects has proved slower than anticipated, two projects approved last fiscal year, one in Argentina and one in Mexico—both to improve and expand water and wastewater services—have met with considerable success and are having an important demonstration effect. Two environmental projects were approved this year, including a second investment in the Argentina project.

In the area of the global environment, the IFC, in cooperation with GEF and the Multilateral Fund for the Montreal Protocol, is preparing five projects, two of which have already been approved by IFC management. Three of these, in Egypt, the Slovak Republic, and Turkey, will help reduce chlorofluorocarbon emissions; a fourth will support the manufacture of compact fluorescent light bulbs in Poland; and the fifth will provide investments through financial intermediaries to small and medium-size firms for work on climate change or biodiversity.

In addition, the IFC assists small and medium-size companies with training and capacity building to introduce them to environmental management systems and techniques for avoiding and minimizing waste and pollution, as well as to IFC's environmental requirements.

ORGANIZATION AND PROCEDURES. Since the Rio Earth Summit, the IFC has made significant changes in the way it organizes its operations to address environmental matters. An Environment Division, which has grown from two members to eighteen in the last three years, supports the IFC's investment departments as well as MIGA. The director of the Technical and Environment Department now reports directly to the IFC's executive vice president. Furthermore, to achieve a better integration of environmental activities within IFC operations, a Vice-President of Operations has assumed corporate oversight for environmental matters. Like the Bank, the IFC screens its operations for their environmental impact, and those that are deemed to have a potentially significant impact on the environment are subject to a full environmental assessment. Since the IFC adopted new requirements on disclosure of environmental information in 1994, information on these and other projects is now available worldwide through the Bank's Public Information Center (PIC). In addition to disclosing environmental information, the IFC also requires sponsors of its category A projects to consult with affected local groups and interested parties during the preparation of the EA.

Notes

1. The World Bank Group, as used in this report, refers to the International Bank for Reconstruction and Development (IBRD) and its affiliates: the International Development Association (IDA), the International Finance Corporation (IFC), and the Multilateral Investment Guarantee Agency (MIGA). IBRD and IDA together are commonly referred to as the World Bank, or simply the Bank.

2. All dollar amounts are current U.S. dollars, except where noted. A billion is 1,000 million.

3. The Desertification Convention is the United Nations Convention to Combat Desertification in Those Countries Experiencing Serious Drought and/or Desertification Particularly in Africa.

PART 1

Part 1 of this report consists of three chapters concerned with Bank activities since the Rio Earth Summit in 1992 specifically aimed at improving environmental management. The first chapter concerns the portfolio of Bank-supported projects with primarily environmental objectives. The second examines activities to address the regional and global environments and includes an account of the Bank's activities as one of three implementing agencies of the Global Environment Facility. The third recounts the Bank's contribution to the intellectual journey toward making development environmentally and socially sustainable.

1. Investing in Environmental Stewardship

WORLD BANK PHOTO/CURT CARNEMARK

In the formerly centralized economies of Eastern Europe many industrial plants, such as this cement factory in Estonia, are both heavily polluting and economically inefficient. During the last decade the Bank has shifted its focus from pollution control to pollution prevention and promotion of cleaner industrial technologies. This year the Bank published the core section of the "Industrial Pollution Prevention and Abatement Handbook," which takes a major step forward by setting quantitative targets for the reduction of pollution from both the production processes and emissions.

The Bank's portfolio of projects with primarily environmental objectives now stands at $10 billion for 137 projects, including $1.1 billion for 21 projects approved this year.[1] This represents roughly 10 percent of the Bank's active portfolio approved since the Rio Earth Summit in 1992. These projects include those aimed at improving natural resource management (the so-called green projects), those aimed at reducing pollution and improving the urban environment (brown projects), and those designed to strengthen environmental institutions (institutional projects). In addition to this large, expanding portfolio of projects targeted specifically at improving environmental management, a growing number of other projects, now totaling more than 200, include environmental components.

The Changing Portfolio of Environment Projects

Among the most notable trends in the Bank's active lending portfolio is the dramatic increase in projects with primarily environmental objectives (hereafter called environment projects) over the last decade and particularly since the 1992 United Nations Conference on Environment and Development (UNCED), held in Rio de Janeiro, Brazil. Seventy new environment projects were approved in the seven years from fiscal 1986 to the end of fiscal 1992, and another seventy were approved just in the three years since the summit in Rio.[2]

This growth in the Bank's portfolio of environment projects reflects a trend in Bank lending away from projects that include solely specific sectoral activities, such as power generation or agricultural production, toward an increased focus on the cross-sectoral issues of poverty alleviation, environmentally and socially sustainable development, and support to the private sector.

More fundamentally, there has been an increasing integration of environmental concerns and components in operations with a variety of other primary objectives—in short, a "greening" of the Bank's portfolio as a whole. Bank staff in various country departments report that, in the future, there may well be fewer stand-alone environment projects as their efforts become increasingly directed toward incorporating environmental considerations into projects in other sectors. Related to this is the growing integration of environmental concerns into Bank country assistance programs and departmental multiyear business plans, such as the plans developed for the Middle Eastern countries, discussed in chapter 3, and West African countries. One example of the progressive greening of the portfolio can be drawn from the projected lending program for some of the Bank's newest member countries in the former

Soviet Union and Eastern Europe over the next several years. Prospective lending operations in these countries include the following:

- Agricultural projects in Estonia, Moldova, and Ukraine that are building capacity to undertake social assessment and will introduce integrated pest management and soil conservation measures.
- A municipal services project in Latvia that may incorporate a municipal development fund to support small local environmental investments and possible similar projects in Belarus and Lithuania.
- A water and wastewater treatment project in Lithuania that includes an environmental component to support management of the Lielupe River Basin by both Latvia and Lithuania.
- Several energy sector projects in Ukraine that will offer important benefits in terms of energy conservation and pollution abatement.
- Energy efficiency and housing projects in Estonia, Lithuania, and Ukraine that emphasize energy conservation and involve close interaction with homeowners' associations and other urban residents, possibly in parallel with support for cultural preservation of older sections of selected cities.

All of these projects are consistent with the objectives of the *Environmental Action Programme for Central and Eastern Europe* (World Bank and OECD forthcoming) which entered the implementation stage in fiscal 1994. The premise of this program is that because of the scarcity of financial resources, human health impacts must be regarded as the primary criterion for setting environmental priorities. The strategy focuses mainly on pollution problems that affect both cities and the surrounding countryside and that are common to all countries of Central and Eastern Europe and the former Soviet Union.

Other examples of this integrated environmental approach are presented in part 2, which describes how projects that are not specifically environmental are seeking to include environmentally beneficial features in their design. In the agricultural services projects, for instance, efforts are being made to improve the sustainability of activities to increase agricultural and livestock production, to use lower quantities of chemical fertilizers and pesticides, and to introduce improved agricultural and land management practices that halt or reduce the loss of soil and vegetation. Such practices include soil conservation, water harvesting, contour planting, minimum tillage, composting, agroforestry, and better integration of crops and livestock. Extension projects, in turn, are increasingly conveying messages on the benefits of conservation. Household energy projects based on the use of fuelwood are concentrating on the sustainable management of natural forests rather than on forest mining and on natural regeneration rather than on plantation development. In the water sector, finally, the Bank is actively pursuing new approaches to move beyond traditional management practices, as box 1.1 illustrates.

New Environmental Lending

Bank-financed environment projects involve a variety of approaches and instruments and now cover sixty-eight countries in all six operational regions. New environmental borrowers in fiscal 1995 included Honduras, Latvia, Lebanon, Lithuania, the Russian Federation, Thailand, Trinidad and Tobago, and the members of the Organization of Eastern Caribbean States (OECS).[3] The largest individual borrowers for environment projects are Brazil, China, India, Indonesia, the Republic of Korea, and Mexico. These countries are also among the Bank's biggest borrowers overall. In Sub-Saharan Africa, South Asia, and the Middle East and North Africa, environmental portfolios are dominated by natural resource management projects; in Europe and Central Asia, pollution and urban environment projects predominate; and in East Asia and Latin America and the Caribbean, green, brown, and institutional projects are all well represented.

Nearly half of the 137 environment projects under implementation in July 1995 involve natural resource management, another two-fifths address pollution or urban environmental issues, and the remainder are primarily concerned with building national environmental institutions. Many of the institution-building operations are directly derived from national environmental action plans (NEAPs), described in chapter 3. In fiscal 1995 the portfolio of environment projects expanded particularly in the former Soviet Union and Eastern Europe and Central Asia, where pollution issues have a high priority, explaining in part the predominance of brown projects approved this fiscal year. This geographical shift is evidence of the growing diversity of Bank borrowers interested in environment-related projects, together with the fact that the former Soviet republics are comparatively recent Bank members.

In terms of total financial commitments and the number of projects, Bank lending for new environment projects declined in fiscal 1995 relative to the immediately preceding years. The number of projects addressing pollution and urban environmental problems rose, but the average size fell, reflecting the expansion of the portfolio into smaller countries. The number of new projects addressing natural resource management fell, in part because such projects are already under way in a large number of countries and there is a determination to ensure

Box 1.1. A New Approach for the Water Sector

Water Pervades Society. Water is an issue which pervades society—it is critical for long-term economic development; for social welfare, especially that of the poor; and for ensuring environmental sustainability. More than 1 billion people lack access to an adequate supply of safe water, and 1.7 billion people do not have adequate sanitation. Contaminated water causes millions of preventable deaths every year, especially among children. Water resources management must, therefore, help to alleviate poverty and ensure that the poor are the beneficiaries of effective decisions and policies rather than the victims of bad ones.

Emerging Trends. Review of current trends indicates that the world is approaching a water crisis in several regions, most notably in the Middle East and North Africa. But in many countries, perceived water problems stem not from a shortage of water, but rather from inefficient use, degradation of available water due to pollution, and unsustainable use of groundwater resources. Massive urban and industrial growth is creating unprecedented demands for water, often at the expense of agriculture, aquatic ecosystems, and the rural poor.

Failure of Current Policies. Although the problems are many and diverse, they all stem from four principal policy failures: refusal to treat water as an economic good; excessive reliance on the government for water and wastewater services; fragmented management of water between sectors and institutions, with little regard for conflicts or complementarities between social, economic, and environmental objectives; and inadequate recognition of the health and environmental concerns associated with current practices.

Moving beyond Traditional Water Management. The new approach is water resource management that

- Addresses quantity and quality concerns through an integrated approach
- Integrally links land use management with sustainable water management
- Recognizes freshwater, coastal, and marine environments as a management continuum
- Recognizes water as an economic good and promotes cost-effective interventions
- Supports innovative and participatory approaches
- Focuses on actions that improve the lives of people and the quality of their environment.
- All types of water, in freshwater, coastal, and marine environments, should be considered as a management continuum with significant

implications for strategy, planning, management, and investment actions. These systems must be viewed as intimately linked, and a much broader range of downstream effects from human interventions and development activities must be recognized. The management of river basins, coastal zones, and the marine environment becomes a complementary issue. The quantity and quality of water—historically treated as separate issues—must now be seen as a global concern requiring a unified management approach.

Implementation of the new approach requires four essential elements: strategies, interventions, investments, and innovations.

- *Move from segmented to comprehensive strategies.* Water issues need to be treated in a systemic manner. Rather than manage water sectorally by its separate uses, policymakers must develop a comprehensive framework for water resources management.
- *Move from curative to preventive interventions.* The new approach emphasizes interventions that move from curative to preventive. This prevents expensive problems from occurring and allows for the effective application of resources. It also promotes sustainable use of diverse and fragile resources and minimizes requirements for remediation, mitigation, and restoration.
- *Move from incremental to strategic investments.* Investments, balanced between preventive measures for avoiding further degradation and curative measures for rehabilitating degraded ecosystems, must be part of long-term public and private sector development strategies. Special attention should be given to ensuring that long-term environmental costs are not neglected in the desire to obtain short-term benefits. In this regard, the importance of increasing user participation in program and project design is critical, especially to ensure the internalization of measures for promoting the use of economic incentives. Given the need to mobilize resources, improve efficiency, and increase the quality of services for users, the participation of the private sector in water management should be encouraged.
- *Move from pilot to mainstream innovations.* Effective adoption and implementation of the new approach demands changes in principles and practices of water resources management programs. Grants should be used strategically to promote and test pilot innovations. Measures should be taken to effectively share and disseminate experiences to allow the benefits from new approaches to water management to be realized at the operational level.

effective implementation of these projects before replicating them more broadly.

Nevertheless, country interest in borrowing for environmental improvement remains strong. The large number of first-time borrowers for environment projects in fiscal 1995 is another indication of this continuing trend. Many of these new borrowers are small countries (the Baltic countries, the OECS, Honduras, Lebanon, and Trinidad and Tobago), and the loans reflect the comparative limitation of both their investment needs and their absorptive capacity for external funding for environmental management. The three environment projects in the Baltic countries approved in fiscal 1995, for example, received average Bank loans of just over $4 million each, due in large part to funding from other donors. By comparison, in fiscal 1994, three large sector operations in Mexico alone accounted for nearly $920 million in lending and close to $2 billion in total investment. Bank environmental lending, while focusing primarily on large middle- and lower-income borrowers (such as Brazil, China, India, Indonesia, Korea, Mexico, Pakistan, and Turkey) in the late 1980s and early 1990s, spread to a number of smaller nations over the past year or so.

Pollution and the Urban Environment: The Brown Agenda

The issues of industrial pollution and the urban environment were given considerable prominence both at the Rio Earth Summit and in the Bank's *World Development Report 1992: Environment and Development* (World Bank 1992). Projects in the brown agenda account for the largest share of total Bank lending commitments for the environment (69 percent), and represent the lion's share of the environmental operations approved during the past fiscal year, both in numbers and in dollars.

At the end of fiscal 1995, fifty-five projects designed primarily to address brown issues and involving Bank commitments of more than $6 billion and total investments of more than $16 billion were under implementation in thirty countries (see table 1.1 for projects approved since Rio; see annex C for all those approved in fiscal 1995 and annex E for all projects active in the environmental portfolio).

The Bank's approaches and project design in the brown agenda have changed significantly over the past decade. Bank focus on the environment in industrial projects, for example, has evolved from funding pollution control equipment for state-controlled enterprises to technical assistance for formulating and enforcing industrial policy and financing credit lines for private pollution control facilities. The focus of Bank assistance is also shifting from pollution control to pollution prevention and to promoting cleaner industrial technologies. Box 1.2 describes

Table 1.1. Projects for Urban Environmental Management and Pollution Control, Fiscal 1993–95
(millions of dollars)

Fiscal year and country	Project name	Loan/credit (L/C)	World Bank financing	Total project cost
1993				
Brazil	Water Quality and Pollution Control Project—São Paulo/Paraná	L	245	494
	Minas Gerais Water Quality and Pollution Control Project	L	145	308
China	South Jiangsu Environment Protection Project	L	250	584
Egypt	Private Sector Tourism Project	L	130	784
India	Renewable Resources Development Project	L + C	190	440
Korea, Rep. of	Kuangju and Seoul Sewerage Project	L	110	530
Mexico	Transport Air Quality Management Project	L	220	1,087
Turkey	Bursa Water Supply and Sanitation Project	L	130	258
Total			1,420	4,485
1994				
Algeria	Water Supply and Sewerage Rehabilitation Project	L	110	170
Brazil	Espirito Santo Water Supply and Coastal Pollution Management Project	L	154	308
China	Shanghai Environment Project	L	160	457
Ecuador	Mining Development and Environmental Control—Technical Assistance Project	L	14	24
Estonia	District Heating Rehabilitation Project	L	38	65
Indonesia	Surabaya Urban Development Project	L	175	618
Mexico	Northern Border Environment Project	L	368	762
	Second Solid Waste Management Project	L	200	416
	Water and Sanitation II Project	L	350	770
Togo	Lomé Urban Development Project	L	26	29
Total			1,595	3,619

(Table continues on the following page.)

Table 1.1 *(continued)*

Fiscal year and country	Project name	Loan/credit (L/C)	World Bank financing	Total project cost
1995				
Burkina Faso	Urban Environment Project	C	37	50
China	Liaoning Environment Project	L	110	351
Estonia	Haapsulu and Matsalu Bays Environment Project	L	2	8
India	Industrial Pollution Prevention Project	L + C	168	330
Korea, Rep. of	Ports Development and Environmental Improvement Project	L	100	1,107
	Waste Disposal Project	L	75	305
Latvia	Liepaja Environment Project	L	4	21
Lebanon	Solid Waste/Environmental Management Project	L	55	135
Lithuania	Klaipeda Environment Project	L	7	23
OECS countries	Solid Waste Management Project	L + C	12	51
Poland	Katowice Heat Supply and Conservation Project	L	45	93
Russian Federation	Emergency Oil Spill Recovery Project	L	99	140
Sri Lanka	Colombo Environmental Improvement Project	C	39	49
Thailand	Clean Fuels and Environmental Improvement Project	L	90	370
Total			843	3,033
Total since UNCED, fiscal 1993–95			3,858	11,137
Active projects approved before fiscal 1993			2,217	4,942
Total active portfolio			6,075	16,079

recent experience in the industrial sector in India, where a new Industrial Pollution Prevention Project was approved by the Bank in November 1994. A similar approach is being taken in the Technology Development Project in China, approved in February 1995, which will support reforms in technology policy and institutions that promote development of cleaner, productivity-enhancing technologies. The project will generate significant environmental benefits: two of the engineering research centers to be supported under the project, for example, will develop clean

Box 1. 2. From Pollution Control to Pollution Prevention in the Indian Industrial Sector

During fiscal 1995 the Bank approved the India Industrial Pollution Prevention Project (IPPP) as a follow-up to the earlier Industrial Pollution Control Project (IPCP) approved in May 1991. The earlier project was intended to assist the Indian government's efforts to prevent environmental degradation caused by industrial activities.

Since IPCP became effective, substantial progress has been achieved in attaining its objectives. Already by early 1995 all of the resources made available under the line of credit had been committed, and more than eighty innovative environmental schemes were at different stages of completion. Likewise, twenty common effluent treatment plants had been financed, providing cost-effective treatment to more than 3,500 small- and medium-scale industries, with a combined capacity of about 150,000 tons per day. Considerable progress had also been achieved in implementing the institutional and technical assistance components. On a wider scale, the state pollution control boards supported under IPCP had significantly increased their effectiveness and were demonstrating a renewed effort to get industries to meet statutory requirements.

Given the high costs associated with pollution abatement and the massive efforts required for monitoring and enforcement, the Indian government adopted a policy of pollution prevention and waste minimization by encouraging the use of clean technologies and providing incentives for industry to prevent pollution. The IPPP of fiscal 1995 supports key aspects of this policy. The project will expand the institutional strengthening program initiated under IPCP by adding four states (Andhra Pradesh, Karnataka, Madhya Pradesh, and Rajasthan). The project will help to introduce and operate additional common effluent treatment plants at industrial estates, assist the most polluting industries in adopting cost-effective waste minimization and resource recovery or pollution abatement measures, and help to disseminate information on cleaner production and successful waste minimization methods. For example, the project is financing a cleaner technology network designed to disseminate information and facilitate duplication of innovative, cleaner manufacturing methods. Likewise, the project will support a waste minimization extension service to address the need for technical expertise and information among small-scale industries. Finally, it will help to attract funding from other sources, such as the Japanese Overseas Economic Cooperation Fund and the Nordic Investment Bank, for example, to support pollution prevention.

coal combustion technologies, working with foreign suppliers to adapt internationally available know-how to technical conditions prevailing in China; others will develop pollution prevention technologies and improve the use of available energy feedstocks.

Another example of an innovative project in the portfolio for brown projects is the recently approved emergency loan to contain, clean up, and mitigate the effects of the huge Komi oil spill in Russia. This project, whose preparation involved extensive local participation, is described in box 1.3.

Several trends are evident in urban environmental management projects. One is a growing number of projects and project components involving urban waste management, including both domestic treatment and disposal of sewage and management of solid waste. Examples from this year include an urban waste disposal project in Korea, a solid waste and environmental management project in Lebanon, and three recently approved operations in the Baltics. The Lebanese and Baltic projects also place considerable emphasis on strengthening local environmental and coastal zone management, reflecting a further trend in the design of such projects (see box 1.4). Environmental projects with a similar focus in Algeria, Korea, Mexico (large sector investment loans for water supply and sanitation and solid waste management) and Turkey are now in their second or third year of implementation.

A second trend in urban environmental projects is a city-oriented, cross-sectoral or cross-media approach to dealing with urban environmental pollution, typified by several recent Bank operations in China, including the Liaoning Environment Project approved this year. Previous projects in Beijing, Shanghai, Tianjin, and Southern Jiangsu Province, together with the Northern Border Environmental Project in Mexico, provide examples of a multisectoral approach to urban environmental problems. This approach reflects a broader tendency by the Bank to enhance urban environmental quality by integrating sectoral interventions and linking them to urban development activities, as outlined in chapter 6. This approach also characterizes two pioneering projects approved in fiscal 1993 to reduce water pollution and improve watershed management in three large metropolitan areas in Brazil, which are discussed in box 1.6 later in this chapter. Other recent operations that take an integrated approach include the Urban Environment Project in Burkina Faso and the Colombo Environmental Improvement Project in Sri Lanka, both approved this year, the Surabaya Urban Development Project in Indonesia, and the Lomé Urban Development Project in Togo.

Natural Resource Management: The Green Agenda

At the end of fiscal 1995, sixty-two Bank projects primarily concerned with natural resource management were being implemented in thirty-nine countries. These operations involve more than $3 billion in Bank

Box 1.3. Mitigating the Komi Oil Spill: The Role of Public Participation

Beginning in February 1994 and culminating in more serious failures in September 1994 and January 1995, leaks from the Kharyaga-Usinsk pipeline in the Komi Republic in the north of the Russian Federation resulted in one of the world's largest oil spills. More than 100,000 tons (730,000 barrels) of oil—three times the amount released by the Exxon Valdez—are estimated to be trapped in very difficult to access bogs and creek beds. More than 20,000 tons (140,000 barrels) of oil were released into the Kolva River in autumn 1994, when temporary dikes to contain the oil failed during heavy rains, causing severe damage to downstream communities. Wholesale release of the remaining oil into the river system would expand this ecological disaster, threatening villages downstream that depend on the river for their livelihood, as well as the overall environment of the Pechora River system into which the Kolva and Usa rivers flow.

The Emergency Oil Spill Recovery and Mitigation Project approved in April 1995 includes three main components: (a) spill containment and cleanup and disposal measures, including emergency social expenditures and contingency subprojects for responding to new leaks; (b) rehabilitation of the pipeline; and (c) technical assistance to strengthen and improve institutional capacity to manage the activities necessary to mitigate the effects of the spilled oil. The third component also includes assistance to ensure that participatory and consultative programs are implemented for affected river communities within a 120 kilometer radius of the spill zone.

Involving communities affected by the oil pipeline spills in the Russian Federation is an important component of the project. In February 1995, preliminary consultation by the government to identify emergency needs resulting from oil spills and the cleanup operations already under way involved informal contacts with a major international NGO, consultations with local NGOs, and preliminary interviews with officials in Syktyvkar, Usinsk, and eight affected downstream villages. As part of the interviews in the affected villages, individuals were asked to rank their needs for emergency relief in health, water supply, transportation services, availability of fuel, waste disposal and sanitation, and feed and grazing for domestic livestock. These initial community rankings were used to establish priorities for immediate emergency services. These priorities were supplemented by a more detailed community-based survey of needs, the results of which have been incorporated into mitigation plans for the affected villages. A central concern of the project planning process was to encourage and facilitate discussion with affected communities on alternative mitigation measures that could be implemented as part of the Bank-financed emergency response program. These consultations supported the development of a social assistance program for affected communities to be funded by the project.

Box. 1.4. Lending for Environmental Improvement in the Baltic Countries

Several innovative approaches have been taken in three recently approved environment projects in the Baltic countries. The Baltic Sea is an important source of economic activity and recreation for more than 80 million people who live along the coast and within its drainage area. In addition, the sea provides essential habitat for maintaining biodiversity, in particular a large variety of resident and migratory birds, as well as terrestrial wildlife species rare in other parts of Europe. The Liepaja Environment Project in Latvia, the Klaipeda Environment Project in Lithuania, and the Haapsalu and Matsalu Bays Environment Project in Estonia have combined priority investments in water and wastewater treatment rehabilitation identified under the Baltic Sea Environment Program with environmental management components concerning institutional development, coastal zone management, wetland conservation, and pilot programs to reduce agricultural runoff. All three projects involve very small Bank loans because they have attracted substantial donor grant funding, primarily from the Nordic countries and the European Union's PHARE Program. This funding partnership reflects a major Bank commitment to early involvement of potential donors in the project preparation process, particularly through joint visits to the countries.

commitments and total investments of nearly $6 billion; roughly 85 percent of these projects have been approved since 1990, and around 40 percent since June 1992 (see table 1.2 for projects approved since Rio). Three new green projects were approved for Bank funding during fiscal 1995, and numerous natural resource management operations are at advanced stages of preparation.[4] Green projects currently under implementation cover a broad range of activities including forest management and biodiversity conservation, establishment or strengthening of national parks and other protected areas, integrated pest management, soil conservation, land management, watershed rehabilitation, and water resource management. (For further discussion of Bank support for biodiversity conservation, see box 1.5.) These were supplemented by an expansion of biodiversity projects approved for financing through the Global Environment Facility (GEF; see chapter 2).

Natural resource management projects developed over the past few years have been guided by the Bank's recent policies for forest and water resource management, which give particular emphasis to environmental concerns. In the forestry sector, such projects approved this year include the following:

Table 1.2. Projects for Natural Resources Management, Fiscal 1993–95
(millions of dollars)

Fiscal year and country	Project name	Loan/credit (L/C)	World Bank financing	Total project cost
1993				
Egypt	Matruh Resource Management Project	C	22	31
Gabon	Forestry and Environment Project	L	23	38
India	Uttar Pradesh Sodic Lands Reclamation Project	C	55	80
Indonesia	Integrated Pest Management Project	L	32	53
Pakistan	Northern Resource Management Project	C	29	40
	Fordwah E. Sadiquia Irrigation and Drainage Project	C	54	71
Seychelles	Environment and Transport Project	L	5	7
Tunisia	Second Forestry Development Project	L	69	148
Turkey	Eastern Anatolia Watershed Rehabilitation Project	L	77	121
Total			366	589
1994				
Bhutan	Third Forest Development Project	C	5	9
China	Forest Resource Development and Protection Project	C	200	356
	Loess Plateau Watershed Rehabilitation Project	C	150	259
Colombia	Natural Resource Managment Program	L	39	65
India	Andhra Pradesh Forestry Project	C	77	89
	Forestry Research Education and Extension Project	C	47	56
Indonesia	National Watershed Management and Conservation Project	L	57	488
Lao PDR	Forest Management and Conservation Project	C	9	20
Pakistan	Balochistan Natural Resources Management Project	C	15	18
Paraguay	Natural Resources Management Project	L	50	79
Poland	Forest Development Support Project	L	146	335

(Table continues on the following page.)

Table 1.2 *(continued)*

Fiscal year and country	Project name	Loan/credit (L/C)	World Bank financing	Total project cost
Tunisia	Northwest Mountainous Areas Development Project	L	28	50
Uruguay	Natural Resources Management and Irrigation Project	L	41	74
Total			864	1,898
1995				
India	Madhya Pradesh Forestry Project	C	58	67
Pakistan	Punjab Forest Sector Development Project	C	25	34
Venezuela	INPARQUES Project	L	55	96
Total			138	197
Total since UNCED, fiscal 1993–95			1,368	2,684
Active projects approved before fiscal 1993			1,825	3,079
Total active portfolio			3,193	5,763

- The INPARQUES Project in Venezuela, which strengthens the capacity of the Venezuelan government to manage the country's national and urban parks, natural monuments, and wildlife refuges and reserves.[5] More specifically, the project will conserve and protect vulnerable areas, intensify public environmental research, undertake training and education, and improve the economic sustainability of national parks and other protected areas. Among other innovative features, the project includes various mechanisms for increasing the participation of NGOs and local communities in park management and related activities. It is expected to directly enhance the protection of an area of approximately 100,000 square kilometers and indirectly strengthen the capacity to manage all of Venezuela's protected areas.
- The Punjab Forest Sector Development Project in Pakistan will promote a sectoral approach to forestry development in the most populated and tree-deficient province of Pakistan. It has components in farm forestry and in participatory range and scrub management and a pilot component promoting the conservation role of timber plantations. Beneficial impacts of project activities are

Box 1.5. The Bank's Biodiversity Portfolio

The Bank has had a long and significant history of investment in biodiversity-related components as part of broader investments in its traditional lending sectors, such as agriculture, tourism, forestry, rural development, and energy. These have included, among other things, establishing protected areas and improving institutional capacity and management. A recent review of Bank and GEF projects with biodiversity conservation objectives and components found the following:

- The cumulative financing for Bank-supported biodiversity projects and components approved between fiscal 1988 and fiscal 1995 is $1.3 billion. Of this total, IBRD and IDA account for $525 million, GEF grants for $182 million, Brazilian Rain Forest Trust Fund for $37 million, other donors for $274 million, and governments for $273 million. The relative contribution of Bank resources to the biodiversity portfolio has declined in recent years as a result of the increased availability of grant funding.
- In general the Bank projects are rarely stand-alone operations. Typically, biodiversity components are contained within broader natural resource management or environmental institution building projects. In contrast, a subset of GEF projects and all of the Brazilian Rain Forest Trust Fund grants are exclusively targeted to address the problems of protecting and managing biodiversity.
- The regional breakdown of the biodiversity portfolio reflects the concern for megadiversity in tropical countries. Particularly large shares of total financing are allocated to Brazil, Kenya, Madagascar, Mexico, and Venezuela.
- In terms of the types of activities financed, strengthening the management of existing protected areas has been the top investment priority in most years, accounting for 39 percent of all resources allocated for biodiversity in the projects surveyed. This was followed by expenditures for natural resource management outside protected areas (24 percent); biodiversity-related policy, planning, and institution building (23 percent); establishment of new protected areas (8 percent); and surveys, research and monitoring, and ex-situ conservation and seed banks (6 percent). There has been no marked change in the composition of biodiversity financing over time.

expected to include the conservation of forest resources in Punjab, the enhancement of soil conservation by erosion control and the return of biomass to soils, and the introduction of participatory range management. Increased supply of wood from farm forestry,

moreover, should decrease pressure on the remnants of natural forest in the province.
- The Madhya Pradesh Forestry Project in India aims to develop the necessary human resources for planning, implementing, and monitoring the state forestry strategy; to increase forest cover and productivity through participatory processes of forest resource management and use, taking special account of the interests of indigenous peoples and other disadvantaged groups; to improve incentives for forest management and the cultivation of trees; and to promote biodiversity conservation. The project's biodiversity component will improve the management of twenty-four protected areas and establish an ecodevelopment support fund to be used for sustainable forest management and development of alternative income-generating opportunities in villages located near protected areas.

In addition to these projects financed by Bank lending, the Bank also supports biodiversity conservation through its role as implementing agency of the Global Environment Facility (see chapter 2) and the Pilot Program to Preserve the Brazilian Rain Forest, which this year moved into the implementation phase. Launched at the July 1990 G-7 summit in Houston, Texas, the pilot program supports a set of projects that together aim to reduce the rate of deforestation in Brazil's rain forests. The projects are designed to strengthen the capacity of the public sector to set and enforce sound environmental policy; to improve the management of special protected areas, including parks, extractive reserves, national forests, and indigenous reserves; and to increase knowledge about conservation of the Amazon rain forest and sustainable use of its resources. The first five projects, with a total cost of $161 million, were approved this year and are described briefly in box 1.6. Several other projects, including a pioneering operation for environmental education, are under preparation.

While this section has described stand-alone project support for improved management of the rural environment, of equal importance is the incorporation of environmental components into Bank-financed investments in agriculture, forestry, and rural development. These are discussed in chapter 5.

Institution Building

The third main focus of Bank lending for the environment is to strengthen public sector institutions responsible for environmental protection and management at the national and subnational levels. As of

> **Box 1.6. Grants Approved by the Brazilian Rain Forest Pilot Program in Fiscal 1995**
>
> *Indigenous lands ($20.9 million).* Aims to improve conservation of natural resources in indigenous areas and increase the well-being of indigenous peoples.
>
> *Science centers and directed research ($20.1 million).* Provides support to two internationally renowned scientific institutions in the Amazon region to strengthen their institutional management, support rehabilitation and expansion of research equipment and infrastructure, increase human resource capacity in scientific research, and disseminate research results.
>
> *Demonstration projects ($22.2 million).* Supports sustainable development by encouraging the participation and integration of local communities in efforts to advance the objectives of the pilot program through a small grants program, evaluation and dissemination of subproject results, and strengthening of NGOs.
>
> *Natural resources policy ($88.0 million).* Helps to define and implement pilot models for the integrated environmental management of the Amazon rain forest and for institutional strengthening of state and federal environmental agencies through zoning, monitoring, control, and regulatory enforcement.
>
> *Extractive reserves ($9.7 million).* Supports the legal establishment of extractive reserves for sustainable production of nonwood forest products, strengthens community organizations and infrastructure, develops and disseminates appropriate technologies, refines conservation and sustainable management of reserve areas, and supports participatory administration of the project.

July 1995, twenty such projects, involving commitments of nearly $670 million and total project investments of close to $1.2 billion, were under implementation. All of these projects have been approved since fiscal 1990 and almost two-thirds in the three years since UNCED (see table 1.3 and annexes C and D for projects approved since Rio; for all such projects active in the environmental portfolio, see annex E). Many of these projects support implementation of NEAPs (see chapter 3 for a discussion of NEAPs). While some of these operations include sizable investment components, all of them include significant technical assistance, training, and studies components.

Four new environmental institutions projects were approved in fiscal 1995 involving Bank financing of $135 million for a total investment of more than $220 million. Of these, three are comparatively small technical assistance operations, while the fourth is much larger, combining investment and institutional development components in the Russian Federa-

Table 1.3. Projects for Environmental Institutions, Fiscal 1993–95
(millions of dollars)

Fiscal year and country	Project name	Loan/credit (L/C)	World Bank financing	Total project cost
1993				
Bolivia	Environmental Technical Assistance Project	C	5	5
Chile	Environment Institutions Development Project	L	12	33
China	Environment Technical Assistance Project	C	50	70
Ghana	Environment Resource Management Project	C	18	36
Korea, Rep. of	Environmental Research and Education Project	L	60	97
Total			145	241
1994				
Gambia, The	Capacity Building for Environmental Management—Technical Assistance Project	C	3	5
Korea, Rep. of	Environmental Technology Development Project	L	90	156
Morocco	Environmental Management Project	L	6	11
Total			99	172
1995				
Benin	Environmental Management Project	C	8	9
Honduras	Environmental Development Project	C	11	13
Russian Federation	Environmental Management Project	L	110	195
Trinidad and Tobago	Environmental Management Project	L	6	11
Total			135	228
Total since UNCED, fiscal 1993–95			379	641
Active projects approved before fiscal 1993			289	536
Total active portfolio			668	1,177

tion. The Benin, Honduras, and Trinidad and Tobago operations are described below; the work initiated in the Russian Federation is discussed in box 1.7. In addition, the Institutional Development Fund (IDF) is providing increasing support for activities with an environmental or social focus, as illustrated in box 1.8.

- The Benin Environmental Management Project will support the development of environmental management capacity at the national level and help the government of Benin to implement the NEAP adopted in June 1993. It will pursue capacity building and institutional support, including streamlining and strengthening national environmental responsibilities, reinforcing policy implementation and coordination mechanisms, promoting better preparation and enforcement of the environmental regulatory framework, developing an effective environmental information system, and enhancing environmental monitoring and evaluation capability. The project will also promote public awareness of environmental issues and the integration of environmental considerations in the education system.
- The Honduras Environmental Development Project has three principal sets of objectives: (a) to strengthen government capacity for environmental planning, policy, and regulation, interagency and intersectoral coordination, and monitoring and enforcement of environmental laws and regulations; (b) to assist the Ministry of the Environment in implementing a national and participatory system of EAs and in developing methodologies for their preparation, processing, and review; and (c) to develop environmental management capacity at the municipal level, with greater grassroots participation, and increase financial support for pilot environmental projects at the municipal and community levels as well as for small and microenterprises using the Honduran Social Investment Fund.
- The Trinidad and Tobago Environmental Management Project will also work to establish the necessary institutional arrangements for environmental regulation and management, along with a priority environmental work program based on a NEAP to be formulated under the project. It will include a public awareness program and an environmental training program for the public and private sectors. It will also support the activities of the Environmental Management Agency. During project preparation, the government fostered a major participatory effort to draft legislation for the agency, which was opened up for public review and substantially revised on the basis of comments received before the legislation was introduced into parliament.

Box 1.7. Strengthening Environmental Management in the Russian Federation

Like many other countries in transition to market economies, the Russian Federation has inherited a costly environmental legacy from decades of growth that neglected to take environmental factors into account in national investment decisionmaking. As elsewhere, moreover, the environmental management system is fragmented and uncoordinated, with many government agencies sharing some responsibility for environmental concerns. Because the capital requirements for resolving environmental problems in the country are high, priorities must be set and interventions selected to address these priorities in a cost-effective manner. Among the institutional and financial problems that need to be tackled are the unreliability of much existing environmental data, ineffective laws and regulations for environmental protection, poorly defined management and organizational responsibilities, inadequate budget allocations, a breakdown of the traditional command and control system for pollution abatement and nature protection, inappropriate criteria for emission standards, and the lack of sufficient medium-term investment funds.

To support efforts to address these issues, a loan of $110 million was approved this year by the Bank for the Environmental Management Project to support, among other things, environmental management and institutional strengthening at the federal level and in the North Caucasus, Upper Volga, and Urals regions. More specifically, the project will assist the Russian Federation in establishing an Environmental Framework Program (EFP), estimated to cost a total of $282 million over four to five years whose objectives are to (a) incorporate environmental and natural resource management concerns directly into the economic, social, and political adjustment process at the federal and regional levels of government; (b) strengthen and streamline government institutions for environmental and natural resource management; (c) improve the formulation and implementation of environmental and natural resource policy and strategy; (d) upgrade environmental and natural resource management systems; (e) strengthen financial delivery mechanisms to address priority environmental management investment needs through the setting up and initial capitalization of a National Pollution Abatement Facility; and (f) facilitate the flow of donor and multilateral resources to the environmental protection sector.

In addition to the operations approved in fiscal 1995, the Urban Environmental Management Project in Colombia, currently under preparation, should be noted because of its highly innovative nature. This proposed technical assistance operation capitalizes on the government decentralization currently taking place in Colombia to build insti-

> **Box 1.8. Using the Institutional Development Fund to Improve Environmental Management**
>
> The Institutional Development Fund (IDF) is a grant facility for financing technical assistance for institutional development not directly linked to planned Bank Group lending operations. The IDF enables a quick response for funding small, action-oriented initiatives identified during the Bank's economic and sector work and policy dialogue. The Institutional Development Fund came into operation in 1992, and in the first two years committed nearly $27 million in grants to 101 projects, funding a wide variety of recipients and critical institution-building activities that otherwise might not have been funded.
>
> The IDF's focus is broad, but a number of its grants have social and environmental objectives at their core. For instance, a $190,000 IDF grant was approved to strengthen organizational management in agriculture and natural resources in Malawi; a $100,000 grant was awarded to build capacity for environmental management in São Tomé and Principe; $190,000 was granted for formulating environmental policy and strengthening environmental capacity in the Lao People's Democratic Republic (PDR); and $430,000 was awarded for a local environmental management program in the Donetsk Oblast, Ukraine, which includes an air quality management program and a public awareness component as a first step in Ukraine's budding environmental program. Other grants awarded by the IDF since 1992 have been used to carry out innovative institution-strengthening programs for indigenous peoples in Bolivia, Chile, and Guatemala; to manage national cultural property in Albania; and to provide assistance to China's Ministry of Water Resources and India's Ministry of Forestry and Environment.

tutional structures for managing environmental problems in four major urban centers: Barranquilla, Bogotá, Cali, and Medellín. This will be the first Bank project to focus exclusively on environmental institution building at the urban and municipal level. In each of these municipalities, new environmental institutions have been established to address a broad range of urban environmental issues, including water supply and sewerage, water pollution, air pollution, and waste management. The proposed project will support these institutions by focusing on environmental planning, organizational structures, regulatory strengthening, and the provision of training and equipment for the participating cities.

Environmental institution-building projects often face particularly complex implementation challenges due to the cross-sectoral and cross-jurisdictional nature of many environmental problems, the likelihood that many environmental agencies are new or weak, and the critical importance of strong political support for achieving environmental improvement goals. Among such operations, which have been under implementation for several years, important lessons can be learned from the Environmental Management Project in Poland, approved in 1990, which is nearing completion and is one of the most successful environmental institution-building projects to date. Much of this success is due to solid preparation work, which included setting clear priorities and effectively collaborating between Polish and Bank specialists, together with firm government commitment to the project's objectives. Strong local technical and institutional capacity and the continuity of key project personnel on both the borrower and the Bank side have also been important factors, as has been the pragmatic approach taken to project design, which has included consideration of procurement arrangements from the earliest stages of preparation. From the very beginning, moreover, several large but heavily polluted municipalities (Katowice and Krakow among others) have been formally involved in project activities, together with the central environmental agency, reflecting the project's serious commitment to decentralization. Flexibility during implementation has likewise been a significant element in the project's highly satisfactory performance.

Managing the Environmental Portfolio

The majority of projects in the Bank's environmental portfolio are performing well and experiencing only minor implementation problems. Their performance, in fact, is not significantly different from that of other Bank projects, although some environmental projects are being implemented more slowly than expected.

Many of the implementation challenges facing environmental projects are similar to those facing the Bank's portfolio as a whole: insufficient availability of counterpart funds, difficulties with technical assistance components, and problems with procurement. This is often evidenced by a lack of compliance with one or more covenants in the loan agreements. The frequency of these problems is also consistent with the experience of the Bank portfolio as a whole.

Yet some challenges are peculiar to the environmental portfolio. The multisectoral, cross-media, and interjurisdictional nature of the programs requires special attention. The recency of borrower government efforts to address them means that implementing primarily environmental projects (and project components) is often a significant challenge. These characteristics, often together with weak national and subnational policy, regulatory, and institutional frameworks for environmental management, weak constituencies for environmental reform, and the borrowers' occasional lack of familiarity with Bank procedures, can indeed make project implementation difficult.

Although environmental projects with implementation difficulties exist in all six Bank operational regions and in all three types of projects, these problems tend to occur more often with operations involving forest and natural resource management, particularly in Africa and South Asia. Review of completed projects by the Bank's Operations Evaluation Department (OED), an examination of highly satisfactory projects, and a recent Bank report on perspectives for environmentally sustainable development in Sub-Saharan Africa point to a number of important lessons for successful project implementation, including the following:

- *Foster executing agency ownership, strengthen the quality of staff, and reduce project complexity.* The first Land Management Project in (Paraná State) Brazil, for example, has stabilized its staffing situation, which had jeopardized field operations at the outset. An improved salary policy, together with increased participation of the municipalities and private rural extension firms, has led to performance well beyond project targets. Similarly, the success of the Environmental Management Project in Burkina Faso can be attributed largely to the excellent quality of the field staff. The project continues to have particularly good links with the agricultural and livestock extension services, and in certain provinces the complementarity between the two is producing very positive results. Training provided under the project has also significantly improved the community's receptivity to certain standard extension messages. In the Mali Natural Resource Management Project all of the field staff have received training in participatory rural appraisal, which has increased the effectiveness of this technique. Unlike a number of natural resource management projects that have experienced difficulties, technical assistance components have also proven successful in these operations. Too many or too diverse components included in an effort to be comprehensive or holistic, however, can strain the ability of borrowers to implement operations adequately, even with well-qualified and motivated staff. Involving the executing agency in project design can help to reduce this problem.
- *Seek local community involvement.* Another key to the success of the Mali and Brazil (Paraná) operations has been to involve local communities effectively. In Mali, project activities such as using television and radio to raise public awareness and train villagers have led to a high level of interest, understanding, and commit-

ment on the part of rural communities. In Paraná, more than half of the farmers who had been receiving project assistance for more than two years adopted the recommended soil management practices, a figure that is high in relation to performance worldwide and the project's initial target of 30 percent. Most of the successful projects also experience only minor or temporary problems with counterpart funding, procurement, and disbursements, while possessing comparatively strong and highly committed management teams.

- *Create a broad consensus for change.* A large part of the satisfactory performance of several environmental projects in Korea, for example, is due to strong government support. All projects proposed for government financing in Korea are approved by the National Assembly as part of the annual Foreign Borrowing Program. Such parliamentary approval firmly commits the implementing ministries and the Ministry of Finance to the success of the project. Project staff in the executing agencies are generally also of high quality and possess a full range of skills for effective project management and implementation. This contrasts with the experience of natural resource management projects in countries as diverse as Algeria, Brazil, and Nepal where insufficient political support and political-administrative changes have contributed to less than satisfactory performance. Inadequate technical and institutional capacity, often exacerbated by the failure of borrowers to implement technical assistance components, or poor inter-institutional coordination have adversely affected implementation of green projects in a number of countries. Weak project management, in turn, is often associated with frequent turnover in administrative and technical staff, low salaries, wages unrelated to performance, inefficient management systems, and inadequate material and logistic support.

- *Ensure good financial performance and strong project management.* Highly satisfactory pollution abatement projects in Chile, Cyprus, Korea, and Mauritania have all been financially successful, mainly by being able to raise water, effluent, and sewer tariffs to the levels required for financial self-sufficiency. In some projects, however, political pressures have impeded utility agencies from adjusting tariffs to the necessary levels. State government fiscal problems that resulted in delays in counterpart funding and procurement have jeopardized the performance of industrial and urban pollution abatement projects in Brazil and China. Fragmented project management has also been a problem in some cases—in China and Egypt, for example—because the large number of participating provincial and municipal agencies has meant that no single entity has an integrated and comprehensive picture of the project's progress. One of the ways in which the Bank is taking up the challenge of improving implementation performance of the environmental portfolio is by providing guidance to regions and borrowers for social assessment. Social assessment is both a tool and a process. As a tool, it identifies, prioritizes, and addresses key social issues that affect Bank lending and that, in the past, have often been dealt with on a fragmentary or ad hoc basis. As a process, it facilitates getting key stakeholders, such as directly affected local groups, NGOs, private companies, and government agencies, involved in project design and implementation; it strengthens institutional capacity to sustain project investments after completion; and it builds consensus for the selection of projects and their components by creating a participatory process of public consultation. It is the process elements of social assessments that reinforce these lessons on how to improve project performance as the Bank and borrowers seek to foster ownership and local community involvement and create a consensus for change.

- *Ensure flexibility in design and operation.* In most of the more marginal regions, especially semi-arid areas, local populations are attempting to manage the resource base under conditions of great economic and social (and sometimes climatic) change. In these circumstances their success will be dependent on their ability to adapt their use patterns and practices to the changing circumstances. The OED review of three pastoral livestock projects in the Central African Republic, Niger, and Senegal indicated the importance of flexible project design and of continued monitoring and evaluation to ensure the continuing relevance of a project's activities. A rigid project blueprint may be rapidly overtaken by events.

Creating Partnerships

International cooperation on environmental policy has become an increasingly vital part of the Bank's work program. This includes links with other agencies and with NGOs and local groups on the Bank's internal policies and project quality. Below are a few examples of recent cooperative activities.

Conference on Environmentally Sustainable Development

Since 1993 the Bank has sponsored an annual Conference on Environmentally Sustainable Development. The first of these conferences addressed the issue of "Valuing the Environment," and the second looked at the "Human Face of the Urban Environment." The third annual World Bank Conference on Environmentally Sustainable Development, to be held in Washington, D.C. on October 4 to 6, 1995, will be the first international gathering calling together members of all stakeholder communities in development and the environment, bringing key opinion- and policymakers in the private and public sectors, investment, international development, and NGOs to the same table to discuss "Effective Financing of Environmentally Sustainable Development." The conference will consist of a series of panels and roundtables addressing such topics as the emerging partnerships between the public and private sectors. Industry leaders and NGOs will examine the latest corporate actions for promoting green technologies and will explore the scope for practices that are both environmentally responsible and financially profitable. Finance and environment ministers will discuss government leadership, emphasizing actions needed to attain environmentally sustainable development objectives through fiscal, monetary, and trade and pricing policies at the national, regional and local levels, as well as financial issues in the context of national environmental action plans and other national strategies. In addition, associated events will be held that address natural resource accounting, environmental indicators, health and the environment in sustainable human development, ethics and spiritual values, and the promotion of environmentally sustainable development. These events will engage other organizations, including the Earth Council, the World Wildlife Fund, the Pan American Health Organization, and the Center for Respect of Life and Environment.

Interagency Activities

Within the United Nations system, the Bank is collaborating on international environmental policy through the United Nations Commission on Sustainable Development and the Inter-Agency Committee on Sustainable Development. In particular, the Bank has provided input and expert advice on the issues of financing for sustainable development, with senior environmental managers attending expert working group meetings as well as the third annual meeting of the commission.[6] In addition, the Bank and the UNDP are launching a major initiative to address issues related to water, described in box 1.9.

Bilateral Collaboration

Over the last three years, bilateral agencies' commitment to the Bank's environmental work has increased, as is indicated by a dramatic increase in trust fund commitments. Together, bilateral and consultant trust fund commitments for environmental initiatives increased 64 percent during the past year alone—from $188 million to $308 million, all for borrower-executed activities. Bilateral assistance financed 40 percent of the work of the Bank's Environment Department, enabling the operation of the GEF coordination unit and providing vital inputs to work on issues of natural resource management and international waters.

The Bank continues to receive a significant share of bilateral support through consultant trust funds. Donors maintain some six consultant trust funds specially earmarked for environmental purposes. During the last fiscal year, for example, Canada, the Netherlands, Norway, and Sweden replenished general environment trust funds; Norway and Sweden also replenished trust funds set up exclusively for environmental work in Eastern Europe and environment-related technical assistance activities.

Nongovernmental Organizations

The Bank's operational collaboration with NGOs has increased significantly in recent years, and the environment has been one of the leading sectors of this collaboration. Although NGO involvement in environmental issues and projects extends throughout the project cycle, an increasing number of NGOs are involved in the early stages (identification and design) of the project cycle. One such example is Egypt's Matruh Natural Resource Management Project, in which NGOs provided crucial background information on social and environmental conditions during the identification mission. At the design stage, NGO involvement in the assessment of potential environmental and social impacts has helped to ensure that the views of people who will be directly affected by projects are taken into account. For example, in Pakistan's Balochistan Natural Resource Management Project, NGOs are working with local communities to prioritize and develop an action plan to overcome community problems, while involving the communities in the design and management of natural resource development. Consultation with NGOs during the environmental assessment process has also improved project design. In Argentina's Yacireta II Project, an NGO helped to identify mitigation measures not anticipated by the EA team, which led to the creation of protected habitats. In some cases, NGOs have been contracted to conduct EAs themselves.

Box 1.9. Global Water Partnership

Water scarcity and water pollution increasingly jeopardize the lives of millions of people in developing countries. The crisis will worsen unless countries improve their management of this essential and precious resource. Fortunately, an international consensus has emerged on the fundamental principles for improving water management. These principles have been endorsed at conferences on water and the environment in Dublin and Rio de Janeiro, both in 1992. They include the following:

- Water is a scarce resource and should be treated as both a social and an economic good.
- Water should be managed at the lowest appropriate level, using demand-based approaches and involving stakeholders, particularly women, in decisionmaking.
- Water should be managed within a comprehensive framework, taking cross-sectoral considerations into account.

An Invitation. Calls for improved approaches have been coming both from individual countries and from the international community. In response, the UNDP and the World Bank invite other partners to join in the establishment of a Global Water Partnership that would support more coherent and integrated approaches in the years ahead. The partnership aims to achieve a dual objective: to support country-level activities adopting internationally endorsed principles and to bring a global perspective to these activities. The scope of many of the challenges is clear, but the final design of the partnership is yet to be determined. Consultations will be held to bring together key participants from developing countries and the international community to plan the partnership

The partnership would consolidate the existing UNDP–World Bank programs and bring together key partners, not just from water supply and sanitation, but from irrigation, the environment, and other subsectors. It would help pool resources for upstream development, thereby contribut-

Another important trend is the increased involvement of NGOs in the Bank's economic and sector work. In the environmental field, NGOs participate in the preparation of national environmental action plans. In Guinea, the government officially designated a national NGO (Guinée Ecologie) to prepare the country's NEAP, and in Burkina Faso, NGOs are drafting the NEAP together with the government.

In the area of policy dialogue, increasing numbers of consultations with a broader range of organizations have been held during the last several years. Starting in February 1994, the Vice Presidency for Environmentally Sustainable Development established a regularized meeting to more effective country-level programs and projects. It would also identify strategic gaps and develop tools, expertise, and specialized programs to address them. More effective use of water will occur as the result of actions at all levels. The partnership will provide knowledge and assistance and help countries make the critical linkages necessary to bring about often difficult reforms. The partnership will start with the field structure of the UNDP–World Bank Water and Sanitation Program but will later expand the scope of services, activities, and products in response to demand.

Features of the Global Water Partnership. The partnership will have four main features:

- *Integrated programs at the regional and national levels.* The key to success of the Partnership will be its ability to promote and support high-quality, integrated programs at the regional and national levels that adopt the Dublin and Rio principles.
- *Capacity building.* Capacity building involves policies, institutions, and people. At the policy level, the partnership will help countries to improve the rules governing the water sector in its broadest context. The partnership will assist institutions in improving the ways in which they operate and collaborate. Training will be offered.
- *Sustainable investments.* The partnership will support the preparation and testing of innovative, integrated approaches to sustainable investments. A key concern will be planning projects that deal with competing demands for water from various user groups.
- *Global orientation for learning across frontiers.* The partnership's global orientation offers significant opportunities for learning across frontiers. The lessons from the regional, national, and local levels will be disseminated to target audiences through a variety of traditional and innovative, user-friendly mechanisms.

ing calendar with NGOs to discuss issues related to environmentally sustainable development and the environment. During late 1994 the Bank and the World Conservation Union (IUCN) conducted a series of meetings to review past collaboration between the two institutions and to guide a joint initiative to develop closer links and coordination on specific environmental policy issues and programs (box 1.10). In May 1994, many developing-country NGOs participated in a consultation to discuss the "Review of Implementation of the Forest Sector Policy" (World Bank 1994i), and a seven-country dissemination mission through Europe and Asia was undertaken to obtain feedback on the draft "World

Box 1.10. Building Links with the IUCN

Meetings held between the World Conservation Union (IUCN) and the World Bank this year resulted in an aide-mémoire designed to encourage the staff of each institution to explore new opportunities for collaboration. Although essentially different in their mission and mandates, the Bank and IUCN pursue several common and complementary objectives related to environmentally sustainable development. The IUCN's objective in this initiative is to provide its members and scientific networks active in 125 countries with opportunities to contribute to a policy program dialogue with the Bank and to benefit from the Bank's expertise on development issues. As a union of 68 states, 100 government agencies, and more than 600 NGOs, as well as a network of specialist commissions drawing together more than 5,000 scientists and practitioners, IUCN represents a major resource in conservation and sustainable development. Examples of this collaboration include the joint production of a report on a global system of marine protected areas identified by eighteen regional IUCN working groups, a review of best-practice experiences in ecosystem management, and project specific cooperation in a number of countries. Other issues on which joint initiatives are under way include social policy, biodiversity, national environment strategies, and debt swaps, which have brought the expertise and networks associated with each institution into closer contact.

Bank Participation Sourcebook" (World Bank 1995n) from donor agencies, government officials, NGOs, and members of the academic community. In 1995 the NGO working group of the World Bank held regional meetings in Colombia, Ethiopia, and India in order to extend consultation to a larger group of NGOs from different parts of the world. Throughout fiscal 1995 the Bank organized workshops with NGOs in Argentina, Colombia, Tanzania, and Washington, D.C. on the Bank's activities to encourage their active participation in the Bank's operations. At the same time, a task force, comprised of NGO representatives and Bank staff, was established to identify and address obstacles to Bank-NGO collaboration at the operational level. To assist task managers in better understanding the benefits and challenges of working with NGOs, the Bank's Operations Policy Department published a practical guide entitled "Working with NGOs" (World Bank 1995m), which identifies key issues for successful collaboration with NGOs.

Notes

1. For information on the identification of World Bank Environmental Projects and Components, see annex B.

2. Two projects in the first group of seventy and one in the second group were closed or canceled during the last year (see annex C).

3. World Bank members of OECS are Antigua and Barbuda, the Commonwealth of Dominica, Grenada, St. Kitts and Nevis, St. Lucia, and St. Vincent and the Grenadines. The OECS, which also includes Montserrat (not a Bank member) was formed in 1968 as a common market that falls within the Caribbean Community (CARICOM), a thirteen-country regional organization.

4. In East Africa, for example, natural resource management–related operations under preparation include projects involving rural community funds in Ethiopia, Kenya, and Uganda, river basin management in Kenya and Tanzania, arid land management in Kenya, and protected areas in Uganda, in addition to a GEF-supported regional environmental project for Lake Victoria, involving water hyacinth control, fisheries management, pollution management, and monitoring of wetlands and water quality in rivers and streams feeding into lakes in Kenya, Tanzania, and Uganda.

5. A similar project, the National Parks Management Project, approved in November 1993, was withdrawn in June 1994 because the Venezuelan government had not signed the loan.

6. In the forestry sector the Bank is cooperating with the Food and Agriculture Organization (FAO), the UNDP, and other United Nations organizations through the Forestry Advisors Group, the United Nations Interagency Committee on Sustainable Development in Support of the Open-Ended Intergovernmental Panel on Forests—which was established by the 1995 Conference on Sustainable Development—and direct talks on technical support and in-country cooperation.

2. The Regional and Global Environment

ANDREW YIM

Support for Thailand's promotion of demand-side management in the electricity sector is one example of GEF-supported activities to stabilize greenhouse gas concentrations at a level that would prevent dangerous changes in the climate. Aided by a grant of $9.5 million, the Promotion of Electricity Energy Efficiency Project aims to build institutional capacity in the Electricity Generating Agency of Thailand (EGAT) and to support the development and adoption of energy efficiency programs. One of these programs, out of five launched, aims at encouraging the use of high-efficiency fluorescent tubes, as shown in this public education parade in Sukothai Province. Energy savings might be as high as 1,400 megawatts, or about 10 percent of EGAT's installed capacity, instead of the originally estimated 240 megawatts.

Pursuing poverty alleviation and environmentally sustainable development successfully at the national level depends on preserving the regional and global commons, such as the atmosphere and climate, the diversity of genetic resources and ecosystems, and internationally shared water resources. Although actions need to be taken locally, and should be part of national development strategies and programs, problems that traverse national borders often need to be addressed cooperatively with other nations. For instance, this is true in the case of transboundary water resources, where efforts to preserve quality of water and ecosystems related to such resources require regional solutions to address global concern for sustainable use of water resources.

The challenge for the Bank is to work with governments to ensure that regional and global objectives are integrated into national environment and development policies. The Bank seeks to do this, on the one hand, through its own regular lending programs; for example, in the area of biodiversity conservation, the Bank's support is considerable (see chapter 1). On the other hand, the Bank is the implementing agency of two important global financing mechanisms: the GEF and the Multilateral Fund for the Montreal Protocol (MFMP). Both facilities are designed to transfer resources in such a way as to enable governments to address global environmental concerns that otherwise would be neglected and to assist countries in complying with the provisions of international conventions or protocols that target global environmental problems. These global mechanisms are described in the second part of this chapter, along with efforts to assist developing-country partners in addressing global concerns. The first part addresses regional environmental concerns.

Regional Freshwater, Coastal, and Marine Programs

A majority of the world's people, including many of the poorest, live along rivers and coastlines. As a result, aquatic ecosystems are among the most threatened environments. In the past year, the Bank continued its work of integrating the management of these complex areas into mainstream development planning. Various programs have successfully leveraged assistance to support planning, investment, institutional strengthening, and training. Increased emphasis is being placed on the exchange of lessons learned between the fully operational programs, such as those in the Mediterranean and the Baltic, and newer initiatives, such as those in the Caspian and Red seas. The Bank, supported by GEF financing, also initiated work on management of a series of tropical and temperate lakes, including Lake Malawi and Lake Victoria, which will be the subject of a strategy study to be issued in the near future.

Mediterranean Sea

The Mediterranean Technical Assistance Program (METAP), a program of the EU, the European Investment Bank (EIB), and the UNDP, has since its launching in 1990 made available nearly $30 million in financial support to over 100 activities in the Mediterranean region.[1] As of early 1995 these activities identified or influenced environmental investment projects in the region valued at over $1.4 billion and provided over 5,000 person-days of training on topics that included coastal environmental impact assessment, environmental negotiation and mediation, and environmental communications. METAP has also launched and supported innovative and action-oriented partnerships through its regional networks: the Mediterranean Coastal Cities Network (MEDCITIES), the Mediterranean Protected Areas Network, and the Mediterranean Water Agencies Network.

An external evaluation of the first cycle of METAP's activities found the program highly innovative, achieving results that exceeded the relative magnitude of limited resources. The evaluation also challenged the program to evolve and develop a demand-responsive regional framework through a regional consultative process. METAP partners are now collaborating to launch a new phase of METAP in early 1996 emphasizing a demand-driven approach, broadening the scope of METAP support to include the development of project preparation capacity, and decentralizing some METAP programs and functions in the region. This new phase will focus on taking sustained action on a number of specific environmental investments in the region; increasing environmental management capacity, focusing on monitoring, enforcement, and participation; and establishing and strengthening partnerships with the private sector and NGOs.

Baltic Sea

This year the Baltic Sea Environment Program moved into a phase of active investment in priority actions by the Bank and a wide range of other financial institutions and donors. Cofinancing of projects, particularly with support from the European Union and the Nordic countries, has accelerated actions in many countries. A description of recent Bank activities is provided in box 2.1.

Danube River Basin

The Bank-supported Environmental Program for the Danube River Basin recently completed a strategic action plan aimed at improving the

Box 2.1. Baltic Sea Environment Program

An example of the value of regional programs in promoting a comprehensive regional approach to environmental management is provided by the Baltic Sea Environment Program. The Bank has developed a strong portfolio of complementary projects, with seven program-related projects, either approved or scheduled for approval by the end of 1995, at a cost of $240 million. It is anticipated that they will be complemented by three additional major projects in Poland. Further projects are being developed in Belarus, Estonia, Latvia, Lithuania, the Russian Federation, and Ukraine. The four approved Bank projects are the following:

Estonia—The Haapsalu and Matsalu Bays Environment Project ($8.4 million). Provides support for strengthening the Haapsalu water and wastewater utility, a demonstration program for control of nonpoint source pollution from agriculture and rural settlements, and implementation of the master plan for Matsalu State Nature Reserve.

Latvia—The Liepaja Environment Project ($21.2 million). Provides support for strengthening the Liepaja water and wastewater utility, a comprehensive management plan for adjacent coastal areas and wetlands, and development of nature-based tourism on the Baltic coast of Latvia.

Lithuania—The Klaipeda Environment Project ($23.1 million). Provides support for strengthening the Klaipeda water and wastewater utility, a comprehensive management plan for the Kursiu Lagoon, coastal zone management, and development of nature-based tourism.

Russian Federation—The Housing Project ($20.0 million for component). Includes a major component for upgrading the water and wastewater services in the northern portion of St. Petersburg, including investment for completion of the Northern Wastewater Treatment Plant and extension of the wastewater collection network.

The World Wide Fund for Nature is undertaking locally based programs, as an integral element of these projects, for the management of Matsalu Bay in Estonia, a Ramsar Convention site; Lake Pape and the town of Jurkalne in Latvia; and the Kursiu Lagoon and Nemunas River Delta in Lithuania. Complementary project activities include integrated coastal zone management plans for the Baltic coast of Latvia and Lithuania.

---

quality and availability of water in the Danube Basin and reducing the negative impact of human activities on the basins and the Black Sea's ecosystems. The plan is organized around collaborative efforts on the part of the Bank and other development organizations aimed at ensuring follow-up actions at identified hot spots. One of the most promising results of the program is the Convention on Cooperation for the Protection and Sustainable Use of the Danube River, signed in June 1995, along with investments supporting wastewater treatment systems in hot spots in Bulgaria, Hungary, and Romania; studies on the negative effects of Moldova's agriculture sector on the water quality of the Danube and its tributaries and how best to negate these effects; and management training for municipal water authorities in the Danube Basin. A complementary GEF-funded Danube Delta Biodiversity Program between Romania and Ukraine links the Danube River and Black Sea Environment Programs and provides an opportunity to develop a model for cooperative management and restoration of delta ecosystems.

Black Sea

The Bank continues its commitment to the Black Sea Environment Program, which provides the sea's coastal countries—Bulgaria, Georgia, Romania, the Russian Federation, Turkey, and Ukraine—with a solid basis for developing long-term policies and investment programs. Jointly funded by the Bank, the GEF, the European Bank for Reconstruction and Development, and several bilateral donors, support for investment operations in the region continues to come from the Urgent Investment Portfolio developed last year, which has direct links to current Bank project development activities. These activities include an $18 million Municipal Services Project in Georgia; a survey of the Black Sea coast to identify potential areas for sustainable aquaculture; creation of national and regional integrated coastal zone management networks and plans of action; and publication of a booklet on the Black Sea wetlands that resulted in a grant to help preserve them. In fiscal 1995 the Bank also began a collaborative effort with participating country governments to prepare a Black Sea environmental priorities plan to address regional investment priorities, on the macro scale, for dealing with the environmental problems of the Black Sea.

Aral Sea

Following their independence, the Aral Sea Basin republics—Kazakhstan, the Kyrgyz Republic, Tajikistan, Turkmenistan, and Uzbekistan—requested assistance from the international community in addressing the crisis in the Aral Sea Basin. Because of the rapid expansion of irrigated agriculture, the Aral Sea has shrunk in size, and the result has been the loss of fisheries, extensive pollution, human health problems, and salt and dust storms. In cooperation with the UNDP and

UNEP, the World Bank helped to prepare a plan of action to mitigate the impacts of environmental degradation, to develop sustainable water management strategies, and to develop regional institutions with the capacity to implement the Aral Sea Basin Program. Following endorsement of the program by the five heads of state, as well as the international community of donors and NGOs, seven priority programs (consisting of nineteen projects) were identified. Program preparation has begun with commitments of $31 million on grant terms from the donor community, as well as from the basin states, and implementation is expected to begin early in 1996.

Institution building is a cornerstone of the program, and the heads of state established two apex institutions, one to serve as a management organization, the other to operate as a financing institution. Additional technical institutions—including an Ecology Commission as well as individual technical groups supporting each program component—are also in place and actively involved in program implementation. The capacity-building efforts are proceeding favorably, aided with substantial support from GEF project preparation funds from the pilot phase, UNDP, and other donors. The individual projects are moving forward steadily, particularly the regional water resources management strategy, which is in many ways the centerpiece of the entire program. Also advancing are the water quality improvement projects; a wetlands restoration project; a drainage project; studies in biodiversity, salt and dust, and limnology and climate change; and the water supply, sanitation, and health projects in Kazakhstan, Turkmenistan, and Uzbekistan.

Red Sea and Gulf of Aden

In the Red Sea and Gulf of Aden, where an exceptionally high level of endemism is found in coral reef systems, and where environmental degradation is still largely limited to areas of intensive coastal development and offshore oil production and transport, the timely introduction of preventive measures is regarded as a highly cost-effective approach to reducing future risks of major environmental impacts. Within this context, the Bank, in collaboration with its GEF partners, the UNDP and UNEP, recently embarked on a regionally coordinated strategic action program for protecting and managing the Red Sea and Gulf of Aden. The initiative aims to support the Program for the Environment of the Red Sea and the Gulf of Aden (PERSGA), established by the Jeddah Convention. PERSGA seeks to identify priority actions for protecting and managing the region's international waters and coastal ecosystems and to facilitate their implementation by cooperating governments.

Caspian Sea

In response to a recent initiative of the Caspian Sea littoral governments, the Bank is collaborating on development of an environmental program for the Caspian Sea. The proposed program aims to develop a comprehensive long-term strategy for protecting and managing the Caspian environment and will be modeled after the existing regional sea and river basin programs mentioned above. Building institutional capacity at the national and regional levels will be an important focus of the program, along with developing national policies to reduce the pollution load of the Caspian Basin with clearly defined priorities for establishing a system of regional monitoring, protecting biodiversity, improving management of coastal zone and wetland areas, and developing a regional system for the self-financing of management requirements.

Lake Victoria

The Lake Victoria Environmental Management Program is the first major international lake management initiative undertaken by the Bank, and is supported by GEF funding. Discussions to broaden regional cooperation covering the Lake Victoria Basin were initiated in late 1992 by Kenya, Tanzania, and Uganda. In May 1994 the three governments decided to enter into an agreement to undertake the program jointly. Addressing a complex set of managerial, scientific, technical, and institutional issues, the program will provide the three nations with necessary skills, information, technical and financial resources, and the institutional and legal framework to successfully manage fisheries, pollution, and land use in the wetland and catchment and will strengthen the national institutions required to support regional institutions in implementing the program. The program will provide the basis for national investment programs and projects related to managing the resources of the Lake Victoria Basin.

New Global Marine Initiatives

In addition to its work on a regional scale, the Bank also supports a number of global initiatives for coastal and marine resources management. The Bank has supported, in cooperation with the Great Barrier Reef Marine Park Authority of Australia and the World Conservation Union (IUCN), preparation of *A Global Representative System of Marine Protected Areas* (World Bank, IUCN, and Great Barrier Reef Marine Park Authority 1995), which identifies important areas for conservation and provides a framework for management actions (see box 2.2). The Bank

Box 2.2. Development of a Global Representative System of Marine Protected Areas

The Bank has supported, in cooperation with the Great Barrier Reef Marine Park Authority of Australia and the IUCN, the preparation of a four-volume study and accompanying map entitled *A Global Representative System of Marine Protected Areas* (World Bank, IUCN, and Great Barrier Reef Park Authority 1995). This study is the culmination of work by the marine working groups of the IUCN's Commission on National Parks and Protected Areas to provide a systematic basis for developing a global system of marine protected areas (MPAs) to conserve representative examples of the world's rich marine biodiversity. Within a biogeographic classification scheme developed for each of the world's eighteen marine regions, the study maps show all marine protected areas around the world.

Among the study's major findings is that in most marine regions, the existing system of MPAs is not adequate to ensure the protection and management of the marine biodiversity within that region. Many MPAs are threatened by activities outside their boundaries, including land-based sources of pollution and habitat conversion, that are beyond the control of existing management. The need for integrated coastal zone management as a larger framework for establishing and managing MPAs is therefore critical. Of the 155 sites identified as being of regional priority for the conservation of marine biodiversity, nearly half are already designated as MPAs but are essentially "paper parks" without adequate support to meet their management objectives.

The study identifies major gaps in the biogeographic representation of marine biodiversity within this global system of MPAs and makes recommendations about how to fill these gaps. Using a comprehensive set of ecological, socioeconomic, and feasibility criteria, the commission working groups identified priority sites at the national and regional levels for the establishment of new protected areas as well as for existing MPAs in urgent need of management support to meet their conservation objectives. Through this systematic analysis, the study provides strategic guidance to the Global Environment Facility, multilateral financial institutions, and other donors for investments in the conservation of marine biodiversity. The highest priority will be in the development phase of the global MPA initiative beginning in January 1996.

has agreed to contribute core administrative resources to the project development phase of this initiative, which plans to prepare at least two priority marine protected area projects for GEF and other assistance in each of the next two years. The Bank is also an active member of the International Coral Reef Initiative and has an advisory role on the executive planning committee (see box 2.3).

Box 2.3. The International Coral Reef Initiative: Protecting the "Forests of the Sea"

The Bank is a partner in the International Coral Reef Initiative (ICRI) and has an advisory role on the Executive Planning Committee. The initiative grew out of recognition that coral reefs are in serious decline globally, and, in contrast to the momentum now building to save the world's tropical forests, efforts to conserve coral reefs, and the outstanding marine biodiversity and life-support functions they maintain, are inadequate. The ICRI focuses on four major objectives: improved coastal management, capacity building, research and monitoring to inform management decisions, and periodic review of the efficacy of interventions to manage coral reefs sustainably. Addressing these issues, a global partnership among coral reef nations and international organizations is being forged to conserve the world's coral reef ecosystems.

As part of its support for ICRI, the Bank sponsored a Workshop on Sustainable Financing Mechanisms for Coral Reef Conservation in June 1995. Consistent with the objectives of ICRI, the Bank is supporting preparation of the proposed Coral Reef Rehabilitation and Management Project (COREMAP) in Indonesia, which will be presented for GEF assistance in 1996. The project will improve the use and conservation of coral reefs and related ecosystems in a variety of sites throughout the Indonesian archipelago—the epicenter of the world's marine biodiversity. Because human activities are the primary cause of coral reef degradation, the project focuses on mechanisms to encourage more sustainable use of coral reef ecosystems through economic incentives, including ecoenterprises and alternative livelihoods for reef-dependent communities; through enhanced regulatory and enforcement capabilities; and through management information networks, increased public awareness, and policy and institutional reforms that support these efforts. Community-based management will be the principal focus and operational modality of the project.

The Global Environment

Ratification of the U.N. Framework Convention for Climate Change (FCCC), the Convention on Biological Diversity (CBD), and the Desertification Convention demonstrated countries' commitment to the global environmental concerns expressed at UNCED.[2] Since then, GEF has been confirmed as the operating entity of the respective FCCC and CBD conventions, and it will remain the interim funding mechanism for both (see box 2.4). Under convention terms, only developing countries that have ratified the document are eligible for GEF funding. As one of three implementing agencies for the GEF, the Bank is able to expand its program that provides grant resources and concessional funding to developing countries. In addition, the Bank is one of four implementing agencies for the MFMP, established in 1991 as the financial mechanism for the Montreal Protocol on Substances That Deplete the Ozone Layer, which assists developing countries to institute measures that eliminate the production and consumption of ozone-depleting substances.

Bank Funding for the Global Environment

While the GEF- and MPMF-funded assistance that the Bank channels to developing countries plays a catalytic role in integrating the global and national environmental dimensions of sustainable development in the Bank's country assistance, in dollar terms it represents a small proportion of overall Bank assistance for global environment conservation. In lending terms, from fiscal 1988 to fiscal 1995, Bank assistance for biodiversity apart from GEF topped $500 million. The cumulative value of the portfolio, which includes client governments and other donor contributions for biodiversity in the same projects, is approximately $860 million. Between fiscal 1992 and fiscal 1995 the GEF pilot phase brought an additional $237 million to bear on biodiversity issues. Of that total, $182 million were from GEF grants, with the remaining $55 million from client governments and other donors. Finally, the Pilot Program to Conserve the Brazilian Rainforest approved $161 million in assistance in fiscal 1995; $37 million from the Bank-administered Rain Forest Trust Fund, $103 million from bilateral cofinanciers, and $21 million from Brazilian counterparts.

The Bank, GEF, and Brazilian Rainforest Trust Fund together represent a total Bank-managed biodiversity portfolio of $1.26 billion. The Bank's IDA and IBRD biodiversity assistance is typically incorporated into broader projects for natural resources management, environmental institution building, or pollution prevention. Therefore, the total value of the Bank's environmental portfolio includes the $500 million mentioned above.[3]

It is also arguable that most Bank assistance for energy sector development is supportive of the climate convention in that it leads to improved economic efficiency and hence more efficient use of resources and lower greenhouse gas emissions per unit of energy consumption. In addition, the Bank's direct support for supply- and demand-side efficiency is growing, as is its support for renewable energy sources, particularly under the aegis of the Bank's new Solar Initiative. As the Bank begins to address the global environment impact of other real sector development and macroeconomic reform, its development assistance

Box 2.4. Global Environmental Conventions—Recent Developments

United Nations Framework Convention for Climate Change (FCCC). The FCCCs goal is to stabilize atmospheric greenhouse gas concentrations at a level that prevents dangerous human interference with the climate system. The convention has now been ratified by 136 countries. At the first meeting of the Conference of the Parties, held in Berlin in March 1995, the main question was the adequacy of current commitments of member states to achieve the conventions main goal. In response, the agreed Berlin Mandate starts a negotiation process, to be concluded by 1997, to set limitation and reduction objectives for greenhouse gases within a specified time frame. On the subject of joint implementation, wherein one country can contract for an emissions reduction in another country, the agreement calls for a pilot phase to be established, with participation open to all interested countries. Finally, this agreement paves the way for the Bank to meet requests, including those from private investors, for expanded Bank and GEF financing of joint implementation activities.

The Convention on Biological Diversity. The Convention on Biological Diversity calls for the conservation of biological diversity, the sustainable use of its components, and the fair and equitable sharing of the benefits arising from its use. As of April 5, 1995, it had been ratified by 117 countries and the European Union. The first meeting of the conference of the parties to the Convention on Biological Diversity was held in Nassau, The Bahamas, in late 1994. The meeting highlighted the need for both enabling activities and investment projects and provided a list of program priorities and eligibility criteria. These priorities include the following:

- Developing integrated national strategies and projects that address national priorities
- Strengthening conservation, management, and sustainable use of ecosystems, habitats (especially marine and coastal), and arid and semiarid lands and mountain ecosystems
- Identifying and monitoring wild and domesticated biodiversity
- Investing in capacity building, technology transfer, and development
- Involving local and indigenous people
- Conserving and sustaining the use of endemic species
- Promoting sustainable benefits and providing access to other national, international, and private sector efforts.

programs should be increasingly supportive of improved management of the global environment.

Although the Bank's level of funding for global environmental issues is clearly significant, perhaps of greater importance is its role as an

Using this guidance the Bank has been able to assist countries in preparing national strategies and action plans and a range of investment priorities.

The Desertification Convention. The Desertification Convention seeks to mobilize international action on desertification, relying on national, bilateral, and multilateral funding sources to support the implementation of national action programs. As of July 1995, 105 countries had signed the convention, which is expected to enter into force by mid-1996. In addition to the main convention and its four regional annexes, the negotiating committee agreed on two resolutions: an interim arrangement before the convention enters into force and an urgent action program for Africa, both of which have since been approved by the U.N. General Assembly. The next meeting of the Negotiating Committee, scheduled for August 1995, is expected to formulate concrete recommendations on two outstanding issues: the establishment of the convention's Permanent Secretariat and selection of a global financial mechanism. The Bank has been actively supporting the negotiations of the convention. It sees its further role as working with member countries through policy dialogue and providing assistance in national and sectoral planning as well as investment programs and projects. This will involve examining existing national frameworks for environmental management (national environmental action plans and their equivalents) to address desertification issues, reorienting natural resource management projects to include desertification concerns, and supporting national and local capacity building in the field of desertification control.

In addition, under the auspices of the Middle East Peace Process Working Group on Environment, the Bank has been instrumental in facilitating preparation and launch in June 1995 of the Initiative for Collaboration to Control Natural Resource Degradation (Desertification) of Arid Lands in the Middle East (Desertification Initiative). The Bank is contributing Special Grants Program (SGP) grant funding of $1.8 million to this regional program, which includes the participation of Egypt, Israel, Jordan, Tunisia, and the West Bank and Gaza. The program, which is funded by a variety of donors, including the Intergovernmental Negotiating Committee (Desertification Convention) (INCD), will cost $12.6 million over three years. The Desertification Initiative is seen as the key subregional activity to launch the Desertification Convention in the Middle East and North Africa.

implementing agency for external sources of global environmental funding, which has helped to improve the quality and focus of Bank assistance regarding the global environment and to integrate global environmental concerns cost-effectively in Bank country assistance.

Administering Global Environment Funds

Over the last four years, GEF and the MFMP have emerged as important instruments for enabling developing countries to address global environmental concerns. Launched as a pilot activity in March 1991 (the first project was approved in May 1991), the GEF supports capacity building, research, and investment dealing with four global areas: climate change, biodiversity, international waters, and ozone layer protection, with assistance to land degradation mitigation consistent with other thematic areas.

In its pilot phase, the GEF committed 115 grants totaling $735 million to developing countries for projects and programs that address global environmental problems. The majority of these projects were designed to strengthen local institutions' capacity to address global environmental concerns or to test new technologies for reducing or containing global environmental degradation. Similarly, the Executive Committee of the MFMP has allocated $248 million for 283 investment projects (or subprojects) to phase out 52,000 tons of ozone-depleting substances.

Under the GEF, the Bank's role is to ensure that investment projects address each global environment area while catalyzing additional financing and actions toward sustainable development. In so doing, the Bank complements the work of the UNDP, which supports technical assistance and capacity building, and of UNEP, which provides expertise in environmental disciplines and supports research. Under the MFMP, the Bank, together with the UNDP, UNEP, and the United Nations Industrial Development Organization (UNIDO), assists developing countries in building development capacity and implementing specific actions aimed at reducing the production and consumption of ozone-depleting substances.

While the MFMP continues to operate under its original mandate and governance structure, GEF has undergone a transition from pilot to regular program. In March 1994, representatives of more than seventy countries reached an agreement to restructure GEF and replenish the trust fund at a level of $2 billion. The new GEF, the first replenishment of which is called GEF 1, provides for universal membership, greater transparency and participation in the conduct of its affairs, and assumption of the role of financial mechanism for the conventions on climate change and biodiversity. As in the pilot phase, the responsibility for implementing GEF-financed activities will continue to be shared by the Bank, the UNDP, and UNEP. Each agency will retain its pilot phase responsibility for investment, technical assistance and capacity building, and research activities, respectively. The Bank will continue to serve as trustee of the Global Environment Facility Trust Fund. The new governance structure includes an assembly of the representatives of all participating countries; a council, constituting the main body, composed of thirty-two representatives of constituencies of the participating governments; and a functionally independent secretariat headed by a chief executive officer who serves as chairperson of GEF.

Between July 1994 and May 1995, the council approved a new GEF project cycle; a Project Development and Preparation Facility that provides grants for, among others, project concept development and preinvestment work; the fiscal 1995 and 1996 GEF budgets; an approach for calculating incremental costs; and a work program of projects totaling $134 million, of which projects valued at $103 million will be managed by the Bank. In October 1995 the council is expected to approve a comprehensive operational strategy covering each focal area. Thus the Bank's GEF portfolio has grown to $557 million over the last four years. Simultaneously, its portfolio of investment projects under the MFMP has reached $87 million.

Channeling GEF Resources

The World Bank's GEF portfolio dates from May 1991 with the first pilot phase work program. As of the end of fiscal 1995, projects approved by the council for inclusion in the project pipeline included sixty-three projects totaling $557 million.[4] Fifty-two of these projects, worth $454 million in GEF grants, are from the pilot phase, and eleven new projects, totaling $103 million in GEF grants, have been approved by the GEF council for inclusion in the Bank's GEF portfolio.

The cumulative growth in projects approved by the GEF as they are allocated across thematic areas is shown in figure 2.1. Allocations vary considerably between regions, with the East Asia and the Pacific region leading with 26 percent of approved funds, followed by Eastern Europe at 22 percent, Latin America at 20 percent, South Asia at 12 percent, Africa at 11 percent, and Middle East and North Africa at 8 percent.

As shown in table 2.1 (and annex G), Bank and IFC managements approved a total of thirteen pilot phase projects during fiscal 1995 for a total GEF funding of $99.7 million. This brought the total number of GEF projects approved by the Bank and IFC to forty-four, with total grant funding of $380 million. Of the thirteen projects approved in fiscal 1995, six addressed biodiversity conservation, five climate change, one international waters protection, and one the phaseout of ozone-depleting substances. Two of the projects (the Peru and the Uganda Biodiversity Projects) established trust funds with private asset managers. In addition, the Poland Efficient Lighting Project was the first private sector GEF operation approved by the IFC. Processing of the remaining pilot phase

Figure 2.1. GEF Investment Portfolio Development, Overview

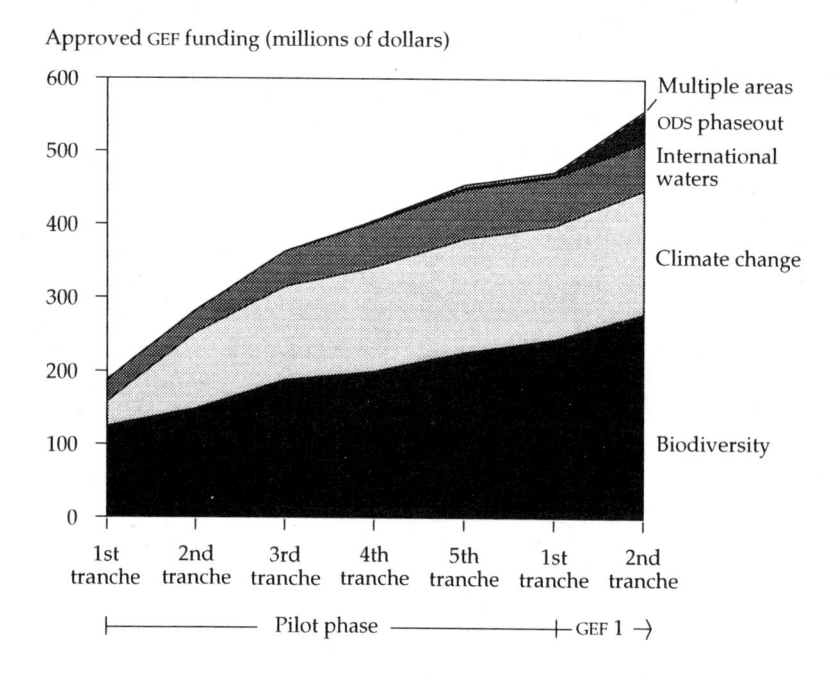

Approved GEF funding (millions of dollars)

Categories (top to bottom): Multiple areas, ODS phaseout, International waters, Climate change, Biodiversity

X-axis: 1st tranche, 2nd tranche, 3rd tranche, 4th tranche, 5th tranche (Pilot phase), 1st tranche, 2nd tranche (GEF 1)

projects is under way, with the last nine projects expected to be submitted for Bank approval during fiscal 1996.

Of the eleven new projects approved in fiscal 1995, five were in support of phasing out ozone-depleting substances in Eastern Europe and the Russian Federation, four were biodiversity conservation projects (China, India, Indonesia, and Mauritius), and two were climate change–related projects (adaptation to climate change in the Caribbean and reduction of greenhouse gas emissions in Lithuania).

The Bank emphasizes the importance of country-driven project preparation. To this end, the GEF recently began, under GEF 1, making preparatory funding available through GEF's Project Development Facility, and similar resources are available from UNDP's GEF Pilot Phase Pre-Investment Facility. By the end of June 1995, the aggregate approved funding under these arrangements had reached $22 million for forty-three projects. By the end of fiscal 1995, approximately 55 to 60 percent of all approved preparatory resources had been disbursed.

Table 2.1. GEF and MFMP Projects Approved by World Bank Group Management, Fiscal 1995
(millions of dollars)

Country	Project	Approved amount
GEF		
Cameroon	Biodiversity Conservation and Management Project	6.0
China	Nature Reserves Management Project	17.9
Czech Republic	Phaseout of Ozone-Depleting Substance Project	2.3
Malawi	SADC Lake Malawi/Nyasa Biodiversity Conservation Project	5.0
Mali	Household Energy Project	2.5
Morocco	Repowering of Power Plant Project	6.0
OECS countries	Ship-Generated Waste Management Project	12.5
Peru	Trust Fund for Parks and Protected Areas Project	5.0
Poland	Efficient Lighting Project (IFC)	5.0
	Coal-to-Gas Convention	25.0
Romania	Danube Delta Biodiversity Project	4.5
Tunisia	Solar Water Heating Project	4.0
Uganda	Conservation of the Bwindi Impenetrable National Park and the Mgahinga Gorilla National Park Project	4.0
Total		99.7
Montreal Protocol		
China	Ozone-Depleting Substances III Project	29.45
Egypt	MCMC Compressor Project (IFC)	2.1
India	Ozone-Depleting Substances I Project	1.25
	Ozone-Depleting Substances II Project	8.12
Indonesia	Ozone-Depleting Substances I Project	17.00
Philippines	Ozone-Depleting Substances I Project	11.73
Thailand	Ozone-Depleting Substances Phaseout I Project	12.5
Uruguay	Ozone-Depleting Substances I Project	1.23
Venezuela	Chiller Retrofits Project	0.25
	FAACA Project	3.1
Total		86.73

Funding under the GEF is based on countries' incurring costs for global environmental benefits incremental to those acceptable as part of regular national policies and programs. Hence it is natural for many GEF operations to be linked to Bank operations, with the latter providing nonincremental funding for baseline support of project implementation without GEF. Over the course of the pilot phase, 40 percent of Bank/GEF–supported projects (accounting for 60 percent of funds) were formally associated with Bank operations. GEF cofunding has led to significant policy gains, which have further increased the impact of GEF operations. Also, Bank-administered GEF funding generated additional funding from multilateral and bilateral donors, NGOs, and private foundations.

Evaluating and Improving GEF Performance

After two years of pilot phase operation, GEF participants initiated a process of independent evaluation conducted by the internal audit departments of the three implementing agencies and overseen by a panel representing GEF participants. On operational matters the evaluation identified, among others, the need to strengthen the strategic framework for GEF operations and ensure that the framework was country-driven and integrated GEF operations into sustainable development; to identify and consult effectively with local communities, NGOs, and other stakeholders; and to improve project-specific and GEF systemwide monitoring and evaluation. While the new GEF council has been active in establishing long-term overarching and thematic operational strategies for the GEF, and a systemwide approach to monitoring and evaluation, the Bank has been proactive in strengthening arrangements for social assessment and public participation and for monitoring and evaluation in each key global environment problem area.

Supporting the Montreal Protocol

World Bank Group–supported Multilateral Fund for the Implementation of the Montreal Protocol (MFMP) activities have grown to 24 projects (involving a total of 160 subprojects) in 20 developing countries, with a total funding of $145 million approved by the executive committee of the convention. Ten of these projects, costing $78 million, were approved by the Bank Group management in fiscal 1995. Project-related disbursements have grown from $900,000 in fiscal 1993 to $22.2 million as of June 30, 1995.

With a 55 percent share of MFMP investment projects, the Bank is active in all major sectors that consume ozone-depleting substances (aerosols, foams, refrigeration, fire protection, solvents, mobile air conditioning) and has taken the lead in both the aerosol and production sectors. All environment projects approved by Bank and IFC managements to date are listed and described in annex G. In addition, the average cost-effectiveness of phaseout in World Bank–supported projects is $3,630 per ozone-depleting potential ton as compared with the average for the MFMP of $4,750 per ozone-depleting potential ton.

The Bank Group's current portfolio of MFMP-supported investment projects will help phase out an additional 35,000 ozone-depleting potential tons of annual consumption over the next two years. Although progress on actual phaseout of ODS was initially slow, the recent upward trend is significant. Over 3,000 tons, more than three-quarters of the total phased out by all implementing agencies, have already been phased out, and this number will escalate to more than 10,000 tons by early next year, when large aerosol sector projects in China will be completed. Three innovative features of the Bank's MFMP program involve the use of umbrella grant agreements, the adoption of a sectoral approach to ODS phaseouts, and the use of market-based instruments. These features are discussed in box 2.5.

An independent evaluation of the MFMP found that the institutional framework of the financial mechanisms system of development, review, and approval of projects is successful in producing an increasing flow of ODS phaseout projects. In fact, the current set of projects in the pipeline exceeds the level of resources available to the fund. However, the main issue facing the MFMP is its ability to implement approved projects expeditiously. The independent study team offered recommendations aimed at improving the effectiveness of the mechanism, identifying priorities for improving implementation and monitoring of projects, taking a programmatic and strategic approach to project preparation and approval, and finding new ways of mobilizing financial resources.

The Bank's Assistance Strategy

Providing financial resources for individual investment projects to mitigate global environmental degradation is only one dimension of the Bank's strategy. Other elements central to this strategy include to

- Support governments, through enabling activities, in implementing their commitments to global environment conventions
- Assist countries in integrating global environmental objectives in national and sector policies and programs (mainstreaming the global environment)
- Leverage financial resources, including those of the private sector, to fund pollution abatement and global environment protection measures
- Work with client governments to ensure that local measures to help address global environmental problems involve stakeholders and the public and have their support
- Support systems for monitoring and evaluation that provide feedback on performance and progress under national action pro-

Box 2.5. New Approaches to ODS Phaseout

Umbrella grant agreements. In early 1993, the Bank developed umbrella grant agreements as a method of minimizing the legal formalities of processing projects while maintaining fiduciary responsibility. These agreements, made between countries eligible to receive Montreal Protocol resources and the Bank, establish the framework for transferring funds over a minimum two-to-three-year period. Before umbrella agreements, the Bank entered into sometimes lengthy negotiations with recipient governments for each set of subprojects submitted to the convention's Executive Committee for approval. This new arrangement saves significant time between Executive Committee approval and Bank commitment. Brazil was the first country to sign an umbrella grant agreement with the Bank. Umbrella agreements are now also in place with China, India, Indonesia, the Philippines, Thailand, and Uruguay and are in the final stages of negotiation in Argentina, Jordan, Malaysia, and Turkey.

Sectoral approach to ozone-depletion phaseout in a resource-constrained environment. With strong support from the Montreal Protocol Executive Committee, the Bank and the government of China have initiated work to develop a sector-based approach to ODS phaseout projects in fiscal 1996. This initiative will further reduce administrative and unit abatement costs; it will expedite phaseout by moving away from project-by-project approvals, compensating for sectorwide phaseout motivated at the enterprise level by policy and regulatory incentives, information on technology change, and declining costs. Enterprises would compete for further funds by bidding with low-cost ODS phaseout proposals, because it would become more expensive for them to continue to use ODS over time. Selection of and compensation for consuming enterprises will be made by governments instead of the Bank and Executive Committee.

Use of market-based instruments to support ozone-depleting substance phaseout. The Montreal Protocol project being implemented in Chile involves a flat compensation payment of $2 per kilogram of ozone-depletion phaseout. This approach captures the lowest-cost conversion projects and encourages enterprises to adopt low-cost phaseout options. Over time, higher compensation per kilogram of ozone-depletion phaseout will be offered until the phaseout is complete. This approach is easy to manage and minimizes administrative overhead because the Bank is not involved in enterprise phaseout decisions. A Bank study is under way to further evaluate the usefulness of market-based instruments in supporting a national ODS phaseout strategy.

grams and projects and help to improve the effectiveness of the Bank's own efforts to assist client governments.

SUPPORTING ENABLING ACTIVITIES. As parties to the global conventions, the governments of developing countries are committed to taking action on global environmental problems. To deliver on these commitments, they need to take preparatory measures such as inventories of resources and baseline surveys, compilation and analyses of existing information, analysis of policies, and preparation of national strategies and action plans. The Bank provides support for such enabling activities, including helping countries to build the required capacity to plan and implement programs and projects that address global environmental objectives.

In the area of climate change, the Bank has supported strategy formulation in China and the Caribbean. In China, the strategy includes evaluating emission reductions options in various subsectors and strategies for implementing least-cost abatement strategies; in the Caribbean, a study focused upon possible impacts of climate change on small island states and policy options for adaptation and appropriate capacity building.

With regard to biodiversity conservation, the Bank responded to requests for assistance from about twenty countries over the past year. These requests included incorporating global biodiversity into national strategic frameworks for environmental management, formulating national biodiversity conservation strategies and action plans, and undertaking sectoral biodiversity conservation programs and special studies. In China and Indonesia, where such studies have been completed, quick follow-up action was taken in the form of investments in priority areas for biodiversity conservation (see box 2.6).

Formulating an effective biodiversity strategy requires conserving representative areas of major habitat and ecosystems in all the world's biogeographic regions. Such protection will help to ensure not only conservation of the greatest number of species but also their long-term survival. An important Bank goal, therefore, is to help countries to develop and apply techniques for identifying and prioritizing areas for biodiversity conservation at the national level. One method is to use rapid appraisal of techniques and tools to collect and analyze data on biological resources and to bring scientific rigor to the selection of reserves and planning of land and coastal areas. In consultation with NGOs (including Conservation International and The Nature Conservancy), the Bank has commissioned a consortium of Australian institutions led by the Commonwealth Scientific Industrial Research Organization to adapt such tools and techniques for developing countries (see chapter 3). The first phase has resulted in guidelines and spatial modeling and mapping tools ready to be field tested in Papua New Guinea in Phase II.

MAINSTREAMING THE GLOBAL ENVIRONMENT. National strategies and action plans for biodiversity conservation or climate change are important steps in incorporating global environmental concerns at the country level. Yet important development decisions are also made at the sector

> **Box 2.6. Biodiversity Strategies Leading to Action**
>
> *Indonesia.* In 1991 the Bank helped the government of Indonesia to prepare a biodiversity strategy and action plan. The plan was developed under the auspices of a steering committee made up of representatives of government agencies and ministries concerned with biodiversity management, the World Bank, the World Wildlife Fund, local NGOs, and academic institutions. Workshops and consultations were held with provincial authorities, international NGOs, and the international donor community. The plan addressed institutional, legal, and regulatory frameworks and identified a number of projects and activities as national priorities. The government is now using the document to set priorities for international assistance for biodiversity conservation. Several of these priority activities have subsequently been funded by the donor community. For example, the GEF is providing support for the Indonesia Biodiversity Collections Project and the Kerinci-Seblat Integrated Conservation and Development Project, as well as partial support for a coral reef project being prepared. Other donors such as Japan, the European Union, the Asian Development Bank, and international NGOs are helping the government to forward priority projects identified in the plan.
>
> *China.* A similar process was undertaken in China involving national, provincial, and local government agencies; academic institutions; NGOs; and international experts. The China action plan identifies a range of activities as national priorities for conservation and sustainable use of biodiversity; many of these activities are consistent with China's obligations under the Convention on Biological Diversity. The plan has already facilitated approval of the China Nature Reserves Management Project, under which GEF support is provided to a number of conservation areas with globally significant biodiversity. Other priority projects are receiving assistance from donors, and the UNDP is preparing a wetlands project for future GEF funding.

level, where it is critical that global environmental concerns are likewise taken into account. This need is recognized by the Convention on Biological Diversity as well as by the Framework Convention for Climate Change.

In addition to its support for strategic and action planning in the areas of biodiversity and climate change, the Bank has begun extending sectoral policy analysis and planning into other areas of environmental concern.[5] These extensions, referred to as global overlays, typically involve three basic steps: first, an analysis of the causes, nature, and magnitude of the effects on the global environment caused by each sector management and development; second, an evaluation of how policies and institutions affect the global environs; and third, an examination of the cost-effectiveness of various investment options in mitigating the negative effects. Such an analysis initially focuses on actions that are in the country's own interest and that capture global environmental benefits (so-called win-win actions). Policies and measures for energy efficiency, for example, typically reduce fuel consumption and lower sulfur dioxide, nitrogen oxides, and particulate emissions. However, going beyond the win-win options implies incurring the incremental costs of additional global benefits, thereby justifying concessional international funding sources such as the GEF.

The Bank's activities concentrated on climate change. They focused on developing tools and methods to apply greenhouse gas accounting at the individual investment level, where the effects of global problems are important to project selection (see box 2.7). In addition the Bank has begun supporting countries that were applying climate change overlays in the energy (Mexico and Ukraine) and forestry (Argentina) sectors.

In following through on these early initiatives, the Bank is developing partnerships with other donor agencies and representatives of the NGO community with a view toward expanding the Bank's assistance to developing countries and making it more effective. The agenda is fourfold: developing analytical tools and methodologies beyond the area of climate change, mobilizing and increasing resources to meet country requests for global overlays, supporting the capacity-building requirements of mainstreaming, and monitoring and evaluating the effectiveness of the program.

In summary, the Bank is prepared to support client governments' efforts to mainstream the global environment through four avenues: first, at its macro level of country dialogue, particularly through its Country Assistance Strategies; second, through supporting client governments in implementing their commitments under the global environment conventions; third, through assisting client countries directly or through Bank economic and sector work; and finally, through project analysis, where it requires, wherever possible, that global externalities caused by the design or scale of proposed activities be measured in economic terms.

LEVERAGING FINANCIAL RESOURCES. The challenge of protecting the global commons has spurred new approaches for directing resource flows. In climate change, even the more optimistic engineering-economic abatement models predict that controlling global emissions of greenhouse gases will be expensive. Concerning biodiversity, cost estimates for protecting identified hot spots and other globally significant

Box 2.7. Tools and Early Applications in Global Environmental Analysis in Climate Change

Methodology development at the project level has progressed rapidly, aided in great measure by the standards developed by IPCC/OECD for greenhouse gas inventory work. Tools include the following:

- The "Greenhouse Gas Assessment Methodology" (Mintzer, von Hippel, and Kolar 1994), a personal computer-based tool for the quantification of greenhouse gas emissions resulting from various energy technologies
- A "Handbook on Greenhouse Gas Assessment Methodologies" (World Bank forthcoming a) for use by Bank project teams, which is expected to be completed in 1995.

Tracking *ex post* carbon emissions performance is a particular concern for Bank-GEF global warming investment projects, where new technology and implementation risks introduce abnormal uncertainties about operation in the field. For this purpose:

- A special greenhouse emissions reporting section has been promulgated for the Supervision Reports of Bank-GEF global warming projects
- Guidance on identifying and monitoring verifiable greenhouse gas performance indicators is found in the Bank and GEF "Greenhouse Gas Abatement Investment Project Monitoring and Evaluation Guidelines" (World Bank and GEF forthcoming).

At the sectoral level, methodology development has focused on laying the groundwork for *global overlays* for greenhouse gas mitigation. Global overlays, which integrate greenhouse gas emissions into regular Bank sectoral work, provide at least three important advantages: (a) analytical economies of scale and scope, (b) strengthened rationale for exploitation of "win-win" opportunities, and (c) identification of GEF project opportunities. Prototype overlays include the following:

- The completed "Ukraine Energy Options Global Environment Analysis," which built on the findings of a World Bank Energy Sector Review, identified the cost-effectiveness of four main mitigation options in the Ukrainian energy sector, and drew conclusions regarding the nature of incremental costs (positive or negative) for each of these options
- An ongoing "Argentina Forest Carbon Sink Enhancement Study," which examines the cost-effectiveness of carbon sequestration options in natural forest protection and timber plantations using different planting regimes
- An ongoing "Mexico Greenhouse Gas Study," which looks at greenhouse gas reduction with respect to power demand and supply-side options as well as efficiency improvements in the oil and gas sectors.

ecosystems are likewise expensive. Unfortunately, additional resources from official sources cannot fund all worthwhile emissions-reduction, biodiversity protection, ozone layer protection, and other global environment projects. Leveraging private sector technologies, management skills, and funds, as well as redirecting private sector capital flows to globally benign uses, can offset this gap. The World Bank Group, particularly its affiliate, the IFC, is well placed to mobilize private sector resources to respond to global environmental concerns. Box 2.8 highlights creative and high-leverage techniques being applied.

Joint implementation under the Framework Convention on Climate Change is another approach to stimulating private investment flows for global environmental needs. In this instance, parties in one or more countries contract with parties in another country to implement an activity that reduces greenhouse gas emissions. The contracting parties can then seek recognition or "credit" for these reductions in emissions.

To provide a practical demonstration of joint implementation, the Bank entered into a cofinancing agreement with Norway in 1992. The cofinancing grant provides support both for two GEF global warming projects—one in Mexico and one in Poland—and for analysis, in the context of these two projects, of some of the issues that could arise if projects like these were considered as possible vehicles for joint implementation under the Climate Change Convention.[6] The summary paper prepared by the Bank (Anderson 1995) describes four issues that arise in designing joint implementation projects: (a) determining the net abatement effect, (b) establishing the price or compensation due in payment for joint implementation projects, (c) identifying performance issues such as verification and treatment of risk, and (d) working through procedural issues, including the nature of contracts and records.

A second phase of this collaboration on joint implementation demonstration with the government of Norway is now under regulation for fiscal 1996–98, and is intended to simulate negotiations in a real-world context of joint implementation transactions, first between governments, and then between private sector industrial and developing country partners.

ENSURING LOCAL PARTICIPATION. GEF operations, and particularly biodiversity conservation projects, often involve complex participation issues. Guidelines for social assessment in Bank/GEF–supported biodiversity projects were issued in 1994 and are being completed for the other focal areas, such as climate change mitigation, international waters protection, and ozone layer protection. These guidelines are meant to alert project planners and managers to social factors that are central to the GEF mission and to social issues that may arise in the context of

> **Box 2.8. Multiplying GEF and MFMP Resources through Private Sector Leveraging**
>
> The competition for GEF grants is keen, and funds have to be apportioned among many projects. Using the GEF to leverage private sector capital helps to multiply rather than divide GEF funds. Examples include the following:
>
> - *Biodiversity Protection Trust Funds* offer a new alternative for combining public and private resources to cofinance conservation and sustainable use subprojects. Trusts can be structured to accept, manage, and disburse additional grants from a variety of sources, including domestic and international public and private foundations. Establishment of a trust may be contingent on contributions from these cofinancing sources, requiring the recipient government and partners to solicit donations. In Bhutan, recipient of the first of ten Bank/GEF-supported trust funds supporting conservation activities in thirteen countries, disbursement of initial funds to the trust was conditional on the trust's receiving matching contributions, and in Brazil, the last of the GEF pilot phase trust funds to be negotiated, GEF trust funds directly leverage private sector funding of biodiversity activities.
> - *Private Sector Financing of ODS Phaseout.* Private enterprises are the dominant users of ODS in both industrial and developing countries. They find themselves increasingly under pressure to respond cost-effectively to environmental expectations. Markets for their products are often global in nature as well as highly competitive. ODS conversion investments are frequently associated with modernization and plant expansion. Consequently, private companies often perceive ODS phaseout as an opportunity to improve products and performance.
>
> IFC interventions, such as the IFC/GEF Poland Efficient Lighting Project and the IFC/GEF Small and Medium-Scale Enterprises Project are discussed in chapter 7.

specific projects. They outline methods and tools for early identification of stakeholders (individuals or groups), for carrying out social analysis in the project cycle, and for increasing stakeholder participation.

To provide lessons from operational applications of social assessment and public participation under GEF-supported projects, the Bank is undertaking two review activities. First, a review of the treatment of stakeholder identification and participation in the GEF portfolio will provide baseline information for the development of an action plan for implementing the social assessment guidelines. Second, an in-depth structured learning study of three GEF biodiversity projects is under way. The study evaluates how well the social assessment guidelines for biodiversity projects are being applied, with the purpose of developing best practices for addressing social and participation issues in Bank- GEF operations.

The Bank has developed methodologies for monitoring and evaluating the effects of broad participation for biodiversity, climate change, and ozone reduction projects, and methodologies are nearly complete for international waters projects. These guidelines will provide the means of measuring the success of participatory processes for achieving the overall environmental and social goals of the projects.

STRENGTHENING MONITORING AND EVALUATION. The Bank recognizes the important role it will play in evaluating whether, and in what respects, initiatives to address global issues are working effectively. The time frame for addressing these issues and for monitoring effects and progress will extend beyond the Bank-defined project implementation period. Furthermore, monitoring and evaluation will require setting up systems and indicators meaningful for the diverse GEF constituencies. In response, guidelines have been developed to give methodological and technical support to task managers who will oversee the identification, design, and implementation of these elements in GEF-supported Bank operations.

In fiscal 1995, monitoring and evaluation guidelines were being prepared for the areas of international waters and ozone protection. Both are in final draft stage, with completion expected by the end of calendar year 1995. These complement guidelines issued earlier for biodiversity (December 1992) and greenhouse gas abatement projects (June 1994). Common to all Bank guidelines for its GEF portfolio is the emphasis on moving monitoring and evaluation from a "downstream" activity to its rightful place in early project design. Not only should this produce a better result and be more cost-effective, it will also focus project objectives and help to reconcile expectations for a project's success.

The next step is implementation of monitoring and evaluation guidelines for operations in global environment areas to review their effectiveness under applications by Bank teams and in-country counterparts, and to convert these initially GEF-linked guidelines to Bank-wide guidance for such operations, regardless of the source of project funding.

Notes

1. METAP, the Environmental Program for the Danube River Basin, and the Aral Sea Capacity Building Project are also funded through the Bank's Special Grants Program. This program is the Bank's instrument for contributing to programs that address significant global or regional development issues but are not suitable for Bank loans, IDA credits, or country-focused operational programs funded by the Bank's administrative budget.

2. The Bank has followed and supported these developments. At the Bahamas conference-of-parties meeting on the Biodiversity Convention (November–December 1994), the Bank presented a paper entitled "Implementing the Convention on Biological Diversity: toward a Strategy for World Bank Assistance" (World Bank 1995e). In connection with the FCCC conference-of-parties meeting in Berlin in March 1995, the Bank introduced a paper entitled "The World Bank and the U.N. Framework Convention on Climate Change" (World Bank 1995o). Similarly, the Bank outlined its role vis-à-vis implementation of the Desertification Convention in the document "Desertification: Implementing the Convention. A World Bank View" (World Bank 1994b).

3. The Land and Water Division of the World Bank Environment Department is completing a comprehensive analysis of cumulative direct and indirect Bank lending for biodiversity conservation, including GEF assistance.

4. The GEF council approves funding from the trust fund during the preparation of projects; the Bank approves projects once they are fully prepared.

5. The Bank's OP 10.04 on economic evaluation of investment operations states that global externalities are identified in sector analysis or environmental assessment work.

6. According to the terms of the bilateral cofinancing documents, the agreement of the governments of Mexico and Poland to Norwegian cofinancing of these two projects is in no way prejudicial to the positions they might take in relation to the role of joint implementation under the FCCC.

3. The Intellectual Journey

WORLD BANK PHOTO/CURT CARNEMARK

Since UNCED the Bank has strengthened its commitment to incorporating social and cultural concerns into its development paradigm by using more widely such tools as social assessment, beneficiary assessment, and stakeholder participation. For example, the government of Morocco requested the Bank's assistance for a project to rehabilitate the old city (*medina*) of Fez, the religious and cultural cradle of the kingdom and a World Heritage Site. In addition to supporting the country's cultural heritage through the restoration and upgrading of the medina's monuments, the project is ensuring that the city and its 150,000 people continue to thrive. The Bank has supported a series of workshops and key surveys to involve ordinary residents, merchants and artisans, and all other stakeholders in decisionmaking.

Supporting the activities described in the previous two chapters is the World Bank's rapidly expanding body of analytical work on the environment. Most of this work addresses three broad questions:

- How to set priorities for action
- How to design cost-effective interventions
- How to remove obstacles and build capacity for effective implementation.

In turn, these questions are being addressed at three levels—through country and regional studies, through the development of best practice and World Bank policies from cross-country analysis, and through the development of new analytical tools and indicators for wider application. This chapter describes each of these in turn and concludes with a discussion of how lessons and techniques emerging from this work are being disseminated through training within the Bank, the wider development community, and the Bank's developing-country clients.

Country and Regional Environmental Strategies

The past three years have witnessed the rapid expansion of national and regional environmental strategies. One important instrument for this at the national level is the national environmental action plan (NEAP), which describes a country's major environmental concerns, identifies the principal causes of environmental problems, and sets priorities for action. Whereas NEAPs are national documents prepared by the countries themselves (sometimes with Bank assistance), the Bank itself also prepares country economic memoranda and country assistance strategies that address a broader range of issues.

National Environmental Action Plans: A Key Tool for Project Design

The Bank has advocated and supported the preparation and implementation of NEAPs since 1992. Responsibility for doing so, however, rests with the government, although the Bank often provides analytical support and assistance in mobilizing resources for the effort. In turn, the Bank draws on the NEAPs in designing its own environmental assistance strategies for the country and encourages governments to consider the concerns of interested parties (including nongovernmental organizations) and to integrate the findings into sectoral and national development plans. For many borrowers, the NEAP offers the first opportunity to assess systematically, and set priorities for, the full range of environmental problems facing a country. It also helps to define needed policies, investments, and institutional reforms.

As of the end of fiscal 1995, initial NEAPs had been completed for sixty-three countries (forty-seven IDA and sixteen IBRD). NEAPs were also at various stages of preparation for a number of new Bank members (such as in the former Soviet Union), as well as for some older (but in some cases inactive) borrowers such as Algeria, Costa Rica, Haiti, Jordan, and Lebanon. Countries preparing NEAPs during the past year include various small island states in the Caribbean as well as Guatemala, the Kyrgyz Republic, Moldova, and Viet Nam. Previous plans were updated recently in Bulgaria (described in box 3.1), Sri Lanka, and Tunisia. Numerous NEAPs, moreover, are now being implemented through Bank-supported environmental institution-building, natural resource management, and urban environmental projects (especially in Sub-Saharan Africa).

Box 3.1. Implementing National Strategies: The Case of Bulgaria

An environmental strategy study carried out in Bulgaria in 1991–92 concluded that past economic and management policies were a major cause of environmental degradation. The study outlined the institutional, legislative, and regulatory reforms needed to implement the policy recommended and stressed the importance of taking a decentralized and participatory approach to environmental management. Since 1992 the government of Bulgaria has tried to follow the action plan laid out in the study, progressing in such areas as developing environmental legislation and regulations, strengthening environmental institutions (including the Ministry of Environment), improving the system of environmental monitoring, and establishing mechanisms for funding environmental protection. As a result, environmental quality is better, pollution levels are lower in the hot spots identified by the study, and the overall framework for environmental management is better designed to undertake future environmental measures.

An update and follow-up of the study were completed this year at the request of the government of Bulgaria. The update recommended the next set of priority issues: industrial air emissions, leaded gasoline, and water and food contamination from heavy metals and toxic organic compounds. It helped to form the basis for a pollution abatement project now being prepared and a debt-for-environment swap funded by Switzerland. The latter allows Bulgaria to invest 20 percent of its Swiss debt in its Pollution Abatement Fund, which will be used for environmental projects, audits and feasibility studies, and small-scale "win-win" lending.

Several important innovations have been introduced in recent NEAPs. The Moldova NEAP, for instance, was one of the first to employ economic valuation to rank environmental priorities across media and sectors. The Viet Nam NEAP, which will be finalized shortly, provides an in-depth analysis of sectoral environmental impacts and establishes strategic implementation plans on the basis of subsector priorities. In Viet Nam, preparation of the NEAP was a participatory process, in which various working groups, including NGOs, carried out most of the analysis and established priorities. Key features of the Kyrgyz NEAP, which is organized around the themes identified in the Environmental Action Programme for Central and Eastern Europe, are indicated in box 3.2.

In April 1995, the Bank published a report reviewing the experience with the process of producing a NEAP. "National Environmental Strategies: Learning from Experience" (World Bank 1995j) identifies good practice and draws lessons from NEAPs and similar documents prepared in more than thirty countries over the past decade. Environmental strategies are living documents that need to change as new problems arise, and the diversity of national problems requires each country to tailor its strategy to reflect national conditions and capacities. Nevertheless, several common patterns emerged from the review:

- Successful strategies involve three key elements: identifying priority problems, defining priority actions, and ensuring effective implementation.
- For environmental strategies to be successfully implemented, technical and economic analysis needs to be sound and skillfully tempered by the active participation and commitment of key stakeholders.
- Effective environmental management requires national and global environmental objectives that are realistic, transparent, and integrated into broad political, economic, and social concerns.

Developing Regional Strategies

In some cases, analytical work and strategic planning benefit from a regional perspective. In the past three years, the Bank has supported and led the preparation of major regional environmental strategies for East Asia, Eastern Europe and the former Soviet Union, North Africa and the Middle East, and Sub-Saharan Africa.

"Toward Environmentally Sustainable Development in Sub-Saharan Africa" (World Bank 1995k), completed this year, helps the Bank to define a medium- and long-term agenda for the region by asking three key questions: What are the key current and future environmental

Box 3.2. Kyrgyz Republic National Environmental Action Plan

The Kyrgyz NEAP, which is based on a cooperative effort between the government of the Kyrgyz Republic and the World Bank, is designed to be updated on a regular basis to reflect changing national conditions and priorities. Among the environmental problems highlighted by the NEAP are the unsustainable use of natural resources—inefficient water resource management, land degradation, overexploitation of forest resources, the threat of irreversible biodiversity loss, and inefficient mining and refining practices—and the impact of water and air pollution on human health. Policy, institutional, and human resource constraints were also identified.

The NEAP is notable for its attention to four important areas:

- *Priority setting.* The NEAP identifies key environmental concerns (water, land, air pollution, and environmental issues related to mining and metallurgy) on the basis of an analysis of health impacts and extensive public participation.
- *Public participation.* As part of the NEAP process, NGOs and the general public were involved in discussing environmental priorities, drafting the NEAP report, and disseminating information on the plan's objectives and expected outcomes. In addition, a public participation program was launched in October 1994 by a local environmental NGO, which serves as a vehicle for ongoing consultations with local NGOs during the final stage of preparation and subsequent implementation of the NEAP.
- *Framework for donor investment.* The NEAP forms a basis for donor support of environmental actions and will be presented to the next Kyrgyz Republic donors' conference. Indeed, its preparation has already led to identification of a regional GEF biodiversity project as well as of an environment and water supply and sanitation project.
- *Institutional arrangements for follow-up.* The NEAP outlines institutional arrangements for implementing and updating the plan. To undertake these revisions, a small NEAP implementation office was set up to ensure monitoring and evaluation, to provide a link between NGOs and the government, and to develop training activities and coordinate donor programs in the country.

challenges in Sub-Saharan Africa? How has the Bank responded so far to those challenges? What should be the Bank's future priorities to assist African countries in integrating environmental concerns into the development process? While acknowledging the formidable difficulties facing many African countries, the paper conveys a strong optimism for environmentally sound development by drawing out lessons from experience and outlining future directions. Implementing this agenda will require the Bank to expand environmental partnerships and networks within a broad range of external institutions, such as United Nations agencies, multilateral and bilateral donors, academic and research institutions, and NGOs.

The Bank took the lead in the development of the Environmental Action Programme for Central and Eastern Europe (EAP), which was adopted at the 1993 Lucerne Environment for Europe ministerial conference. The EAP provides a framework that allows the countries in the region to prioritize their environmental problems and address them in the context of economic transition. Since 1993 the Bank has focused on the implementation of the EAP through its lending operations and policy support. The Bank is particularly active in building partnerships with the Central and Eastern European governments to promote policy changes, institutional improvements, and financially viable investments with tangible environmental and health benefits. To date the Bank has assisted eleven of the twenty-five countries in the region in developing environmental strategies and NEAPs, and in three more countries work is under way.

For the last five years the Bank has provided a total of $1.3 billion for environmental projects in the region. The Bank has taken a major role in the Project Preparation Committee, created after the 1993 Lucerne ministerial conference to coordinate donor assistance for promoting investments with tangible environmental and health improvements in the short to medium term. The Project Preparation Committee is an effective vehicle for designing innovative financial packages to blend loans and grants for high-priority environmental investments. Through the committee, the Bank has secured roughly $50 million in donor commitments for technical assistance or cofinancing for projects in the region. The Bank also contributes to the activities of the task force responsible for the implementation of the EAP.

Two other initiatives are the recently completed environmental strategy for the Middle East and North Africa region and an environmental business plan for Egypt, Jordan, Lebanon, and the Yemen Republic. The former identifies existing and emerging environmental problems of strategic importance, focusing in particular on the economic and public health costs of environmental degradation and natural resource scarcity. It uses an innovative approach of social cost evaluation, priority setting, and a call for action based on a judicious mix of institutional and policy reform and targeted investments. The country-specific environmental business plans, which define the Country Department's operational strategy to address priority environmental issues over the next three years (fiscal 1996–98), and the Mediterranean Environmental Technical Assistance Program, described in chapter 2, operate within the overall vision and agenda set forth in the regional strategy. The main objectives of this approach are to establish an active policy dialogue on environment and sustainable development with the Bank's clients in the Middle East; enhance the environmental content of the current and future Bank portfolio; and strengthen environmental management capabilities among both the Bank's clients and its staff.

Integrating the Environment into Country Assistance Strategies and Economic Studies

The findings of national environmental strategies are increasingly reflected in the country assistance strategies (CASs) and other documents that guide World Bank support to its client countries.

The CAS is the principal statement of the Bank's overall development strategy in a borrowing country. The CAS is, by definition, a concise document (no more than twenty pages) that defines the level and composition of the Bank's assistance. It is not designed to address all the development problems facing a country but focuses instead on four or five of the most critical issues identified by the Bank in collaboration with the country. Environmental considerations are included as a sectoral objective, and discussion of environmental issues is supported by major conclusions from the NEAP and other sector work.

During fiscal 1995, CAS documents were reviewed by the Bank's Board for forty countries, including major borrowers such as Brazil, China, India, Indonesia, and Mexico. CAS reports for many countries of the former Soviet Union, including the Russian Federation and Ukraine, were also presented. Virtually all of these reports contain some description of the environmental challenges facing the country in question. In some cases, considerable attention is given to environmental problems and their underlying causes (such as natural resource or energy price distortions). Other reports emphasize government efforts to address environmental issues at the country level. Recent examples include the CASs for Chile, China, Hungary, Latvia, Niger, Senegal, Swaziland, and Thailand. In Senegal, for instance, where the main focus is on stimulating economic growth, the environment is listed as one of five problem areas that need specific attention.

The focus of CAS reports in relation to the environment varies substantially by region. Soil and land degradation are singled out most frequently in Africa, industrial pollution and energy efficiency are highlighted in Eastern and Central Europe, and both natural resource management and urban environmental issues are prominent in Asia and Latin America. Comparatively little attention is given to global concerns, even though Global Environment Facility (GEF) and Montreal Protocol projects, where they exist, are normally listed among ongoing and proposed lending operations. The links between poverty and environment and between the environment and macroeconomic policies also receive little explicit attention.

Improved environmental and natural resource management generally figures as a key objective in both government development strategies and Bank assistance strategies, although other goals often receive equal or greater priority. Those few CAS reports that do not propose environmental improvement as a prime objective of Bank assistance (such as Mexico's report, which focuses on regaining macroeconomic and financial stability) nevertheless usually include environmental projects or sector work in the future agenda. Environmental issues are also featured in CAS discussions of sectoral policies and lending programs, particularly those involving water resource management (for example, Brazil, India, FYR Macedonia, and Peru), urban sanitation (most countries), energy efficiency (China and various countries in Eastern and Central Europe), industrial pollution control (Brazil, China, Ghana, and Thailand), mining (Estonia, Ghana, Peru, and Poland, among others), and agriculture (especially countries in Africa and Latin America). The need to strengthen national environmental institutions is also highlighted in several CAS reports, as are Bank projects and technical assistance to achieve this objective. Regional initiatives, including the GEF-funded Lake Victoria Environmental Management Plan, described in chapter 4, involving Kenya, Tanzania, and Uganda, are also mentioned.

In addition to the CAS, country economic memoranda (CEMs) advise the Bank's management and Board of Directors on economic prospects, issues, and policies in borrowing countries. The CEM is the Bank's primary comprehensive economic assessment of a country and serves as a basis for communicating with the government on key development issues. CEMs are not required to include environmental concerns, although many do. Recent CEMs in countries as diverse as Egypt, Eritrea, India, Indonesia, the Maldives, and Tunisia have focused on the environment (see box 3.3 for a description of Tunisia's CEM).

Enhancing Country-Focused Economic and Sector Work

More and more Bank resources are being devoted to the analysis of environmental issues. An important part of this effort goes into country-focused environmental economic and sector work (ESW), which helps to identify priorities for Bank lending operations. The results of ESW are used in preparing national strategies. Table 3.1 lists representative ESW studies from the past three years.

> **Box 3.3. Tunisia Country Economic Memorandum: Pricing Resource Use and Degradation**
>
> The natural beauty of Tunisia, its vulnerability to climatic variations, and the importance of environmentally sensitive tourism in the economy have heightened the need to take the environment into account. Recognizing this, the government is revising past policies, including pricing policies, to incorporate the economic value of resources, to minimize haphazard coastal zone planning, and to explore the fiscal and financial consequences of erosion, water scarcity, and pollution. The country economic memorandum (CEM) for Tunisia also has integrated environmental concerns into the country's macroeconomic framework by explicitly linking fiscal and trade policy, as well as by assessing the environmental and social implications of sectoral pricing policies.
>
> Despite recent progress, the CEM points out that Tunisia's environmental program can be strengthened in a number of ways: (a) ensuring that the costs of environmental degradation are borne by resource users and polluters; (b) promoting community-based actions and developing the central and local capacity to monitor progress; and (c) ensuring that the government's development strategy in agriculture, industry, and tourism is based on the economic value (including externalities) of natural resources, in particular those of land and water. Tackling these problems will require additional resources that can, in part, be generated through pollution charges, cost recovery, and efficient use of resources.

Given the growing importance of cities, considerable work has focused on urban environmental problems, as seen in recent pollution-related studies in both Argentina and Chile. The work in Argentina analyzed health, productivity, amenity, and other costs associated with different forms of pollution (focusing on water resource contamination, air pollution, hazardous wastes, solid waste, and noise problems). It also assessed options for addressing these problems based on their comparative cost-effectiveness and recommended a plan of action. The Chile study analyzed the health effects of air and water pollution in Santiago. National officials selected these problems from a short list of potential topics, and Bank staff and Chilean researchers collaborated on the subsequent research. As a result of the full participation of the government of Chile and local researchers in the task of identifying environmental problems, new analytical techniques were introduced to the country, and Chilean experts who took part in the exercise are feeding the results of the work directly into the policy process. Greater Bank-

Table 3.1. Representative Environmental Economic and Sector Work, Fiscal 1993–95

Sector and work	Region or country and fiscal year completed
Pollution and the urban environment	
Atmospheric emissions strategy study	Asia region (1993)
Energy conservation and environment	China (1993), Indonesia (1993)
Mining sector	Angola (1993)
Water and sewerage review and institutions	Colombia (1993), Turkey (1993)
Urban sector and urban environment review	Russian Federation (1994), Senegal (1995)
Hazardous waste management	Nigeria (1995)
Integrated pollution management	Mexico (1995)
Environmental design of roads	Europe, Middle East, and North Africa region (1993)
Natural resource management	
Forestry action plan	Ethiopia (1993)
Forestry sector review	India (1993), Indonesia (1993), Myanmar (1993), Zimbabwe (1993), Costa Rica (1994), El Salvador (1994), Mexico (1994, 1995)
Deforestation practices	Costa Rica (1993)
Water sector issues	Nepal (1993)
Sahel pest management	Africa region (1993)
Minimum tillage agriculture	Europe and Central Asia region (1993)
Fisheries	Mauritania (1994)
River basin study	Jordan (1994)
Institutional development	
National environmental strategy or action plan	Albania (1993), Hungary (1993), Romania (1993), Tanzania (1993), Uganda (1993), Ethiopia (1994), Lao PDR (1994), Malawi (1994), Mauritania (1994), Mozambique (1994), Senegal (1994), Zambia (1994), Belarus (1995), Bulgaria (1995), Côte d'Ivoire (1995), Equatorial Guinea (1995), Guinea (1995), Islamic Republic of Iran (1995), Kenya (1995), Kyrgyz Republic (1995), Mozambique (1995), Nigeria (1995), Togo (1995), Ukraine (1995), Zimbabwe (1995)

Sector and work	Region or country and fiscal year completed
Institutional development *(continued)*	
Special issues of small island states	Dominica (1994), Grenada (1994), Jamaica (1994), St. Kitts (1994), St. Lucia (1994), St. Vincent (1994)
Regional environmental action plan	Caribbean region (1994)
Environmental policy and management ESW	China (1995), Viet Nam (1995)
Environmental assessment review	Guinea-Bissau (1993), Sierra Leone (1993), Chile (1994)
Environmental information	Africa region (1993)
International waters environment	EMENA region (1993)
Environment sector study	Algeria (1994), Namibia (1995), Tunisia (1995)

country collaboration in identifying and undertaking future environmental ESW is likely to have similar benefits elsewhere.

Recent examples of other Bank research on the urban environment can be found in China, India, and Pakistan. For example, "China: Urban Environmental Service Management" was completed in December 1994 (World Bank 1994a) as a follow-up to the national environmental strategy promulgated in fiscal 1992. This study focuses on environmental regulations and pricing, credit control, and direct investment in China's urban environmental sectors. An Indian study developed a decision-making tool with which government officials and institutions can evaluate alternatives for power sector development, taking explicit account of environmental impacts as well as the financial and economic implications of the options considered. An innovative study in Pakistan, whose findings are included in the country's long-term national development strategy, assesses the economywide costs of environmental degradation. This involved back-of-the-envelope calculations to quantify and value environmental costs on the basis of existing data and problems identified in the country's national conservation strategy. The study estimated that environmental degradation amounts to about 3 percent of Pakistan's gross domestic product, due mainly to degradation of water quality, soil degradation, and air pollution. A second study assessed the government's strategy to alleviate shortfalls in energy supply and identified a set of policy and price reforms to promote supply-side efficiency, demand-side management and conservation, and institutional strengthening of energy operations, including monitoring and enforcement of environmental regulations in the power sector. Long-term energy supply options were also evaluated according to economic criteria, including a comprehensive assessment of their environmental costs and benefits.

Although these examples focus on pollution and the urban environment, natural resource management issues still make up the majority of environmental ESW carried out during the past five years. A recent study in Bangladesh, for example, produced a much more complete picture of the environmental problems associated with intensive agriculture than had been available before, pulling existing data into a coherent framework. The report concluded that, in general, environmental problems caused by the increased use of agrochemicals were much less severe than usually thought, although the sustainability of intensive agriculture as currently practiced is in doubt. The study changed the nature and content of research to be carried out under the planned Agricultural Research Management Project. In Chile, the recently completed environ-

Box 3.4. Lessons from Successful Environmental Institutions in Latin America and East Asia

The Bank's Environment Unit for Latin America and the Caribbean recently completed a study of successful environmental institutions, including case studies of effective institutions in Brazil and Colombia. The Colombia case examined regional development corporations that are responsible for river basin management in specified areas. It examined their performance in addressing water quality issues and revealed that these institutions have achieved environmental objectives in part because their work is integrated into the overall process of development planning and in part because it can influence the actual execution of development plans. The second case study described the characteristics and incentives of local planning institutions in Curitiba, Brazil. These institutions made possible the implementation of an urban plan that favored mass transportation corridors (over roads for private vehicles and other alternatives) and managed city growth by gradually introducing land-use controls. As a result, Curitiba has less congestion and air pollution than most agglomerations of its size in the developing world.

One of the key elements associated with successful institutions identified by the reports is the ability to bring a cross-sectoral and multidisciplinary approach to environmental issues, together with assured access to needed resources. Effective institutions are innovative, frequently are directly involved in implementing and planning both development and environmental protection measures, and may—as in the Colombian case—be asked to mediate local conflicts over the use of land, water, and other natural resources. These attributes, together with their technical capacity and catalytic role in local and regional development, are condu-

mental ESW study included an examination of native forest management options. The study identified the excessive costs of overprotecting existing native forests and presented a methodology whereby both biodiversity protection and forestry production goals can be met.

ESW has grown more slowly on institutional development issues than on specific environmental problems. Nevertheless several important institutional analyses have taken place over the past few years. Among them are studies conducted in fiscal 1995 on successful environmental institutions in Brazil, Colombia, and the newly industrialized East Asian countries. Both are described in box 3.4.

Identifying Best Practice and Defining Bank Policies

The tremendous investment in Bank analytical work over the past three years has resulted in a growing body of examples of best practice.

---

cive to gaining public support, thus enhancing effectiveness. The study also concluded that building successful institutions requires legal frameworks that allow agencies to influence the allocation of resources as well as enjoy sustained political support (such as that provided by the three-time mayor of Curitiba). It recognized that achieving strategic objectives takes time; programs to strengthen environmental institutions, accordingly, require a long time horizon.

A Bank study is also examining environmental management, specifically pollution abatement in the industrial sector, in two of East Asia's newly industrializing countries. It surveys 180 plants in Korea and Singapore to determine their responses to regulatory actions, incentives, and public pressure for pollution abatement. As in the Latin American examples, institution building took time and responded to internal and external factors (including the Olympic and Asia games in the Korean case). In Korea, administrative mechanisms were dominant, including frequent, unannounced inspections and stiff fines for noncompliance with environmental regulations. Public investment for environmental purposes was a strong stimulus to private pollution control investments. Decentralized decisionmaking by environmental inspectors and autonomy from the courts also contributed to the credibility of official environmental institutions. Moreover, strong public support for and government commitment to environmental improvement, adequate financial resources, a high degree of technical competence, and continuity of mid-level management with a consistent vision of institutional goals despite administrative changes at the top were key factors.

Whether the concern is urban pollution, rural resource management, or social assessment and participation, there is a large (and rapidly growing) literature to draw on. These examples form the basis of both best practice documents and the policy statements and training programs designed to ensure that the lessons learned are incorporated into Bank and borrower activities.

Urban and Industrial Pollution Management

With rapid urban and industrial growth, pollution has become a key environmental concern in many of the world's large cities. Recent work is identifying priorities and finding cost-effective approaches to dealing with pollution from municipal and industrial sources. More and more evidence points toward air pollution as a major health threat. At the same time, large numbers of poor people do not receive safe drinking water, and badly polluted watercourses impose growing productivity and amenity costs.

The Bank has played a leading role in developing an analytical methodology for estimating the human health impacts of exposure to pollution—especially air pollution—in developing countries, where the availability of data is very limited. The methodology has been successfully applied to determine environmental priorities in major cities including Bombay, Jakarta, Mexico City, and Santiago. A Bank-organized workshop in June 1995 that brought together leading epidemiologists, environmental health experts, and practitioners acknowledged the achievements made, endorsed the methodology, and recommended further refinements.

Addressing air pollution adequately means intervening across sectors and institutions and coordinating a policy response with both government and the private sector. In Asia, the Bank has responded to the problem of air pollution with three linked cross-country and multicity programs developed over the past few years: (a) the Urban Air Quality Management Program has developed strategies and sectoral action plans to address air pollution associated with transport, industry, residential, and other sources in Bombay, Jakarta, Katmandu, and metropolitan Manila, (b) RAINS ASIA, a policy analysis model based on acid rain scenarios developed in Europe, is helping to guide long-term industry and energy investments and location strategies, and (c) a clean technology initiative is highlighting opportunities for introducing cleaner technologies in the context of rapid economic and industrial growth. Country status reports are being prepared for China, India, Indonesia, the Philippines, and Viet Nam.

In preparation for the forthcoming environment ministerial conference in Sofia, Bulgaria, the Bank is analyzing progress in implementing the Environmental Action Programme for Central and Eastern Europe, which was endorsed by fifty countries at the last ministerial conference in 1993 in Lucerne, Switzerland. This program had a major influence on setting priorities for effective pollution management, such as the elimination of lead from gasoline. Future work in this area deals with emerging priorities such as the growth of traffic.

The improved understanding of pollution issues emerging from the extensive operational work in different parts of the world is being incorporated in a consistent set of new guidelines. The earlier approach focused on reducing the emission of pollutants through end-of-pipe controls that were often expensive and did not necessarily yield corresponding environmental benefits. Above all, performance was often far from consistent. The new approach is particularly suited to countries that are experiencing rapid industrial growth but lack influential environmental institutions; it is based on the practical incorporation of the concepts of sustainable development and cleaner production, together with an emphasis on good management. Results show that this approach can reduce the resources required and the wastes generated at lower costs than the traditional command and control approach.

The Bank is encouraging the adoption of these cleaner production methods; the new *Industrial Pollution Prevention and Abatement Handbook* (World Bank 1995g) takes a major step forward by setting numerical targets for the reduction in pollution loads generated during production as well as for final emissions. Expansion of the handbook is continuing, drawing on information from agencies such as UNEP, United Nations Industrial Development Organization, and the World Health Organization, as well as industry sources. It will be refined as it is put to practical use.

Natural Resource Management

In 1992, the Bank adopted a new forest policy to address tropical deforestation and inadequate investment in forest planting and management. Over the past three years, this policy has led to increased support for institutional cooperation and reform of sectoral policies and institutions, as well as stakeholder participation. It has brought a more realistic assessment of resource values into the decisionmaking process and led to greater Bank efforts to preserve parks and protected areas and to manage watersheds. This year, the Bank reviewed its forest policy, which is discussed in greater detail in chapter 5, and elaborated on lessons learned for future Bank support of the forestry sector. The review found that if properly valued, regulated, and managed, forests can contribute significantly to reducing rural poverty and that sustained forest resources can be created based on community benefits. This will require some reconciling of competing pressures for conservation and use, as well as increased investment in the sector through policy and market reforms.

Biodiversity is an important component of integrated forest management. In the past year, the Bank developed technology for rapid assessment of biological diversity, as described in box 3.5. Elsewhere, work

---

Box 3.5. Rapid Assessment of Biodiversity Priority Areas: Lessons from the Pilot Phase

There is an urgent need to identify quickly the places that should be primarily managed to protect biodiversity. Recently, the Bank developed guidelines for the rapid assessment of biodiversity priorities (RAP). Based on methods being adopted for use in developing countries by a consortium of Australian scientists, the World Bank, and the GEF, these guidelines incorporate current ecological theory and best scientific practice in light of three realities. First, there is a limit to the amount of land and water that will be managed primarily for biodiversity protection; second, creating complete inventories of all species and genotypes is not an achievable goal in the near future; and third, land and coastal use will continue to change as people use biological resources to meet their needs. In light of these realities, the guidelines suggest that:

- RAP methods have to be explicit, cost-efficient, and flexible and must attempt to deal with the problem of inadequate knowledge. The guidelines enable users to make an explicit statement of different areas' relative contribution to overall biodiversity protection. Initiatives can then be taken to protect areas that make a significant contribution.
- Competing land uses pose severe constraints on biodiversity protection, and RAP must have maximum flexibility in locating priority areas to facilitate negotiation while ensuring protection of unique areas.
- RAP data bases must be derived from raw data with a consistent level of detail across regions, because identifying priority areas requires making comparisons across regions. The guidelines include methods for designing efficient biological surveys and are accompanied by software tools for data base management and spatial modeling.

Box 3.6. Integrated Coastal Zone Management in Africa

Home to two-thirds of the world's population, coastal areas and their natural resources are coming under increasing stress from urbanization, industrialization, and environmental transformation. In Africa, the lack of systematic policy, planning, and management structures for dealing with complex issues highlights the need for regional and cross-sectoral management. Integrated coastal zone management (ICZM) is widely perceived as an effective means for planning and orchestrating development to meet the needs of resource users while maintaining the productivity of coastal systems.

To support development of an ICZM strategy, the Bank recently completed "Africa: A Framework for Integrated Coastal Zone Management" (World Bank 1995d). The report profiles the coastal zones of East and West Africa, reviews past efforts by the Bank, other donors, and NGOs, and presents a framework for promoting ICZM as part of an overall regional investment strategy for the Bank. The framework is set in the context of an ideal future scenario for African coastal areas in which ICZM plays a key role in the transition to sustainable development over the next thirty years. A long-term goal is to put in place a system for integrated and participatory development planning and natural resource management by 2025. This system would optimize the benefits to individuals and society from coastal resources by reducing conflicts between users, mitigating adverse development effects, and enhancing coastal ecosystem productivity.

---

carried out jointly with the Asian Development Bank concentrates on deforestation and the associated loss of biodiversity in East Asia, the region with the highest global rates of tropical rain forest losses. A program of studies and technical assistance is under way to look at policy and management measures that increase forest-related revenue and produce sustainable management of forests in Indonesia. Other studies in the program focus on explicit valuation of forests' environmental benefits and on transboundary issues affecting deforestation and timber harvesting in Northeast Asia.

Integrated coastal zone management (ICZM) is another area receiving priority attention in fiscal 1995. The Bank has assisted in developing environmental management strategies in several Asian coastal metropolitan areas under the Metropolitan Environmental Improvement Program. Future work will focus on the broader links between urban growth and the coastal and marine environment. ICZM is also the subject of a recent major Bank strategy study for Sub-Saharan Africa (World Bank 1995d), as described in box 3.6. Other Bank support for coastal zone management, including collaboration on the International Coral Reef Initiative, is discussed in chapter 2.

Participation

Participation contributes to social capital by strengthening awareness, commitment, and social accountability. The Bank-wide Learning Group on Participatory Development, functioning since 1991, produced two major documents in the past fiscal year. The first is "The World Bank and Participation" (World Bank 1994k), which presents compelling evidence that participation can, in many circumstances, improve the quality, effectiveness, and sustainability of projects and strengthen owner-

---

Box 3.7. How Participatory Approaches Improve Projects and Economic and Sector Work

Albania, Rural Poverty Alleviation Project. An urgent need exists to inject cash into impoverished mountain areas and provide employment opportunities. Albanian consultants worked with rural farming communities to design credit delivery mechanisms suitable for the poor. Sixty-three village credit funds have been created as a result.

Brazil, Urban Development Project. Three years into project implementation, the participatory design of a subproject saved a large loan component targeted at the poor from cancellation. A new procurement approach bound engineering firms and social organizers into joint ventures. Engineers and social organizers negotiated the design and management of subprojects with slum dwellers. Women provided leadership in the slums. The Bank integrated structured learning into the project.

India, Forestry Project. The Bank is helping to mainstream the Forest Protection Committee approach initiated in West Bengal. Through this approach, foresters shift out of a policing role and into a social role that provides income to poor people and regenerates the forest. Workshops brought various government stakeholders together to identity the institutional changes needed to support participatory forestry.

Morocco, Women-in-Development Strategy. Through meetings and orientation workshops in participatory methods, the Bank convinced skeptical government officials to allow local women to participate in the formulation of a women-in-development strategy. The government agreed but stipulated that the task must be carried out by Moroccans. Government and NGO personnel received intensive training to undertake participatory rapid appraisal in rural villages. Rural women are preparing their own recommendations for inclusion in the sector report.

ship and commitment of government and stakeholders (see box 3.7). Community participation strategies are particularly important in reaching the poor. The report proposed an action plan for mainstreaming participation.

These recommendations were accepted by Bank management and endorsed by the Board of Directors. As a result, the following activities were begun:

- A vice-presidential committee was established to oversee implementation of the recommendations.
- This committee asked every regional and central vice-presidency to prepare its own action plan, which includes a status report on current participatory activities and concrete steps to strengthen and expand these efforts over the next two years.
- The Interagency Learning Group on Participation was set up to promote continuous learning and sharing of experiences among development institutions and to encourage operational collaboration on specific activities in order to produce better results on the ground. The group's membership consists of representatives from governmental and nongovernmental organizations, project implementing agencies, academia, and donor institutions.
- The Bank allocated resources to support innovation, learning, and mainstreaming of participation through its regular budget process and through creation of the $2 million Fund for Innovative Approaches to Human and Social Development (FIAHS). Forty-seven Bank-funded projects received FIAHS allocations ranging from $8,250 to $40,000, and fourteen additional social scientists joined the Bank.

The second major product, the "Participation Sourcebook" (World Bank 1995n), documents Bank practice on participation, shares how-to lessons with task managers across regions of the Bank, and constitutes the basis of current technical knowledge on participatory development in the Bank. All told, more than 200 Bank staff and consultants contributed directly to the contents of the sourcebook, and several hundred reviewers both inside and outside the Bank provided comments and feedback. Twenty technical papers on participation were prepared as background material, reflecting sectoral and cross-cutting issues. They have been published separately by the Environment Department.

Social Assessment

Just as environmental assessments identify important environmental issues, social assessments (SAs) analyze the social factors that affect development. As with EAs, SAs improve the design and delivery of Bank-assisted projects and analytical work. They also provide a framework for analyzing social factors and for giving a social content to Bank projects and economic and sector work. Social assessment is carried out in order to (a) identify key stakeholders and establish an appropriate framework for their participation in project selection, design, and implementation; (b) ensure that project objectives and incentives for change are acceptable to the range of people intended to benefit and that gender and other social differences are reflected in project design; (c) assess the social impact of investment projects and, where adverse impacts are identified, determine how they can be overcome or at least substantially mitigated; and (d) develop capacity at the appropriate level to enable participation, resolve conflict, permit service delivery, and carry out mitigation measures, as required. Moreover, SA is now mandatory on GEF projects (see chapter 2).

Incorporating SA into the Bank's project cycle requires increasing the involvement of stakeholders. In some cases, this can be done during project preparation, but in more and more situations such as for biodiversity or capacity-building projects—structured learning and SA participation are being built into the project itself. For example, as described in box 3.8, the SA in Baku in Azerbaijan led to important initiatives to ensure adequate access to water in that capital city and should markedly contribute to project success.

Some of the best practice lessons from the Bank's recent experience with social assessment are the following:

- SAs must be selective and strategic and focus on issues of operational relevance. Given the range of social factors that potentially affect a project's success, SAs must be tailored to specific problems and situations.
- Good SA involves consulting with stakeholders and affected groups and collecting other forms of data. In some cases, stakeholders simply provide initial information, and no further interaction is foreseen. But often projects are improved when issues are jointly assessed and agreed, or when beneficiaries are given responsibility for identifying problems and solutions. Where local participation in project design and implementation is expected, participatory collection and analysis of data can build trust and mutual understanding early in the project cycle.
- SA design is influenced by the degree of stakeholder involvement required and the complexity of the issues addressed. Where social factors are complex and social impacts or risks are significant, formal studies generally need to be carried out as part of project preparation. Where initial uncertainty is considerable because of

Box 3.8. Social Assessment in Azerbaijan

The Baku Water Supply Project is the first Bank lending operation in Azerbaijan. A social assessment (SA) was included to identify socioeconomic factors that affect the project's design and implementation and to determine the potential impacts of the project on residents of Baku, the capital city and home to a third of the country's population. The Baku SA was also intended to initiate dialogue between the Baku Water Department and its clients. Originally including 400 household surveys, the SA process was later expanded to include five separate studies and a public seminar on the results. Among other things, the SA found that public water service is inadequate throughout Baku and that most households have developed some sort of strategy to cope with the unreliable water supply. In the process, however, households spend up to seventeen times the cost of their monthly water bill on alternative water supplies, while an estimated 40 to 60 percent of public water is not paid for. Many households said they would be willing to pay more than their monthly water charge to receive better public water service. In addition, there are important geographic and socioeconomic variations in the distribution of water and the way users deal with an unreliable public water supply, with low-income groups suffering the most from the current situation.

The Baku SA made significant contributions by identifying the need for (a) improved governance and an autonomous water agency; (b) an equitable and economically viable water pricing policy that encourages water conservation and is accompanied by the installation of properly functioning water meters to allow a quantity-based tariff structure; (c) effective monitoring of both private wells and illegal water vending, a potential health risk; and (d) mechanisms to take into account the specific needs of the different consumer groups.

---

lack of awareness, commitment, or capacity, SAs contribute to the design of projects that are flexible and responsive to change.
- Task managers need technical and financial support for SA. Social issues are invariably complex, and task managers need appropriate financial and technical support so that the participatory process and social analysis do not become a source of frustration and delay.

Of the participatory activities or social assessments that received support from FIAHS during the last fiscal year, 79 percent were undertaken in the context of institutional strengthening, capacity building, and decentralization; 17 percent were for activities related to environmental sustainability and natural resource management; and the remaining 4 percent supported private sector development objectives. In another example, the assessment in Fez, Morocco, took place early in project preparation and produced new ideas for using sites, for changing regulations, and for minimizing the impacts of resettlement. By raising local awareness of the project, the assessment also encouraged broader local interest in upgrading and maintaining this historic city.

Beneficiary Assessment

Fiscal 1995 may be heralded as the year in which qualitative assessment came of age in the World Bank. This was the first year in which systematic client consultation was recommended for all departments in the Africa Region by the regional vice president; it was also the year in which the Latin America and Caribbean Region developed its own policies strongly advocating listening to key stakeholders as a systematic, integral part of its project and policy work. The key tool used in qualitative assessment throughout the Bank is beneficiary assessment (BA), and the primary expression of this approach directed toward policy formation is the participatory poverty assessment (PPA).

Two initiatives involving BA stood out during this year: the assessment conducted in Senegal on agricultural extension, recently completed, and the assessment on education and poverty in three regions of Brazil, just beginning. The Senegalese BA revealed that the project had a positive impact on farmer productivity where the message was correctly transmitted and understood, but that it also suffered from serious flaws in communication involving both the contact farmers and the extension agents. Similar assessments are now planned for Mali and Guinea next year.

In total, the Bank has undertaken nineteen participatory poverty assessments, and these have brought out useful information on the perspectives of key actors in the countries that would not have been learned through more conventional questionnaire surveys. In Cameroon and Mexico, the assessment brought to light the severe incentive problems stemming from the underpayment of teachers and health workers, who did not consider themselves to be equipped to serve people well, contributing to low attendance in classes and low use of health facilities. Of particular importance is the finding of participatory poverty assessments on the role of local institutions in fostering self-reliance and on the pervasive mistrust toward government.

Resettlement

Involuntary resettlement has been a companion of development throughout history, indelibly written into the evolution of industrial as well as developing countries. Over the past decade, approximately 80 million to 90 million people have been resettled as a result of infrastructure programs for dam construction, sanitation, urban upgrading, and transportation improvements. World Bank–financed programs account for a small, but significant, share of this total: for example, roughly 3 percent of the resettlement caused by dam construction and 1 percent of that caused by urban and transportation worldwide.

Although limited in relative terms, the Bank's involvement in resettlement operations is nonetheless significant, and the Bank has sought to work with governments to promote better policies and legal frameworks for resettlement, at and beyond the project level. The World Bank's influence in policy matters is far-reaching and is being used to improve the conditions of persons who are involuntarily displaced.

The World Bank's resettlement policy evolved through three successive policy documents from 1980 to the current policy, adopted in 1990. Built on an extensive review of Bank experience, this policy promotes two fundamental objectives: first, to minimize or avoid resettlement wherever possible, and, second, to enable persons who are resettled to recover fully at least their prior income and living standards by participating in the benefits of the project that obliges them to move.

Over time, specific components have been incorporated into the Bank's policy to improve the likelihood of reaching these goals. For instance, the policy lists eleven specific components that are required of resettlement plans. These include ensuring that the affected individuals and communities participate in their own resettlement, that vulnerable individuals and communities receive special attention, that cultural property such as cemeteries and religious shrines are moved or rededicated, and that people have multiple options as they move on to new lives.

At the request of the Bank's Board of Directors, in 1990 the Operations Evaluation Department (OED) examined Bank-supported projects with involuntary resettlement to investigate the facts, assess the adequacy of guidelines, and identify lessons for future lending. It soon became clear that the information on resettlement in general, and on incomes of resettled people in particular, was weak. In response, OED undertook a series of four impact evaluations to examine the outcomes of resettlement in completed projects. Impact evaluations are undertaken when projects are at or near full development—that is, late enough to determine the extent to which rehabilitation has been achieved and whether the resettlement is sustainable. The projects studied were the Khao Laen Hydroelectric Project in Thailand, the Kpong Hydroelectric Project in Ghana, and the Karnataka Irrigation Project and the Second Maharashtra Project in India. Specially commissioned socioeconomic surveys yielded data on changes in incomes and living standards and, just as important, rehabilitation and adaptation of individuals to their new life. The two impact evaluations in India also included studies of people who had been displaced. The findings of the impact evaluations were distilled in "Overview: Early Experience with Involuntary Resettlement" (World Bank 1993b). This report analyzed the factors explaining resettlement outcomes and recommended that, although the policy was appropriate, its implementation and monitoring should be improved.

Meanwhile, since 1990, parallel efforts within the Bank have shifted from enhancing the policy to improving performance in resettlement operations. Technical advice and tools have improved as more resettlement experts have been involved in planning, supervision, and evaluation of projects. However, problems in a number of resettlement operations, which are also noted in the continuing OED work, led to creation of the Task Force on Involuntary Resettlement in 1992. The Bank-wide review, "Resettlement and Development: The Bankwide Review of Projects Involving Involuntary Resettlement 1986–93" (World Bank 1994h), heightened the focus on resettlement work and led to more frequent project supervision, remedial work on individual cases, policy dialogue with major borrowers, a training program for government and implementing agency personnel, and better operational understanding of resettlement both inside and outside the Bank.

Since the Bank-wide review was published, activities have included two further reports to the Bank's Board of Directors on Bank-wide efforts to improve implementation of the resettlement policy and on corrective actions in projects not in full compliance with the policy. These reports generated more awareness of and commitment to the Bank's resettlement policy.

Improving Methodologies and Indicators

The past three years have seen a sharp expansion of the Bank's research and analytical work directed toward improving the methodological tool kit available to environmental specialists and policymakers. These methodological initiatives can be broadly categorized as those that improve the diagnostic and design capacity for environmental policymaking and those that develop environmental indicators and innovative techniques for data analysis.

New Methodologies and Diagnostic Tools

The following paragraphs describe a few of these innovations. Others are described in subsequent chapters.

Analyzing the impact of infrastructure and natural habitats. As part of a broad effort to understand the causes and consequences of tropical deforestation, the Policy Research Department has recently developed a methodology to explore the tradeoffs between development and environmental damage posed by road building. By understanding the incentives and constraints affecting the conversion of natural habitats to agriculture in Africa, Latin America, and Southeast Asia, the researchers will examine the effects of macroeconomic, sectoral, and regional policies on the forest and on the persons who depend on it.

Identifying pollution pressures. A major focus of Bank analytical work is industrial pollution, including abatement costs, benefits, and regulatory options for industrial pollution. This work stresses cost-effective regulation and implementation of market-based pollution control instruments wherever feasible. Because few environmental protection institutions can undertake the needed firm-level cost-benefit analysis (due to lack of data on industrial emissions and abatement costs), appropriate estimation methods need to be employed. The Industrial Pollution Projection System (IPPS) is a comprehensive response to this need. The first prototype of IPPS covers approximately 1,500 industrial product categories, all operating technologies, and hundreds of pollutants. It can separately project air, water, and solid waste emissions, including criteria for air pollutants, toxins, bio-accumulative metals, and commonly used water pollutants, and it can provide conservative benchmark abatement costs. IPPS emissions and cost parameters are currently being used for a comprehensive cost-benefit analysis of the impact of industrial pollution in Mexico.

Addressing pollution priorities. The Decision Support System for Industrial Pollution Control (DSS/IPC) was developed within the Environment Department of the Bank as a personal computer–based tool for rapidly assessing the major contributors to pollution in a geographical area, the reduction options, and associated costs, all based on an inventory of economic activities. The system serves a variety of operational and policy research needs; it can be used as a tool to organize information and also to provide analytical support in the formulation of policy options and pollution control strategies. The system can incorporate transport, municipal, industrial, and energy sources of pollution and can estimate the geographical impacts of each.

The system comprises several functional modules: production activities, pollution loads, pollution concentrations, selection of priority pollutants, and control measures and technologies, with costs. Each of these modules can be adjusted for local conditions, and costs and modules can be used separately. A version of the system is available with a generalized default data base, and it continues to be refined in the course of operational support work.

Creating public demand for improved performance. In Indonesia, the Bank's Research and Indonesia Departments, working closely with BAPEDAL, the Indonesian Environment Agency, have designed an innovative public information tool for pollution control. The approach ranks plants by environmental performance, and public announcement of these rankings is expected to increase the public pressure on polluters to clean up their operations. A related project will use information on the stock market in twenty developing countries to trace the impact of different levels of corporate pollution on market valuation.

Estimating the costs of pollution reduction. Future Bank research includes a two-year study of the economics of industrial pollution control in developing countries. This project will deepen the Bank's involvement with environmental regulatory authorities in Brazil, China, India, Indonesia, Mexico, the Philippines, and South Africa. It will specifically address the costs of pollution reduction in these countries, examine successful regulatory strategies, and analyze the factors that explain the variation in performance across plants. Finally, to assess the health impact of pollution, researchers are undertaking a retrospective study of the effect of air pollution on daily mortality in Delhi between 1991 and 1994.

The methodological work described above will contribute to an integrated effort to understand how macroeconomic policies simultaneously affect growth, poverty alleviation, and environmental protection and the tradeoffs and complementarities among these three goals. The strategy is to understand how industrial firms, farms, and urban households respond to macroeconomic signals in ways that affect poverty, growth, and the environment. With this understanding, policymakers can seek macroeconomic, sectoral, and regulatory policies that protect the environment while promoting economic and social development.

Analyzing the links between economywide policies and the environment. Elsewhere in the Bank, there is also continuing work to improve the formal integration of environmental issues in economywide policy analysis and dialogue. In several detailed country studies, the analysis of economic policy interventions and their likely effects on the key environmental problems of a country is being facilitated with the use of the action impact matrix, which relates proposed government policy *actions* to their likely environmental *impacts*. In the action impact matrix, analysis of the links between the current program of economywide policy reforms and the priority environmental concerns can be broken down into a three-step process.

In the first step, the Bank discusses the economic reform agenda with both the economic planning and environmental authorities. The process of involving economic planners and environmental managers in discussions of relevant interactions between the economy and the environment is as important as the analytical end product of the exercise. In the second step, the priority environmental problems (identified by country documents, such as the national environmental action plan) are identified. As much quantification as possible should be introduced at this stage. For example, indicators for each of the main environmental concerns may be presented both in biophysical and economic terms.

The *underlying* causes of the environmental problems are then highlighted (in contrast to their proximate causes). This illustrates how underlying causes, including both existing policies that distort incentives (for example, subsidized prices), and the absence of policies to address market failures (for example, effluent charges), lead to inappropriate incentives for resource use. In addition to economic factors, the role of institutional factors, such as the conditions of access to natural resources, may also be important.

Finally, in the third step, the information from the two previous steps is combined in the action impact matrix to focus on the possible interactions between economywide policy reforms and priority environmental concerns.

As a first assessment, constructing these tables helps to identify problems, because the matrix illustrates broad relationships, without necessarily specifying the magnitude of impacts. In current applications, the matrix has proved useful to both economic and environmental decisionmakers, even at this initial stage:

- First, it provides an integrated overview of economic conditions and programs of reforms and their potential impacts on key sustainability issues.
- Second, it can help to identify important links that should be incorporated in policy dialogue.

Subsequent work can then be undertaken to examine these links in more detail. This process enables closer coordination between economic and environmental decisionmakers, thus strengthening the consensus on development programs.

For initiating policy discussions and dialogue, the action impact matrix provides the initial assessment of potentially relevant links between the economy and the environment. The approach is proving useful in operational work. The Bank's Board endorsed more in-depth work to promote policy reforms in the area of environment, and since October, several country applications have begun. Current efforts focus on applying the action impact matrix approach to include environmental issues in the policy dialogue that the Bank undertakes with member countries. Collaborative efforts are now being completed in Bolivia, Ghana, and Sri

Lanka, and a fourth one is being initiated in the Philippines. In these initiatives, the Environment Department, in cooperation with Bank regional staff, is working with environmental and economic planning ministries to integrate environmental and natural resource management concerns directly in policy dialogue.

Developing Environmental Data and Indicators

The Bank is both a producer and a consumer of data. Using environmental data to give insights and provide policy guidance is a constant challenge, and considerable progress has been made in this area during the past three years. The Bank is pursuing two initiatives. The first, at the broadest level, is marked by the publication this year of the first edition of *Monitoring Environmental Progress* (World Bank 1995i). This volume poses compelling questions that environmentally sustainable development indicators should help to answer. The first edition does not seek solutions; rather it tests the strengths and weaknesses of available environmentally sustainable development indicators and explores how such indicators could yield analytical insight and establish near-term priorities for basic research, including the compilation and modeling of data.

A workshop convened in September 1994 brought together experts on environmental indicators and others working on the topic from international agencies (United Nations Commission on Sustainable Development, the UNDP, United Nations Statistical Division, UNEP, FAO, and the International Center for Tropical Research), countries, and NGOs. This workshop made progress in improving the coordination of the efforts of major international organizations and in promoting the sharing of data and information. The first draft of *Monitoring Environmental Progress* (World Bank 1995i) was presented at the April 1995 meeting of the United Nations Commission on Sustainable Development and was successful in getting people to agree to a framework (presented in the technical notes to the volume). This first edition seeks to contribute to and channel the continuing discussion.

Bearing in mind the need for timely—if imperfect—indicators, *Monitoring Environmental Progress* constitutes a first attempt at measuring wealth and also reports on a short-cut approach to green national accounts (see box 3.9). This approach adjusts the saving residual for drawing down natural capital to arrive at a genuine saving measure. This demonstrates how a miscalculation of the saving residual can lead to a mistaken view of how well an economy is preparing for the future. Figure 3.1 illustrates these preliminary estimates for nonfuel primary exporters. The issues considered are by no means exhaustive, and future editions will continue to report progress on this front. In addition, the Bank has, for some time, been implementing initiatives in integrated

Box 3.9. Where Is the Wealth of Nations?

First estimates of human resources, natural capital, and produced assets show that human resourcefulness is our most important form of wealth. Further, nations differ in their endowment of wealth. The figure indicates significant differences in the composition of wealth between high-income and developing economies, where developing economies are subdivided into those most dependent on exporting raw materials and those more oriented toward exporting manufactures, services, and so forth. Although the pies are not drawn to scale, they suggest the disparities in global distribution of wealth. With less than 16 percent of the worlds population, high-income countries have nearly 80 percent of global wealth. Raw material exporters have almost as many people but less than 5 percent of global wealth. Other developing countries, with nearly 70 percent of the worlds population, have barely 16 percent of global wealth.

Box Figure 3.9. World Distribution of Wealth by Country Group and Resources
(percent)

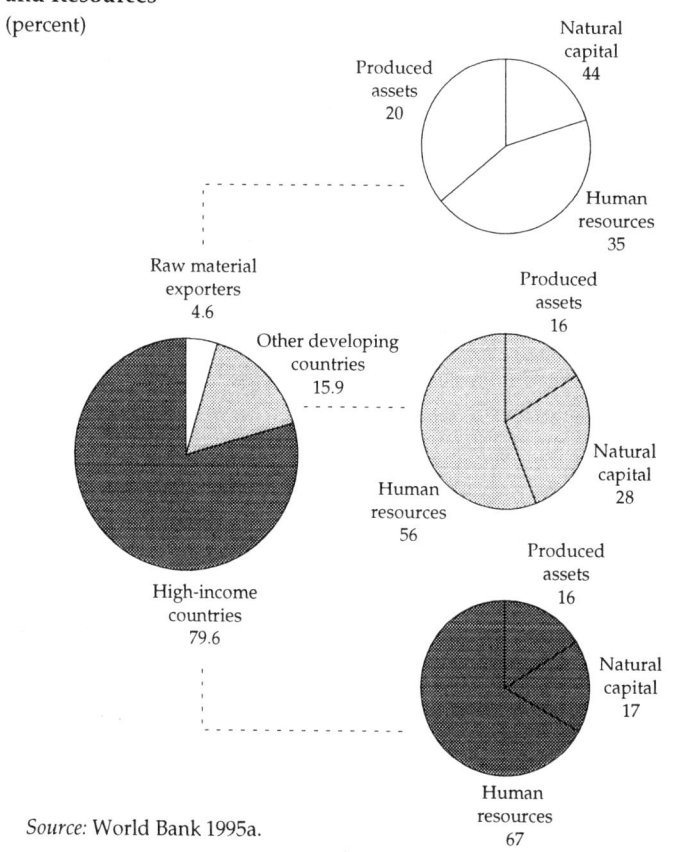

High-income countries 79.6
- Produced assets 20
- Natural capital 44
- Human resources 35

Other developing countries 15.9
- Produced assets 16
- Natural capital 28
- Human resources 56

Raw material exporters 4.6
- Produced assets 16
- Natural capital 17
- Human resources 67

Source: World Bank 1995a.

Figure 3.1. Investment and Savings: Nonfuel Primary Exporters, 1966–91

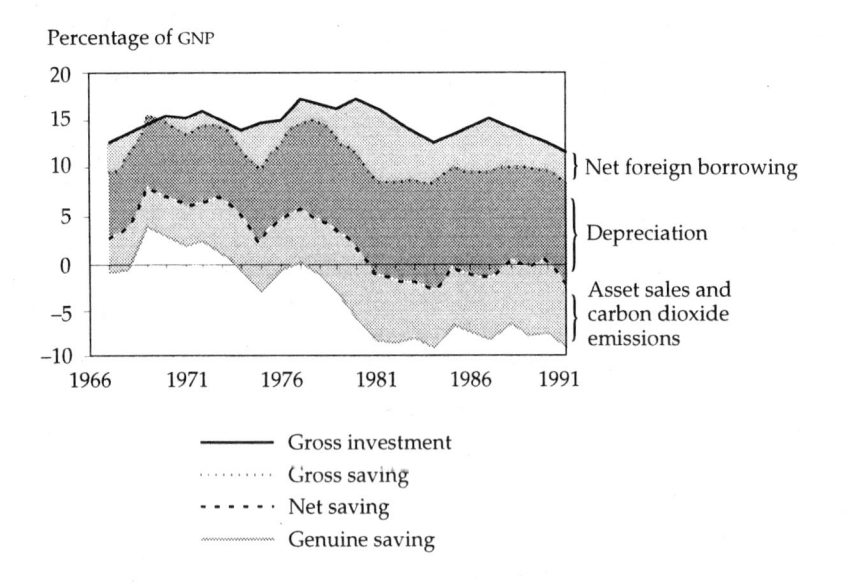

Percentage of GNP

} Net foreign borrowing
} Depreciation
} Asset sales and carbon dioxide emissions

——— Gross investment
·········· Gross saving
- - - - - Net saving
~~~~~~~ Genuine saving

Note: On the basis of accounting identities, subtracting net foreign borrowing from gross domestic investment yields gross saving. Net saving is obtained by subtracting depreciation of produced assets. Netting out an allowance for global damages from carbon dioxide emissions and the drawing down of natural resources yields genuine saving.
Source: World Bank (1995).

environmental and economic accounts, in partnership with the United Nations Statistical Division, and work has been undertaken in Mexico, Papua New Guinea, and Thailand.

In the second initiative, the Bank is examining ways to monitor the effect of its activities on the environment as well as other sectors. This is done through the identification and systematic use of environmental performance indicators for individual projects and forms part of the Bank-wide effort to improve the monitoring of project performance in all sectors. Environmental performance indicators are applicable both to projects that have specific environmental objectives and components (such as industrial pollution prevention or abatement) and to projects that pursue other goals but have potential environmental impacts (such as an infrastructure project that affects local forests). They address both *pressures* on the environment generated by a project, such as the percentage of standing forest cleared, and the *state* of the environmental variable being monitored, for example, the change in ambient concentrations of particulates in particular project areas. They can also be used to monitor the *response* to a given environmental problem, whether it is caused by a project, as in the infrastructure example cited above, or is part of a specific environmental management program, as in the case of freestanding environmental institution-building projects.

Although specific environmental protection indicators need to be defined on a project-by-project basis, the Bank is preparing a guide for task managers on how to go about this process. In doing so, it has outlined an approach to developing monitorable indicators of environmental change on the basis of the pressure-state-response framework mentioned above. Representative indicators are suggested for monitoring both the source and sink functions of the environment, as well as the performance of environmental institutions. Among the source and sink functions, local impacts (land degradation, water pollution) and global impacts (biodiversity loss, climate change, ozone depletion) are distinguished. Specific indicators include changes in forest cover in a given area over time, emissions of carbon dioxide by a particular economic activity, ambient concentrations of particulates, and so on. Because environmental impacts cut across all major investment sectors, environmental protection indicators are intended to complement rather than substitute for sector-specific performance indicators.

Elsewhere, the Bank has supported data collection and analysis efforts to identify priorities for establishing and improving the management of marine protected areas in collaboration with the Great Barrier Reef Marine Park Authority, the World Conservation Union, and the Commission on National Parks and Protected Areas (discussed in chapter 2).

In Latin America, and consistent with the Bank's evolution toward a habitat-oriented strategy for biodiversity conservation, the Bank, together with the World Wildlife Fund, has developed methodologies for assessing and mapping the conservation status of 191 ecoregions in Latin America and the Caribbean (see box 3.9). And in Indonesia, the Bank is experimenting with a methodology to identify vulnerable rural communities. This work is described in box 3.10.

Providing Training and Outreach

More efforts are being devoted to training and dissemination of best practice results, both to Bank staff and to member country officials via the Bank's Economic Development Institute (EDI). These efforts build on past Bank analytical and project work and help to set the agenda for the future.

> **Box 3.10. Conservation Assessment of the Terrestrial Ecoregions of Latin America and the Caribbean**
>
> Habitat loss and degradation are the leading threats to biodiversity in Latin America and the Caribbean. Although the Amazonian rain forests have long been the focus of conservation concerns, they represent only a portion of the region's biodiversity. Other less spectacular or less species-rich ecosystems are often more threatened, but they receive less attention in conservation strategies. *A Conservation Assessment of the Terrestrial Ecoregions of Latin America and the Caribbean* (World Bank, Latin America Technical Department, and World Wildlife Fund 1995) offers guidance on how the conservation status of these habitats can be used to help prioritize actions.
>
> The report proposes a hierarchy of habitat types and defines and maps 191 ecoregions. Marine and freshwater ecoregions are not covered, but the report includes the region's mangrove ecosystems. The conservation status of each ecoregion is determined using landscape features such as the amount of habitat loss, the number and size of remaining blocks of intact habitat, the degree of fragmentation, the rate of conversion, and the degree of protection. The biological distinctiveness of each ecoregion is also defined and, combined with the conservation status, is used to rank ecoregions in terms of urgency for conservation action. Nine maps are bound in the report, and there is an inserted poster map of the ecoregions in Latin America and the Caribbean.
>
> The report builds a solid foundation on which donors, multilateral organizations, and national policymakers can establish their own conservation strategies. In conjunction with advice from national conservation strategies, it will lend critical guidance to all Bank operations involving the protection and management of natural habitats.

Within the Bank, there has been a major increase in the numbers of staff trained, both in environmental and natural resource economics and in sectoral environmental management issues. In fiscal 1995, for instance, the Environment Department sponsored some nineteen courses that reached more than 600 people. Most courses, which were presented by Bank staff, lasted one or two days and drew heavily on Bank projects and economic and sector work. Topics included the fundamentals of environmental management, coastal zone issues, and handling of ozone-depleting substances. Courses offered in the last three years, most more than once, are listed in table 3.2. Formal training is complemented by a series of seminars, lectures, and ad hoc workshops.

At EDI, a major new emphasis on environmental economics and management has resulted in rapidly expanding training efforts, with

Table 3.2. Internal Training Courses for Bank Staff
on Environmental Issues Offered in Fiscal 1993–95

Issue covered	Course
Flagship course	Fundamentals of Environmental Management
Environmental economics and impact analysis	Introduction to Environmental Economics Economic Analysis of Environmental Valuation Economic Analysis of Environmental Impacts Economywide Policies and the Environment
Sector-specific environmental assessment	Separate environmental assessment courses for agriculture, transport, water and sanitation, urban, industry, and energy staff Environmental Assessment for Infrastructure, Industry, and Energy Development Environmental Assessment, Resettlement Action Plans, and Archaeological Surveys in Project Processing
Natural resource management issues	Participatory Forestry Management Water Resources Management Forestry Symposium Water Resources Seminar Protected Areas, Natural Habitats, and Ecosystem Management Using Coastal Resources for Environmentally Sustainable Development Natural Resource Management in Arid Areas
Social issues	Indigenous Peoples and Economic Development Involuntary Resettlement Workshop Legal Issues in Resettlement and Rehabilitation Legal Aspects of Resettlement in Bank Projects Resettlement Workshop for Agriculture and Environment Technical Training in Social Assessment and Participation Social Assessment Resettlement Indigenous People's Knowledge Systems and Institutions
Urban development and pollution issues	Urban Environment Strategies and Action Plans Critical Success Factors for Implementing Energy-Efficiency Improvement Programs Practical Solutions to Environmental Pollution Industrial Pollution Control

(Table continues on the following page.)

Table 3-2 *(continued)*

Issue covered	Course
Other issues	Issues of Environmental Sustainability in Africa
	National Environmental Action Plans: Issues and Options
	National Environmental Action Plans
	Environmental Legal Procedures
	International Environmental Law and the GEF
	GEF 1 Operations Targeting Coordinators and Technical Specialists
	Principles of Environmental Institution Building
	Environmental Information Systems

more courses offered in borrowing countries, particularly in Africa and the former Soviet Union, as well in Washington, D.C. In a recent course for African environmental economists, funded by the European Union, EDI developed a carefully structured two week course with modules addressing both microeconomic and macroeconomic issues. Staff from the Bank's Environment Department worked closely with EDI to prepare and present many of the course modules. In the future, EDI plans to develop closer links with Bank staff, drawing on their project and best practice experience and integrating the lessons into its course materials. The partnership between the Bank and EDI is expected to grow stronger in the coming year. One promising avenue for the future is the joint presentation of training that will include both representatives of borrowing member countries and Bank staff.

Table 3.3. EDI Environmental Training, Fiscal 1994 and 1995 and Projected Fiscal 1996

Broad activity themes	Number of activities			Number of participants		
	1994	1995	1996	1994	1995	1996
Project and portfolio management, project analysis, and procurement	5	11	0	130	286	0
Development management	1	3	3	26	78	78
Water management policy	5	5	19	78	130	494
Environment policy, regulation, and valuation	13	15	31	338	390	806
Involuntary resettlement program	4	7	9	104	182	234
Total	28	41	62	676	1,066	1,612

The number of courses in environmental training for which the EDI has been directly responsible has grown over the past two years and is expected to grow further in the coming year (see table 3.3). In total, sixty-nine courses were conducted, and approximately 1,800 people in borrower countries were trained. These courses stressed environmental policy, regulation, and valuation and water management and policy, primarily in Asia, Africa, and Eastern and Central Europe.

In one example of recent activity, EDI plans to undertake coastal zone management training programs at the field level in the Middle East and North Africa, with courses planned for the Gaza Strip and Jordan in late 1995. EDI also held a series of training courses on water resources management and plans a major training program on river basin management in Africa. These will include presentations on the links between river basins, coastal zones, and marine environment.

PART 2

Part 1 reviewed World Bank activities specifically directed at protecting the environment at the national, regional, and global levels, as well as the intellectual journey the Bank is undertaking in the realm of environmentally sustainable development. Part 2 addresses the question of how Bank activities not specifically addressed at protecting the environment have also evolved since the Rio Earth Summit.

Bank-financed investment not specifically focused on the environment falls into three categories in terms of their environmental impact. The first are activities that are unambiguously benign to the environment. These include education, health, and nutrition projects, for example. The second are activities that could be environmentally benign if properly designed; if improperly designed—that is, if they ignore possible environmental impacts or miss opportunities to benefit the environment—these activities can have an adverse effect on the environment. An example might be an irrigation project: although better irrigation will improve soil yields, thus reducing pressure to convert new land to agriculture, a poorly designed project might not include adequate drainage, leading to soil salinization, or might extract groundwater excessively, damaging natural habitats and causing subsidence. The third type of activity involves a tradeoff between protecting the environment and promoting economic development and reducing poverty. An example might be an energy or a road project. In many cases, such projects are impossible without some adverse impact on the environment. However, energy and roads also prevent worse damage, such as that which can occur as a result of burning wood and dung, for example, or from the grinding poverty that is often the lot of individuals who cannot take the fruits of their labor to market. In these cases especially, the benefits and costs, environmental as well as economic, of different approaches need to weighed carefully, and adverse environmental impacts need to be avoided or mitigated. None of these types of activity is sector-specific; however, certain types tend to predominate in different sectors.

The following chapters look at a selection of sectors: agriculture, energy, transport, and urban development. These sectors represent some 60 percent of Bank activity. Part 2 does not address activities that are unambiguously environmentally benign, nor does it address that portion of the Bank's lending directed at economywide policies. A recent major study, presented to the Bank's Board of Directors during the last fiscal year, found that these latter activities can be both good and bad for the environment. Although they are critical to environmentally sustainable development—because sectoral efforts alone, however generously funded, are unlikely to succeed if the overall policy and regulatory framework gives people incentives to do just the opposite—they often, during the transition period, exacerbate existing problems. This is of particular concern where those who suffer are the very poor, whose marginal existence is made even more perilous, and the environment, where damage can be irreversible. As a result, the Bank is seeking to include environmental concerns more often as an integral part of its adjustment lending.

4. Making a Difference with Environmental Assessments

JUAN DAVID QUINTERO

Since Rio both the number and effectiveness of environmental assessments have increased, and EAs are affecting project design earlier in the project development cycle. The Espirito Santo State Water Project in Brazil, for example, will provide potable water and sewerage services and treatment and prevent further pollution of beaches that are an important recreational area for the poor of the capital city of Vitória, pictured here. Through public participation in the environmental assessment process, two locations were identified where the siting of new treatment plants would seriously affect local populations. One plan would have eliminated clay deposits vital for the subsistence of traditional artisans, the *paneleiras*. Project designers and artisans together decided on mitigatory measures for securing the local artistic tradition, lifestyle, and livelihood of the people.

In the past decade, the Bank introduced a variety of instruments into its lending and advisory activities in an effort to strengthen its environmental performance and to minimize potentially negative effects. These measures now form a solid foundation of environmental policy and best practice directives that guide all of the Bank's work. Among the most influential of these measures is the environmental assessment (EA), which provides policymakers, planners, and analysts with a better understanding of the environmental situation and issues at hand. After presenting a brief history of the evolution of environmental policy at the Bank, this chapter focuses on the Bank's experience with EA since the Rio Earth Summit and presents lessons learned from the recently completed second environmental assessment review of Bank-financed projects.

A Brief History of World Bank Environmental Policy

Environmental concerns became an explicit part of Bank activities in 1970, when the position of environmental adviser was established. Bank environmental policies and assessment procedures evolved slowly during the following fifteen years, and rapidly during the past decade, reflecting the changes in thinking taking place in the international development community. The first internal instruction to Bank staff on the environment concerned with how to approach social issues associated with involuntary resettlement, Operational Manual Statement (OMS) 2.33, was released in February 1980.[1] This was followed by a statement on tribal peoples in Bank operations issued in February 1982 (OMS 2.34, later updated by Operational Directive 4.40 in September 1991).

The first operational policy statement on environmental aspects of the Bank's work (OMS 2.36) was issued in May 1984. This required that environmental considerations be introduced at the time of project identification and preparation and recognized that modification could also occur at the time of appraisal, negotiation, and implementation. With this, the Bank became the first multilateral development agency to screen projects for their environmental consequences and to adopt environmental guidelines for the evaluation of future lending operations. Moreover, by the mid-1980s, the Bank was financing projects containing specific environmental components, including several primarily environmental projects (see annex C for a list of the Bank's portfolio of primarily environmental projects).

Since 1984, and particularly since 1989, Bank policies in relation to the environment have become more and more forceful, expanding to include agricultural pest management (1985), management of wildlands (1986), protection of cultural property (1986), collaboration with NGOs

> **Box 4.1. World Bank Environmental Policies**
>
> *Environmental assessment.* All Bank projects are screened for their potential environmental impacts, and those categorized as A are subject to a full EA.
>
> *Environmental action plans.* This policy outlines Bank support for preparation of country environmental action plans by borrowing governments.
>
> *Agricultural pest management.* The Bank's policy promotes effective and environmentally sound pest management practices and advocates the use of integrated pest management techniques in Bank-supported agricultural development projects.
>
> *Water resources management.* This policy restricts World Bank involvement in water resources management to support for the provision of water, sanitation facilities, flood control, and water for productive activities in a manner that is economically viable, environmentally sustainable, and socially equitable.
>
> *Indigenous people.* This directive recognizes that special action is required where Bank-supported investments affect indigenous peoples, tribes, ethnic minorities, or other groups whose social and economic status restricts their capacity to assert their interests and rights to land and other productive resources.
>
> *Involuntary resettlement.* This directive recognizes that involuntary resettlement may cause severe long-term hardship, impoverishment, and environmental damage unless appropriate measures are planned and carried out.
>
> *Forestry.* World Bank involvement aims to reduce deforestation, enhance the environmental contribution of forested areas, promote afforestation, reduce poverty, and encourage economic development.
>
> *Environmental policy for dam and reservoir projects.* This establishes policy for dam and reservoir projects and codifies best practices, including preparation of preliminary reconnaissance to identify potential environmental effects and ascertain the extent of needed environmental studies and actions.
>
> *Wildlands.* This provides the basic framework for Bank support for the protection, maintenance, and rehabilitation of natural habitats.

(1988), and environmental policy for dam and reservoir projects (1989). See box 4.1 for a list of environment-related Bank policies and annex A for a full description. In addition, in 1987 the Bank implemented a series of structural changes that strengthened environmental policies, procedures, and staff resources; this process culminated in 1989 with the introduction of Operational Directive (OD) 4.00, Annex A: Environmental Assessment (revised in 1991). This directive requires that all Bank investment projects be screened for their potential environmental effects.

All of these instruments have since been, or are in the process of being, updated and strengthened, and more recent directives include ones on indigenous people (1991), water resources management (1993), and forestry (1993). The revised policy for protecting and managing cultural property will soon be released (see box 4.2). The effects of these sectoral policies are reflected in the discussion in the following chapters. In 1993, all existing ODs began to be revised and incorporated into a new system

---

Box 4.2. A Policy for Cultural Heritage

Much of the Bank's work on heritage conservation supports efforts of the Bank's regional departments to identify cultural heritage sites and to incorporate opportunities to conserve them into projects. The Bank also uses environmental assessment requirements as a tool to identify cultural heritage issues.

The Bank recently prepared an operational policy on cultural heritage, which is ready for final review. This operational policy, which builds on the previous operational policy note on cultural property of 1986, reflects the intervening experience with project and environmental assessment. It emphasizes using expert advice, conservation, mitigation of adverse impacts, and community participation.

Environmental assessment work in this area has gradually expanded. The "Environmental Sourcebook Update on Cultural Heritage in Environmental Assessment" (World Bank 1994c) was published in autumn of 1994 and is now translated into Chinese, French, Russian, and Spanish. With the dearth of information on cultural heritage in environmental assessment, this publication has met with considerable enthusiasm from experts and practitioners, and EA training is being provided to a number of national governments. For instance, in June 1995, an EA workshop on highways in China featured discussions of cultural relics, a subject of much interest in many Chinese provinces. An update on cultural heritage in coastal zone management has been prepared and is under final review.

Several new projects with heritage components have been identified in the past year, typically as part of environmental infrastructure or water sector projects. Among new work is the inclusion of cultural heritage conservation in GEF biodiversity projects, such as the project undertaken recently in Ecuador. Heritage conservation sector studies have also been carried out for countries in Africa and Asia.

Fiscal 1995 also marks the first IDF grant allocated for heritage conservation. Albania, the recipient, will use this grant to revise its legislation regarding cultural heritage, develop inventory methods, and formulate a national heritage conservation strategy. Other countries have expressed interest in applying for similar IDF grants.

of operational policies and Bank procedures. The new system comprises three categories of directives: operational policies (OP), Bank procedures (BP), and good practice (GP). A list of Bank policies relating to the environment can be found in annex A.

Using Environmental Assessments to Direct Environmental Lending

Since 1989, and particularly since the Rio Earth Summit in 1992, governments, development institutions, nongovernmental organizations (NGOs), and, increasingly, the private sector, have established EA policies and procedures and are implementing them in a wide range of development projects. Now most major investment decisions are made taking potential environmental consequences into account.

The ultimate purpose of EA is to safeguard ecological functions and ensure responsible use of natural resources. These results can only be

---

Box 4.3. The Environmental Assessment Process

The EA process is built into the Bank's project cycle as an integral part of project design and implementation. Acting as adviser throughout the process, the Bank ensures that the practice and quality of EAs are consistent with EA requirements and that the process feeds effectively into project preparation and implementation. The main EA-related steps in the project cycle are described below.

Screening. To decide the nature and extent of the EA to be carried out, the Bank team determines the nature and magnitude of the proposed projects potential environmental and social impacts and assigns the project to one of three categories. Category A requires a full EA and is assigned to projects whose adverse impacts may be sensitive, irreversible, and diverse. Category B requires some environmental analysis and is assigned to projects whose impacts are less significant and not as sensitive, numerous, major, or diverse. Few, if any, of these impacts are irreversible, and remedial measures can be more easily designed. Category C projects require no EA or other environmental analysis. Projects with multiple components are classified according to the component with the most significant adverse impact.

Scoping and terms of reference. Once a project is categorized, a scoping process defines the project's likely environmental impacts and area of influence more precisely and develops terms of reference for the EA. As part of this process, information about the project and its likely impact is disseminated to local communities and NGOs, followed by consultations that help to focus the EA on issues of concern at the local level.

fully evaluated after a project has been completed, but because many of the Bank-funded investment projects that have undergone EAs are still being implemented, the effectiveness of EAs can best be assessed by looking at their influence on project design, preparation, and implementation (box 4.3 briefly describes the EA process and how it fits into the Bank's project cycle).[2] The Bank's experience is that EAs are contributing significantly to the environmental and social sustainability of Bank-supported development initiatives.

Assessing the EA Portfolio

Between 1989 and 1995, more than 1,000 World Bank projects were screened for their potential environmental impacts: about 600 of these projects have been screened since UNCED, and 228 were screened in fiscal 1995 alone (see table 4.1). Among the investment projects approved by the Bank's Board of Directors in fiscal 1995, 23 projects (10 percent) were

---

Preparing the EA report. A full EA report is comprised of eight components: an executive summary; a concise project description of the geographic, ecological, social, and temporal context of the project; baseline data including assessment of the study area's dimensions and a description of physical, biological, and socioeconomic conditions; an impact assessment that identifies and assesses the likely positive and negative impacts of the project; analysis of alternatives from an environmental perspective; a mitigation or management plan that identifies implementation and operational measures to eliminate, offset, or reduce adverse environmental impacts; an environmental monitoring plan; and public consultation with affected groups and NGOs during the scoping and EA review stages.

EA review and project appraisal. Once the EA draft is complete, the borrower submits it to the Bank for review by environmental specialists. If the EA is satisfactory, the Bank project team can proceed to project appraisal, which includes, for instance, review of the EA that assesses institutional capacity for environmental management and ensures adequate budget for the mitigation plan.

Project implementation. The borrower is responsible for implementing the project according to agreements derived from the EA process. The Bank supervises the implementation of environmental aspects as part of overall project supervision.

Table 4.1. Projects with EA Category Screened since the Rio Earth Summit, Fiscal 1993–95

Project category	Number of projects	Percentage of total
A	67	11
B	242	40
C	289	48
Total	598	100

Note: Percentages may not add to 100 due to rounding.

classified as category A, which require a full environmental assessment; 81 projects (36 percent) were classified as category B, which require some environmental analysis, and the remaining 124 (54 percent) were classified as category C, which require no EA. In fiscal 1995, category A projects were generally concentrated in the agriculture, energy and power, transport, urban, and water and sanitation sectors, reflecting a fairly consistent sectoral distribution over the past three years (see table 4.2). A description of the category A projects approved in fiscal 1995 can be found in annex F.

Making EA Effective

To improve their effectiveness, the Bank has undertaken two reviews of EAs and is integrating the lessons that emerge into its continuing EA practice. In addition, the Bank's Operations Evaluation Department is conducting a process review of the effectiveness of environmental assessments and environmental action programs (EAPs). The purpose of this review is to evaluate (a) the impact of EAs and EAPs on Bank operations and borrower capacity both before and during project implementation, (b) the efficacy of the review process furnished by the EAs/EAPs in meeting the Bank's environmental objectives as reflected in the ODs, and (c) the extent to which the Bank furnishes support to build capacity in emerging environmental initiatives. The review is covering the past five years, since OD 4.00 was issued. The evaluation process is centered on the preparation of eight country case studies and is scheduled to be completed in fiscal 1996. The second review was able to assess the EA process in a more systematic and detailed fashion. It found improvements in the institutional and operational strength of EAs and in the effort to link EA recommendations with project preparation and implementation. The review concluded that the EA process is now firmly rooted in the Bank's normal business activity. An EA's effectiveness in improving the environmental performance of a project largely depends

Table 4.2. Distribution of Category A Projects, by Sector, Fiscal 1993–95

Sector	1993	1994	1995
Agriculture	3	7	4
Energy and power	10	9	7
Industry	0	0	0
Mining	0	1	0
Tourism	1	0	0
Transport	3	4	5
Urban	0	4	4
Water and sanitation	2	0	3
Total number of projects	19	25	23

on two factors: its quality in technical terms and the degree to which it influences a project's conceptualization, design, and implementation.

The Quality Dimension

The second EA review found that as they learn from experience, the Bank and borrower countries are improving the quality of EAs. This has been especially true in the past three years. Direct and site-specific impacts are being identified and evaluated better in EAs for Bank-financed projects within a broad range of sectors and geographical locations. EAs more consistently identify and discuss fully the most relevant issues and impacts, providing a good basis for developing sound mitigation plans and monitoring measures. For example, analysis of environmental impacts was an integral part of Swaziland's Urban Development Project, where alternative locations were evaluated for the water supply, sewerage treatment, and solid waste disposal components. As a result, changes were made in the design criteria, certain options were eliminated because they were environmentally untenable, and further alternatives were accepted. In some cases, project preparation was delayed until impacts had been properly assessed. Box 4.4 provides a further innovative example, in China's Liaoning Province, in which the EA was used to quantify not only the potentially negative, but also the potentially positive impacts.

Cumulative impacts—such as acid rain caused by emissions from power plants and industrial facilities—have proven more difficult to address, because they have indirect or induced impacts such as spontaneous settlement along a road alignment. Most EAs focus on the direct impacts of a specific investment rather than on these second- or third-order effects. Reasons for this may include insufficient guidance and

> **Box 4.4. Quantifying Impacts in China**
>
> The Liaoning Province in northeast China, home to 25 million urban dwellers, is an important industrial region confronting acute problems of water supply and air and water pollution. Following a previous Bank-supported urban infrastructure project that focused on water supply, the Liaoning Environment Project, approved in fiscal 1995, will invest in improvements in water and air quality, industrial pollution control, municipal solid waste management, and environmental management and training. The project is an innovative mix of pollution control measures encompassing different sources and levels, from the city through individual industries.
>
> The Liaoning Environment Project underwent two EAs. The first was to ensure compliance with the country's environmental regulations; the second, to address Bank concerns. The main feature of the second EA was a quantitative assessment of the project's *positive* environmental impacts, such as reductions in pollution loads and improvements in air and water pollution. Exposure of urban populations to environmental pollution weighed heavily in selection of the project components. An urbanwide approach was used to quantify gains from pollution reductions, as well as to form the basis for identifying further pollution control measures needed to reap the full benefits of the project. Because the project focuses on environmental protection, most EA recommendations became part of the project design, with environmental concerns addressed in the project agreements and conditionalities, in supervision and monitoring plans, and in the proposed environmental mitigation plans.

training on how to carry out such analysis, lack of attention to these aspects in preparing EA terms of reference, and legitimate questions about the value of such analysis, considering the extra costs involved and relative uncertainty about the validity of findings. Financial limitations in developing countries may also play a role. Clearly, however, it is important to be aware of these factors and, to the extent possible, to ensure that cumulative, indirect, and induced impacts receive the attention they deserve.

Another important issue in environmental assessment is the need to integrate economic and environmental analysis better. To date, few EAs have attempted to quantify environmental impacts in economic cost-benefit terms. To address this need, the Bank is finalizing guidance on economic analysis in EA, based on the book, *Economic Analysis of Environmental Impacts*, written in part by Bank environmental economists (Dixon and others 1994). Box 4.5 provides an example of how economic analysis has been used to assess and compare impacts.

Box 4.5. Economic Costs of Environmental Impacts

Korea's Ports Development and Environmental Implementation Project involves constructing two new port facilities and an industrial complex, all of which require dredging and reclamation and potentially will generate considerable noise, air pollution, and wastewater. As part of the EA review, alternative sites were analyzed, including an environmental cost-benefit analysis comparing two possible sites for the project. Costs taken into account included construction costs of the wharf, breakwater, terminal, and industrial sites; operation and maintenance costs of the port facilities; and compensation payments for loss of property and income related to fishing and harvesting of seaweed and loss in value of residential properties located near the new port and processing site.

The direct cost difference between the two sites was estimated to be more than $100 million. However, when the environmental costs represented as loss in property values were included, the more costly site in terms of direct costs resulted in *fewer* impacts, valued at $7.3 million. Had the risks of damage to a fragile protected marine ecosystem been included as well, this difference would have been even greater.

Analysis of Alternatives

Beyond simply avoiding and mitigating environmental harm, an EA can enhance project design by considering alternative investments from an environmental perspective. To meet Bank standards, EAs must compare systematically a project's proposed design, site, technology, and operational alternatives for their potential environmental impacts. EAs should also compare capital and recurrent costs of each option, their suitability under local conditions, and their institutional, training, and monitoring requirements. Ideally, EAs should quantify each alternative's environmental costs and benefits to the extent possible and attach economic values where feasible.

Although many of the EAs submitted to the Bank during the past several years provided only a limited analysis of alternatives, more and more now examine alternatives in greater depth. Analysis of alternatives in Indonesia, for instance, prompted a change in the location of a proposed wastewater treatment plant. In Croatia, the EA for the Highway Project considered six options for road alignment on the basis of their likely impact on agricultural land, forest habitat, watercourses, settlements, and air, water, soil, and noise pollution. EA specialists developed a rating system to rank the variants and presented the findings at a public meeting. The final choice was modified to reduce further the potential negative effects on the landscape.

Considering sectoral investment alternatives adequately from an environmental perspective is far more difficult than simply avoiding or minimizing the negative impacts of a proposal. It is complicated by the fact that borrowers rarely require such an analysis of alternatives in their own EAs. An in-depth analysis of alternatives, including economic analysis of environmental costs and benefits, also requires specialized skills on the part of EA consultants, and many countries and local consultants do not yet have this capacity. Finally, timing may be a serious constraint when project preparation is not synchronized with the borrowers' planning process. In practice, many EAs are carried out at a stage when the major design and location decisions have already been made, and the main available alternatives are either to go ahead with the project, perhaps with limited technological or operational changes, or to abandon it completely. Although these "downstream" planning issues are important, because they may alter the nature and significance of environmental impacts, EAs should ideally also influence the "upstream" planning process. To address this need, the Bank is encouraging the use of sectoral and regional EAs to introduce environmental concerns before major decisions are made. These are discussed briefly below.

Mitigation, Monitoring, and Management Plans

The quality of EA mitigation, monitoring, and management plans has improved in the past few years. These plans specify the measures and activities to be undertaken, explain how they will be implemented, indicate their timing and duration, and identify costs, sources of funding, and entities responsible for their implementation. The mitigation plan for China's Sichuan Gas Development and Conservation Project, for instance, includes a system to detect gas leaks and automatic alarm devices. Similarly, an essential component of the monitoring plan for Ethiopia's Calub Gas Development Project includes establishing an environmental monitoring system to track both biophysical and socioeconomic repercussions in areas where they will have an impact.

Many of the problems with these issues have not yet been fully restored, however, and the Bank is making an effort during appraisal and negotiations to finalize adequate plans and, in particular, to resolve the issue of time in some projects. Further progress is likely with stronger borrower EA requirements, improved borrower capacity to carry out EAs, and more targeted follow-up by the Bank and other donors once draft EA reports have been submitted for review.

In some instances, the Bank's requirements have in themselves led to institutional capacity building in preparing EAs and in preparing mitigation, monitoring, and management plans. This is the case, for example, in a series of programmatic loans to Indonesia in the urban and roads sectors, for several water and sanitation projects in Korea, and a wide variety of sectors in China. Only a few years ago, China had virtually no EA experience or expertise. Today, EAs are routinely performed for a large number of projects, primarily by Chinese EA specialists. Over time, the plans developed on the basis of EA work have become more specific and realistic.

Using Public Consultation

Public consultation plays a key role in identifying and assessing environmental impacts, comparing alternatives, designing appropriate mitigation measures, and building local ownership and participation into the development process. More borrowers are including substantive public consultation as part of the EA and are gaining experience in designing meaningful consultation processes. In many projects, consultations are becoming more open and interactive, using public meetings or new approaches such as interactive television or radio. Consultations include not only local NGOs or representatives of directly affected people but also the whole population in a project area. The quality of EA work has improved significantly as a result. In Paraguay's Natural Resources Management Project, for example, following consultation, new areas were demarcated that will protect a vulnerable ethnic group, the Tupi Guarani, and reduce destruction of fragile natural resources. Box 4.6 offers additional examples of public consultation and its effect on project design, while box 4.7 details opportunities for public consultation during various stages of the EA process.

In some projects, however, borrowers have found it easier to consult with local NGOs than with affected communities, in particular with women and the poor. Some EAs, moreover, still do not sufficiently document the consultation process and its results. Public consultation also remains a challenge in countries whose governments have no similar requirements or cultural traditions in this regard or whose local project and EA consultant teams possess insufficient social science expertise. A study within the Bank's Africa Region (Cook and Donelly-Roark 1995), for example, found that one primary factor in the success of EAs that used demonstrable levels of participation was the use of EA consultants who were knowledgeable about participatory techniques.

To consolidate public consultation in EA, the second EA review suggested the following measures:

> **Box 4.6. Public Consultation and Project Design**
>
> EA consultations with affected people or local NGOs have contributed to changes in project design in numerous projects. In Ghana's Environmental Resource Management Project, for instance, public consultations drove the process of project design from the very beginning. Investments under the village-level land and water resource management component were entirely designed by local communities, which diagnosed problems, developed action plans, and are now responsible for implementation. A coastal wetlands component was also largely designed through local consultation. Affected communities and user groups participated in setting the boundaries for ecologically sensitive areas and in determining the levels of resource use and conservation in coastal wetlands. Similarly, the consultation process for Colombia's Power Sector Technical Assistance Project led to changes not only in the design of the project but also in priorities for national policy related to the development of power. And in Brazil's Espirito Santo Water Project, the original design would have negatively affected two communities. By including these communities in the EA process through the disclosure of information and through consultations, satisfactory mitigation measures counterbalanced the impacts and improved local living conditions.

- Implementing agencies in borrowing countries should be strengthened to the point where they have sufficient institutional resources to plan and carry out consultations with stakeholders. This requires a staff of qualified professionals in social and communication sciences and a basic office infrastructure.
- Sufficient funds need to be allocated to finance the consultation process. The implementing agency, not the stakeholders, should pay for the necessary equipment, transport, and per diems. Financing institutions like the Bank may be able to help a borrower country identify sources of funding, if needed.
- The borrower agency or EA team should quickly analyze the project's social context to answer the following questions: Who are the relevant stakeholders? What are the customary institutional forms of decisionmaking in the country? What are the customary forms of communication preceding decisionmaking?
- Borrowers should be encouraged to identify the appropriate areas for and participants in consultation. Not all groups need to be consulted on all details of a project, such as purely technical decisions that do not require public input. However, on decisions that intimately affect local living conditions, the interested com-

> **Box 4.7. Public Consultation at EA Stages**
>
> *Scoping.* Effective scoping involves consulting with representatives of affected people and NGOs to identify key issues and prepare appropriate terms of reference. But in many projects, the EA consultants responsible for making sure that consultations take place are hired only after the terms of reference for the EA have been completed. One alternative would be to help the implementing agency organize initial consultations during scoping. Another would be to adjust the contracting process so that the consultants are already on board at the scoping stage. This could be done, for instance, by selecting EA consultants, paying them an advance to conduct the scoping and prepare the proposed terms of reference, and then negotiating the contract for the actual EA.
>
> *EA preparation:* Many EAs involve consulting affected people at various stages of the process. The most common method of contact is through surveys. These are often undertaken in the context of resettlement or when indigenous peoples are involved.
>
> *Draft EA report.* Consultation on the draft EA report is one of the most important elements of the EA process. The persons consulted should be allowed sufficient time to review the draft conclusions before discussions take place. It is likewise critical that the findings and recommendations be presented in a form that is meaningful to the persons consulted. Sometimes, radio is the best medium for dissemination.
>
> *Project implementation.* It is good practice to extend contacts with local people and NGOs on EA-related matters during project implementation. In some projects, local NGOs play a role in monitoring and implementing the projects environmental impact. In others, participatory sessions with local groups are scheduled for subprojects and components that were not completely defined prior to approval.

munities should take direct part in the decisionmaking process or make the decisions themselves.

Project agencies should work systematically to ensure that stakeholders are consulted at the main stages of project preparation, particularly the scoping stage, before EA terms of references are finalized. The conclusions emerging from these consultations should be fed back to the participants for their verification.

Improving EAs

The second EA review found that, to improve the environmental performance of projects, EAs need to influence overall project preparation and implementation. Even high-quality EAs sometimes lack this dimension and thus have little or no impact on the project. The environmental assessment must be fully integrated with the overall project cycle during project preparation, during negotiation of binding implementation agreements, and during project implementation itself.

Integrate EAs into Project Preparation

To be fully effective, the EA must form an integral part of project preparation and should not be detached from the broader process of project preparation. Some EAs, particularly sectoral and regional EAs and EAs that are project-specific but prepared within a comprehensive environmental policy framework, are more intimately linked to early project design by being part of the diagnostic study process.

However, EAs for environmental management projects are occasionally seen as duplicating or overlapping work already undertaken in other project feasibility studies. In these cases, an early sectoral or regional EA focusing on policy, legal and institutional aspects, and strategic choices may be more useful than a project-specific assessment.

Convert EA Recommendations into Specific Deliverables

Once realistic environmental mitigation, monitoring, and management plans have been prepared, the next step is to convert them into agreed actions to be implemented; to define the procedures, standards, and guidelines to be followed throughout the implementation process; and to ensure that the agreed actions are explicitly reflected in legally binding project, contract, and bidding documents (see box 4.8). Bank experience suggests that when recommendations are fully incorporated into project documents, implementing agencies have clear information on what is expected and may be more committed to following up on the EA. Supervision of environmental performance also becomes more feasible where clear performance criteria are spelled out.

Learn from Project Implementation

In the final analysis, project implementation tests EA effectiveness in two ways. It reveals the extent to which the EA identified and accurately assessed a project's actual environmental impacts. It also reveals the effectiveness of plans and measures intended to avoid or mitigate adverse impacts and to manage and monitor environmental quality. In the process, it demonstrates the performance and capabilities of the institutions responsible for implementing EA-related activities.

> **Box 4.8. Translating EA Recommendations into Project, Contract, and Bidding Documents**
>
> In China's Second Ertan Hydroelectric Project, EA mitigation and monitoring plans were explicitly incorporated into official project documentation, specifying the individuals and agencies responsible for the programs; the general elements such as start-up date, study locations, data collection methods, and type of data analysis; and the budget through the year 2000. The detailed environmental measures represent an important step toward institutionalizing environmental aspects in project design and implementation and increasing the effectiveness of the EA process.
>
> Similarly in Pakistan, EA recommendations were incorporated in the physical works design and bidding documents for the Domestic Energy Resources Development Project. This project involves developing oil and gas fields as a joint venture between state-owned and international companies and constructing a condensate plant and gas pipelines. It includes measures for environmental protection and institutional strengthening. Institutionalization of the EA recommendations played a vital role in selecting contractors for the project. For example, one bid was rejected because it failed to meet an EA requirement, even though it was the most financially competitive.

The second review of EA found that the general performance of Bank-financed category A projects under implementation is above the Bank-wide average for investment projects; this is encouraging, because it suggests that projects subject to full EAs perform better than those not subject to them, even if a direct causal link has yet to be established. Box 4.9 offers three important lessons identified by the second EA review and based on EA experience and project implementation since 1990.

Emerging Challenges

As Bank experience with environmental assessment evolves, important areas of work continue to emerge that require innovative approaches. Among these are Bank work with sectoral and regional EAs, EAs of private sector development projects, and financial intermediary lending.

Sectoral and Regional EAs

Experience has shown repeatedly that sectoral EAs can avoid the inherent limitations of project-specific EAs in addressing issues related to policy, planning, and the broader legal and institutional framework. By

> **Box 4.9. Lessons from EA Experience in Project Implementation**
>
> The accumulating experience is generating important lessons about the preparation of good EAs, especially with regard to environmental mitigation, monitoring, and management measures and to realistic targets and institutional arrangements for implementation:
>
> - Environmental mitigation, management, and monitoring plans have to balance the desire to address a multitude of complex environmental problems and the limitations of local institutions. High-priority objectives may include strengthening local institutional capacity, correcting key policy failures, and developing practical solutions and models to address high-risk problems.
> - Where existing environmental management capacity may be insufficient to address a project's challenges, a strategy should be formulated to establish preconditions for its environmental success, including a stable and qualified implementation unit, adequate counterpart financing, sufficient logistical capacity, and sustained management support. Staffing and logistical requirements should be determined as precisely as possible.
> - If a project implementing agency cannot develop adequate capacity to carry out environmental mitigation, management, and monitoring plans, responsibility for these measures should be contracted out to other organizations. Monitoring, data analysis, management of protected areas, or similar measures may benefit from being contracted out to NGOs, universities, or consulting firms.

moving upstream in the planning process to a stage where major strategic decisions have yet to be made, sectoral EAs offer opportunities both to analyze environmental issues in relation to policies, institutions, and development plans and to support environmentally sound sectorwide investments. Sectoral EAs have recently been prepared to support the Dominican Republic's Power Sector Project and Morocco's Large-Scale Irrigation Project II, as well as Bank-supported projects for urban development (solid waste management), transport (roads, highways), water (rural water resource management), and energy (power development).

Sectoral EAs require a different approach to mitigation, monitoring, and management planning, especially when specific subprojects are not known at the time of project appraisal. Sectoral EAs suggest broad approaches and options, taking into account the constraints and opportunities present in the sector and overall environmental management capacity in the country. For example, sectoral EAs may consider broad mitigation solutions related to production systems as well as end-of-pipe cleaner technologies, or they may develop standard operating procedures. Several sectoral EAs look at such options, such as a road sector project in Indonesia, an irrigation project in Chile, and a series of other resource management projects in India.

Regional environmental assessments, in contrast, examine the cumulative effects of several current, planned, or expected activities in a particular area. They are especially useful when considering major investments in remote or previously undeveloped areas with potentially significant environmental and socioeconomic changes. Projects that develop hydroelectric power development or construct roads, for instance, can set in motion intentional or unanticipated development processes that influence the environment in multiple and cumulative direct and indirect ways. Regional EAs can also be valuable in urban or semiurban settings, such as coastal zones, that normally are subject to a variety of planned and unplanned changes.

To date, only one approved project has been subject to a regional EA: Paraguay's Natural Resources Management Project. A proposed operation, the Biodiversity Conservation Project in Indonesia, has also been subject to regional analysis. There is some indication, however, that regional assessments are becoming more common, as projects establish a sound spatial planning and management framework and follow a spatial approach to mitigation, management, and monitoring. A regional EA is being prepared in Lebanon for a project that focuses on a 16 kilometer wide coastal zone, as well as in Indonesia for the proposed Bali Urban Infrastructure Project. In addition, several projects include studies and plans aimed at strengthening environmental planning on a regional scale—such as river basin management in Brazil, coastal zone management in Egypt, and urban environmental planning in Sri Lanka—although these studies are not referred to as regional EAs. Regional EAs appear to have a strong potential for improving the environmental dimension of regional development planning and for contributing to more sustainable investment patterns and strategies at a regional level. Like sectoral EAs, regional EAs can move environmental analysis upstream in the planning process to a stage where major strategic decisions and policies have yet to be made.

EA and Private Sector Development

Another emerging area for EA is private sector development. The private sector is fast becoming the main engine of economic development in most countries, and the Bank encourages this trend by supporting privatization programs and developing the financial sector in borrowing countries. An important component of this is lending through financial intermediaries, such as commercial banks and rural credit institutions.

Through loans to financial intermediaries in the form of credit lines, the Bank promotes private sector development on a broad basis, reaching investors in various sectors of the economy.

With respect to an EA process for subprojects funded through financial intermediaries, the second EA review suggests two possible courses of action: (a) establish and strengthen environmental screening and review capacity within financial intermediaries or (b) rely on and strengthen the government's EA procedures and requirements. In some cases, a combination of these approaches is most effective. The Bank, in turn, is responsible for appraising environmental capacity at the level of the financial intermediary or government to screen subprojects, obtain expertise needed for EA preparation, review EA reports, and monitor environmental conditions during project implementation.

Several innovative approaches have been adopted in financial intermediary projects. These include a special, parallel credit line exclusively for investments in control and prevention of pollution, and joint government and private sector implementation of detailed EA procedures covering screening, environmental audits, full EAs, and review and clearance functions. Training of professional bankers is also becoming more prevalent. In the past, EA requirements were imposed on financial institutions that saw little advantage in adopting their own environmental procedures or requirements. The new generation of financial intermediary projects emphasizes the role that project environmental screening and review can play in sound credit risk management (see box 4.10).

Box 4.10. Credit Risk Management in the Russian Federation

The Russian Enterprise Support Project aims to modernize and privatize Russian industrial enterprises with funds channeled through participating Russian banks. This unprecedented environmental approach includes a detailed procedure developed by the World Bank in close coordination with the European Bank for Reconstruction and Development. The procedure is intended to help the enterprises undertake their own environmental credit risk management and protect their loan portfolios from being weakened by projects failing to meet Russian environmental regulations.

In the step-by-step procedure, roles and responsibilities for the participating banks, enterprises seeking credit, environmental agencies, and the World Bank are clearly delineated. Guidance is provided on documentation requirements, with checklists of activities requiring analysis, including activities that should not be financed under any circumstances, such as the production of tobacco or radioactive products.

Notes

1. OMS 2.33 on involuntary resettlement was later complemented by Operational Policy Note 10.08 of October 1986 and was replaced by Operational Directive (OD) 4.30 in June 1990.

2. Adjustment loans and credits do not fall under the Bank's EA policy, but consideration of their environmental effects is required under OD 8.60 on adjustment lending.

5. Seeking New Directions: Agriculture and the Environment

WORLD BANK PHOTO/CURT CARNEMARK

Historically, the irrigation sector has been a major engine of agricultural growth in developing countries, but it is now constrained by complex environmental uncertainties and competition for water. Recognizing these constraints, the Bank has stressed the need for a comprehensive framework for subsectors—such as irrigation and drainage—and for innovative approaches. Such an approach is evidenced in Pakistan's Rural Water Supply and Sanitation Project, which is developing a delivery mechanism whereby rural communities, such as these farmers, would provide, operate, and maintain the service.

Feeding the world's growing population while preserving the natural resource base on which it depends presents the agricultural sector with a range of difficult choices. To meet their rising needs, farmers can either expand the area they cultivate or increase the yield from their existing farmland. Agricultural expansion by land-use conversion, for example, or diversion of water resources raises troublesome environmental concerns as natural habitats shrink and become more fragile and as water becomes more scarce in other sectors. At the same time, agricultural intensification through application of chemical and other modern inputs can, if improperly managed, pollute the groundwater, build up pesticide resistance and a dangerous reliance on monocultures, and diminish the range of genetic resources. These challenges affect a resource base that may already be overstressed by poverty, misdirected policies, underinvestment in farmers' training, inadequate dissemination of agricultural research and technology, and generally unresponsive institutions and systems of governance.

Facing the Challenges Ahead

The past thirty years have been an extraordinarily successful period for the agricultural sector in much of the developing world. In Asia, per capita grain production has risen from 215 kilograms to more than 279 kilograms, and the perennial threat of famine has been removed for nearly 200 million people. World grain yields, because of the development of irrigation systems, the availability of high-yielding varieties, and the use of modern inputs, have risen from about 1.8 tons per hectare in 1970 to about 2.7 tons per hectare in 1991. Some areas, however, have not been part of this overall success. In Sub-Saharan Africa, in particular, yields and inputs have stagnated, and grain production per capita has actually fallen in at least twenty-seven countries. Furthermore, agriculture is still vulnerable to the vagaries of storms, floods, droughts, and late rains, which have reduced harvest yields this year, causing world grain stocks to decrease substantially.

Resource Conversion

Throughout most of history, new demands for food have been satisfied by converting natural resources to agricultural uses. Over the past three decades, area expansion accounted for 16 percent of new agricultural output in developing countries; in Sub-Saharan Africa, it accounted for 47 percent. The remaining reserves of natural areas are shrinking, however, and the share of these lands that is suitable for sustainable agriculture is declining even faster. In addition, increased awareness of the global significance of remaining natural habitats as repositories of biodiversity and as carbon sinks is putting the environmental consequences of agricultural expansion into starker perspective.

In addition to the conversion of land, appropriation of water for irrigation is a major source of growth in agricultural output. In 1990 diversion of water for irrigation in developing countries amounted to approximately 839 million cubic meters per year, nearly 80 percent of total water use. However, in many parts of the world, particularly the Middle East and North Africa, but also parts of Asia, growing demand for water from other sectors is forcing the agricultural sector to adopt new growth strategies and new water management practices.

Intensification

Beginning in the 1960s, growth in output on existing farmland began to be a major engine of growth in developing-world agriculture. Part of this growth has come from improved varieties that have greater tolerance for drought, disease, and other stresses. However, a significant part of the growth in yield has resulted from a more intensive use of modern inputs, including chemical fertilizers and pesticides.

Although pollution from overuse of fertilizers has become a problem in industrial countries, including the Netherlands, the United Kingdom, and the United States, in much of the developing world underuse of fertilizers remains a real problem. Inadequate soil nutrition traps farmers at low levels of productivity and often forces them to deplete their soil resources to meet their immediate needs. The problem is intensified when matched with poor soil management practices. In Sub-Saharan Africa, where yields are low, fertilizer use is a mere 14 kilograms per hectare per year (compared with more than 190 kilograms per hectare per year in countries of the Organisation for Economic Co-operation and Development, OECD), and pesticide use is negligible. Training in efficient fertilizer use and integrated pest management will help promote proper use.

In parts of some developing countries, however, such as eastern China, the Punjab of India and Pakistan, and parts of Eastern Europe, use of fertilizers is approaching the levels found in industrial countries. Moreover, in many countries, policymakers have subsidized the prices of agricultural inputs. In Indonesia, for example, this policy, which has been reversed, contributed to a buildup of pesticide resistance in the brown planthopper, which seriously damaged rice harvests in the 1980s. In addition, evidence is accumulating that even intensive and highly productive systems, as currently managed, may be unsustainable. Results from long-term trials at the International Rice Research Institute indicate declining yields of the best varieties. Likewise, in the highly productive areas of the Indo-Gangetic Basin, where rice and wheat are grown in intensive rotation, yields are beginning to stagnate and the response to inputs is declining. The potential significance of these findings for developing countries is troubling. The Bank has been monitoring this issue and examining national systems for evidence of yield stagnation, as, for example, in the work described in box 5.1.

Implementing a New Approach to Agricultural Lending

The Bank's approach to agricultural development has evolved considerably over the past decade. Approaches that emphasize new irrigation infrastructure and land settlement have been gradually supplemented by efforts to increase the output from existing farmland by assisting farmers in adopting intensified production systems involving greater use of modern techniques and high-yielding varieties. Subsequently, as awareness has grown of the need to give more attention to natural resource management, the number of projects incorporating some form of land management has increased. Recently, by adopting new policies on water resources, forests, and agricultural pest management, the Bank has increased its emphasis on improving the quality of resource management (by focusing on operation and management rather than on new construction, for example, and by emphasizing intersectoral links) and on leveraging the complementarities between poverty reduction, better agricultural practices, and improved environmental stewardship.

In the three years since the Rio Earth Summit, Bank financing in agricultural development has totaled more than $10 billion. The Bank's portfolio of agricultural projects now actively pursues opportunities to improve the efficiency of resource use (through, for example, price reforms and involvement of local communities and farmers in the management of their own resources); to promote and better target investment in technology development and adaptation (by involving farmers in research, for example); and to focus on improving conditions of small farmers.

A New Emphasis in Agricultural Subsectors

An overview of the composition of the Bank's agriculture portfolio is provided in table 5.1. Some of the key activities with which the Bank is associated are discussed here.

> **Box 5.1. Bangladesh: Environmental and Natural Resource Degradation from Intensive Agriculture**
>
> Bangladesh has one of the world's most dense populations, making land extremely scarce. Practically no prospects exist for increasing the area under cultivation. Agricultural growth, therefore, has been based on intensification: modern rice varieties now account for almost half of the rice under cultivation, an increasing proportion of land is double- or triple-cropped, the area under irrigation has more than doubled since 1980, and use of chemical fertilizers has doubled since the early 1980s. Due to this intensification, Bangladesh has become foodgrain self-sufficient in good years, a result few observers would have anticipated ten years ago.
>
> Concern is rising, however, that this intensive agriculture may not be sustainable. While the continued conversion from low-yielding local to high-yielding modern varieties has led to rising yields, yields of modern varieties are declining in areas that have been cultivated intensively for many years, despite rising input levels. Yield declines are strongly associated with the length of time that intensive production practices have been employed in each district. Long-term trials conducted by the Bangladesh Rice Research Institute also indicate that intensive rice cultivation can result in declining yields, even under good management and using the full recommended doses of all nutrients applied.
>
> Stagnant or declining yields despite rising inputs indicate that land degradation is reducing productivity; in fact, without increases in input, yields would have fallen even further. This problem is not unique to Bangladesh. Many other green revolution countries have also experienced slowdowns or downturns in the rate of growth of production and yield. There is considerable debate over the exact causes of declining productivity. In Bangladesh, the most likely cause is nutrient imbalances. High-yielding modern varieties are far more demanding of soil nutrients than local varieties are, and this problem is exacerbated by the prevalence of multiple cropping. The use of chemical fertilizers has increased, but not sufficiently to compensate for the higher rates of offtake, and this intense use has been offset by reductions in the application of farmyard manure, which is increasingly used for fuel.
>
> *Source:* Pagiola 1995.

Land

Sustainable land management implies maintaining and enhancing the quality of land resources while providing environmental, economic, and social benefits. Unlike other resource-based industries, agriculture is

Table 5.1. Agriculture Sector Projects Approved, Fiscal 1990–95, by Major Subsector

Subsector	1993 Number of projects	1993 Amount of loan or credit (thousands of dollars)	1994 Number of projects	1994 Amount of loan or credit (thousands of dollars)	1995 Number of projects	1995 Amount of loan or credit (thousands of dollars)
Sector loan	22	1,118	21	1,818	18	994
Fishing	0	0	0	0	1	9
Irrigation and drainage	11	920	8	1,026	9	782
Livestock	1	23	0	0	0	0
Marketing	0	0	0	0	0	0
Agroindustry	2	493	0	0	2	92
Perennial crops	1	92	1	70	0	0
Research and extension	3	53	5	88	7	348
Forestry	2	92	8	565	8	139
Other	3	477	5	340	10	388
Total	45	3,268	48	3,907	55	2,752

made up of millions of small-scale entrepreneurs who make individual decisions on how to manage their resources and invest their scarce capital. Although the land-use decisions of individual farmers may seem to be insignificant, these decisions are repeated over and over again in the landscape and thereby collectively achieve global impact. Thus, government initiatives that rely on expensive and capital-intensive methods beyond the reach of most farmers and not suited to local environments are likely to fail. A misdirected policy framework that leads to improper management of land use is another major cause of environmental degradation. Therefore the Bank is shifting toward three approaches for improving land management:

Move to least-cost, quick-return methods of soil moisture conservation. This has been done in projects ranging from India to Indonesia, Burkina Faso, China, and Mali. The China Loess Plateau Watershed Rehabilitation Project, for example, will strengthen the capacity of the Upper and Middle Reach Bureau of the Yellow River Conservancy as a leading agency for soil and water conservation in the Yellow River Basin and will enable the provinces and prefectures to be better equipped to meet the formidable challenge of developing the Loess Plateau. The project will be implemented largely by the villagers living in the watersheds and will include substantial farmer training. In the Sahel, water-harvesting technologies using rock bunds are being promoted as part of community-based systems for planning resource management, while in China, India, and Indonesia, contour vegetative barriers, often involving vetiver grass (*Vetiveria zizanoides*), are being supported. These technologies are highly flexible and can be implemented by farmers without reliance on government subsidy.

Push for market-based land reform. In Colombia, Jamaica, and South Africa, where projects are under development, Bank sector work has shown how policies that restrict the poor's access to land can have a negative effect on the environment. Rural poverty, inefficient resource allocation, and natural resource degradation are joint phenomena that are often induced by a nexus of policies favoring modernization of large-scale farming at the expense of what are in fact more efficient and employment-intensive family farms. This policy nexus forces impoverished populations onto marginal lands, such as tropical forest frontiers and erodible hillsides (see box 5.2).

Encourage decentralized rural development. This approach would take advantage of local knowledge, earn the support of populations affected by development, and be flexible so as to adapt to local circumstances. In the arid rangeland zones, for example, the last decade has seen a dramatic shift, from the development of inappropriate infrastructure that has often induced land degradation to community-based resource management. The emphasis is now on developing an appropriate institutional framework for resource management—through pastoral associations, for example—before the physical investments in water and rangeland improvement are made. These associations, developed by reinforcing traditional links of the range users and allocating grazing rights to these groups, are important vehicles in developing community-based resource management projects, as demonstrated in the Central African Republic, Egypt, Kenya, and Mali. The Central African Rangeland and Livestock Project also uses these associations to manage buffer zones for game parks. In the potentially higher-productivity areas, the emphasis is on integrating livestock into farming systems, improving nutrient recycling, and reducing reliance on outside inputs such as organic fertilizers and herbicides. Many of the recently approved provincial agricultural development projects in China and the livestock components of agricultural service projects in Africa promote environmentally sustainable farming systems. Simultaneously, in the livestock management sector, for example, Bank support has declined for intensive bioindustry types of production, such as industrial feedlots and pig and poultry operations.

Additionally, providing finance to poor farmers is an important way of breaking the cycle of poverty. Adequate rural finance is a critical aspect of creating the conditions for decentralized rural development.

Box 5.2. Revitalizing Land Reform in Colombia

Bank sector work in Colombia has stressed that putting more land in the hands of small farmers is likely to generate gains in efficiency as well as equity, helping to raise the competitiveness of agriculture. In Colombia, the use of land and labor has been driven in highly inefficient directions by a variety of agricultural, land, and rural finance policies and programs, including a number of policy interventions that have circumscribed the poor's access to land. These have prematurely and dramatically reduced employment opportunities in the sector, increasing the concentration of poor people in rural areas and the degradation of resources on hillsides and on the Amazon frontier. Government interventions to drive up the demand for labor in periods of a temporary downturn will do little to cure the fundamental misallocation of land and labor in Colombian agriculture. Nor will interventions to improve the productivity of hillside agriculture of poor farmers be sufficient. More radical approaches are required.

A strong case can be made for reorienting and revitalizing the Colombian land reform. Three reasons are paramount. First, migration away from the countryside has—contrary to the initial expectations of Colombian policymakers—neither eliminated rural poverty nor reversed the tendency of small farmers to cultivate steep slopes in an unsustainable manner. Farmers need to have access to some of the more fertile bottomland currently used for extensive livestock grazing. Second, putting land into the hands of the rural poor will help to defuse one of the causes of rural violence and may thereby help to promote investment in agriculture. Third, small farmers in Colombia have high productivity if given access to land resources, markets, and agricultural services.

Given the less-than-encouraging record of past and current land reform efforts, it is clear that future land reform must be based on radically new approaches that are cheaper, faster, more decentralized, and more participatory. Market-assisted approaches, which are now possible under new Colombian laws, hold a lot of promise for achieving the goals and targets of land reform.

Bank projects that provide resources to financial institutions for on-lending to farmers and rural enterprises have risen to 16 percent of the portfolio since 1992.

Irrigation, Drainage, and Water Resource Management

During fiscal 1990–95, irrigation has accounted for an average of 26 percent of Bank lending for agriculture. Historically a major engine of agricultural growth in developing countries, this subsector is now confronted with complex environmental uncertainties. Increased crop production in irrigated agriculture accounted for half of global gains in food production in the last three decades, but continued growth is constrained by intersectoral competition for water and the need for improved management. Recognizing these constraints, the Bank has reviewed its approach to the sector in its policy paper on water resources management (World Bank 1993c), which stresses the need for a comprehensive framework uniting subsectors (such as irrigation and drainage). This approach to water management, using river basins as the basic unit of analysis and reforming planning and management to ensure efficient and environmentally sound resource development, has led to three main focuses:

Improve the efficiency of existing irrigation systems before creating new ones. Since 1972, while the Bank has been shifting away from the traditional approach of financing the expansion of irrigated areas through the construction of new infrastructure, issues such as water allocation policy and organization of groups of water users have been relatively minor concerns. Recently, however, the Bank's irrigation portfolio has focused more and more on rehabilitating existing systems and managing them with a view to improving efficiency. Most early Bank irrigation loans to Mexico, for example, were made during a period when the economy was protected, decisionmaking for irrigation investment was centralized, and project lending focused mainly on technical issues. Since the early 1990s, however, the government of Mexico and the Bank have adopted a sector investment approach rather than a project-specific one. In an attempt to improve management and maximize the returns on investment, emphasis has been placed on involving beneficiaries in implementation and operation, training staff to monitor water use, and strengthening institutions. Two recent projects, valued at about $2 billion, focus exclusively on improving water management through major policy and institutional reforms. The Irrigation and Drainage Sector Project emphasizes completion of unfinished works; rehabilitation, modernization, and more efficient use of existing irrigation and drainage infrastructure; improved water management; and operation and maintenance. Similarly, the On-Farm and Minor Irrigation Networks Improvement Project makes the Mexican irrigation sector more efficient and less reliant on government funds because investment is shared by beneficiaries and the government.

Encourage decentralization and local management of water resources. Public sector irrigation agencies are implementing programs to share management and financial burdens with water users with a view to holding irrigation management accountable for the efficient distribution and use of water in the sector. Thirteen of the twenty projects approved by the

Board in the last two years include user participation in project management, and the Bank is disseminating good practice cases. User participation programs are under way in East and South Asia, Latin America, the Middle East, and North Africa. In India, Indonesia, Mexico, and Morocco, among other countries, the Bank is helping to improve management and increase the participation of beneficiaries. The proposed Tamil Nadu Water Resources Consolidation Project, for example, will improve performance of irrigation projects by, among other things, encouraging farmer participation through decentralized management.

Impose charges for using water that reflect its scarcity value. In Morocco, water losses between farm gate and crops are estimated at 30 to 40 percent as a result of inefficient water management on farms due to low water charges and inadequate collection performance. Water losses of this magnitude can lead to a buildup of soil salinity and groundwater pollution and are aggravated by the growing scarcity of water. Under a recent Bank project, water charges will be raised so that the volume charge covers the entire estimated operation and maintenance costs, as well as a reasonable portion of depreciation costs and the land betterment levy.

Forestry

Less than a year before the Rio Earth Summit, the Bank adopted a new forestry policy that addresses the challenges of excessive deforestation in tropical forests and inadequate investments in tree planting and forest management (World Bank 1991a). The policy recognizes the range of competing uses for the forest as a resource, the importance of macroeconomic policies and policies in other sectors for forest management, and the fact that many forest problems result from inappropriate policies and market failures that lead to excessive harvesting and insufficient incentives for planting trees and managing forests sustainably. The policy calls for the reform of policies, institutions, and investment priorities and for significant changes in how forests are valued and used. Since adopting this forest policy, the Bank has increased its support for activities in the sector: ten major pieces of sector work have been undertaken, and during the past four fiscal years the Bank has committed $1.7 billion for an additional twenty-six forestry projects, in contrast to total support of $2.6 billion for ninety-seven projects prior to 1991. The composition of new lending in the sector has also shifted substantially (see table 5.2).

The policy emphasizes the *intersectoral links affecting forests* by encouraging more effective collaboration among traditional forestry services, agricultural extension agencies, and NGOs. Such an approach implies

Table 5.2. Changing Patterns of Investment in Bank-Financed Forestry Projects, 1984–95

	1984–91		1992–95	
Investment category	Amount (millions of dollars)	Share (percentage)	Amount (millions of dollars)	Share (percentage)
Resource expansion	1,081	32	564	22
Resource management (total)	1,041	31	1,120	44
Watershed management	83	3	400	16
Alternative livelihoods	23	1	381	15
Harvesting	268	8	151	6
Road construction and maintenance	318	10	11	0
Forest protection (fire, disease, and so forth)	172	5	25	1
Resource assessment	63	2	62	3
Other management	114	3	91	4
Parks and protected areas	156	5	293	12
Forest tenure	9	0	23	1
Institutional support	366	11	292	12
Technology development and transfer	126	4	106	4
Training	80	2	36	1
Wood industries	139	4	7	0
Policy reform and studies	314	9	19	1
Other	40	1	84	3
Total project costs	3,352	100	2,537	100
Total Bank lending	1,675		1,707	

Note: Percentages may not add up to 100 because of rounding.

that forest policy in rural areas needs to be inextricably linked to the planning and implementation of agricultural, household energy, population, and other sectoral activities. Four additional principles also guide the Bank's work in the sector.

Rectify market and policy failures that encourage deforestation and inhibit sustainable land use. The Bank has promoted the reform of sectoral policies and institutions and has especially sought to bring more realistic assessments of resource values into decisionmaking. Sector studies in Costa Rica, Ethiopia, India, Malaysia, and Mexico call for changes in forest pricing practices, liberalization of international trade restrictions, and revisions in land tenure. Sectorwide forestry projects in Bhutan, India, and Poland assist in a broad range of policy and institutional reforms. In the Forest Management and Conservation Project in Lao PDR, for example, the Bank is helping to reform trade and pricing policies and is investing in forest management, protection activities, and human resource development.

Give special emphasis to expanding public participation in forest resource planning and management and mobilizing private sector resources and skills. The Bank is also encouraging stakeholder participation in forest management, planning, and protection, and lending for alternative livelihoods has increased from 0.7 to 15 percent. In projects in Brazil, India, and Mali, the Bank is supporting agroforestry, joint forest management, and other environmentally sound agricultural and off-farm activities as ways of improving opportunities for the rural poor living at or within forest boundaries.

Expand and intensify the management of areas suitable for sustainable forest production, including establishing plantations to reduce pressures on the existing base of forest resources where the scope to do so is sound from a social, environmental, and economic perspective. In the past three years, the Bank has financed establishment of more than 2 million hectares of plantations, including farm forestry and other noncommercial plantings. In the Forest Resource Development and Conservation Project in China and projects in other countries, the emphasis has been on the technical quality of tree planting and on contracting out work previously undertaken directly by government forestry agencies. The share of forestry lending for resource expansion has fallen from 32 percent in 1984–91 to 23 percent in 1992–94, but the annual dollar amount has increased 12 percent. The Bank has emphasized improving the technical quality of planting stock as a way of maximizing the value of its investment to farmers and the environment. In many projects, especially government-sponsored planting schemes in developing countries, poor-quality planting stock results in low survival rates and poor growth. These result in low returns and significantly reduce farmer interest in planting trees. Through technology improvement components in forestry projects such as the Maharashtra Forestry and Andhra Pradesh Forestry projects in India and the Forest Resource Development and Conservation Project in China, the Bank is helping to introduce technologies such as root trainers, culling, and the use of improved soil mixes. These are all low-cost practices that can be introduced into village-scale private or community nurseries.

Expand the designation of forest areas as parks and reserves by adopting and encouraging borrower governments to use a precautionary approach to forest use, particularly in tropical moist forests. To preserve forest areas intact, the Bank has substantially increased investment in parks and protected areas and in watershed management. The share of lending for protective and restorative purposes has increased from 12 percent in 1984–91 to 28 percent during the last three years. This includes the Protected Areas and Wildlife Services Project in Kenya, which establishes a legal, institutional, and financial framework for wildlife resource management, rehabilitates park infrastructure, and supports community-based wildlife extension services and other activities. In line with the requirements of the forest policy paper (World Bank 1991a), the Bank does not finance commercial logging in primary moist tropical forests. Applying the precautionary principle has also led to a decline in the share of lending for activities, such as road construction, from 10 percent in 1984–91 to just 0.4 percent in 1992–94.

Agricultural Research and Extension

Bank-supported agricultural research also reflects these shifts in approach. One trend has been to expand the scope of agricultural knowledge to emphasize the productivity of scarce natural resources. For instance, information has been substituted for the use of chemicals through developing more cost-effective and sustainable systems for controlling pests and diseases. Much of this work goes under the heading of integrated pest management and promises to become more important in Bank-supported projects for agricultural development (see box 5.3). The same concepts have been expanded to embrace integrated nutrient management, which develops more sustainable land management systems. This expansion of the research and technology-sharing agenda has meant that operations tend to be more complex than the more narrowly focused endeavors of previous decades.

Land quality indicators are critical to achieving better and more sustainable land management. They were developed as a method of assessing the degree to which land is being degraded as a result of agricultural practices, and they are emerging as important standards for monitoring the environmental performance of agricultural and other natural resource management projects. They are also useful for assessing the impact of policies and technologies on the environment and on production at the national and international level. Land quality indicators have direct application in country assistance strategies and national environmental action plans and can be aggregated upward to provide the basis for measuring global trends in loss of fertility and degradation of soil. The Bank, together with the Food and Agriculture Organization and the United Nations Development Programme, is spearheading an initiative to find cost-effective ways to develop international information systems for monitoring and evaluating sustainable land use. Within Bank projects, the methodology will be used to promote better portfolio

> **Box 5.3. A Win-Win Technology: Integrated Pest Management**
>
> Not only is integrated pest management one of the best examples of a "win-win" technology in agriculture, it is also an example of integrated research, extension, and farmers' participation. Misuse and overuse of pesticides can be a safety hazard to farmers and consumers, especially in combination with low levels of literacy and poorly enforced labeling and handling regulations. They can also contribute to the buildup of pesticide resistance in pests and the depletion of desirable predator insect populations. Integrated pest management systems employ measures such as pest scouting to monitor pest populations, along with the use of natural predators, pest-resistant crop varieties, and rotations, as adjuncts and alternatives to chemical pesticides. In the Integrated Pest Management Project in Indonesia, the Bank is supporting extension of a pioneering approach to crop protection that builds on work initiated by the government of Indonesia in cooperation with the Food and Agriculture Organization of the United Nations. By reducing the use of pesticides through a mix of biological and cultivation measures, the project minimizes the cost of protection while ensuring that insect damage does not become economically excessive. In addition to the Indonesian project, integrated pest management techniques are being implemented in twenty-two other Bank-supported agricultural projects.

management by providing an empirical basis for monitoring and evaluating agricultural and environment projects.

The Bank is chairing a multidonor study to assess the interactions between livestock and the environment. This work provides an objective assessment of both the positive and negative roles of livestock development in land degradation, as well as of how to improve livestock production.

Similarly, in irrigation, the Bank has developed the International Program for Technology Research in Irrigation and Drainage (IPTRID). This program promotes innovations to improve the sustainability of irrigated agriculture. It assists developing countries to prepare research projects that address operational problems related to water scarcity, drainage and reuse, water quality, waterlogging, and salinity. IPTRID is active in countries that cover 75 percent of the world's irrigated area, including China, Egypt, India, Mali, Morocco, Niger, Pakistan, and Senegal. The program has helped to prepare more than two dozen action research projects, seven of which, valued at some $60 million, are already being implemented. For example, in Egypt IPTRID is working with the

Cairo Water Research Center, with financing from the African Development Bank, to carry out small- and large-scale trials to establish the effects of poor-quality water on crops, habitat, and public health and to formulate operational guidelines for future projects on reuse of drainage water.

In the area of agricultural extension, three trends reflect the emphasis on sustainable management of natural resources:

- A trend toward increased farmer participation, usually through increased consultation at project design and joint problem-solving during implementation. Although the Bank has paid attention in the past to the supply side of the generation and transfer of technology, more recently it has been seeking ways to balance this with support for farmers' organizations by formulating demand, generating and transferring information and technology, and using new technology in an environmentally responsible way.
- A trend toward projects that make natural resource management more sustainable, usually through support for community-based activities. Typically, extension staff in cooperation with technical specialists assist the local population in making a diagnosis, setting priorities, and planning and provide support when villagers implement the resulting action plan. Such natural resource management projects often seek to improve forests, livestock, cropping, and land-based agriculture.
- A trend toward project components that pilot alternative approaches to extension.

An interesting development, however, is that the Bank is faced with tough challenges in its support of rural advisory services, because agriculture is becoming more knowledge-intensive. This is true for all farmers, rich and poor: integrated pest management is a good example (box 5.3). Support for instructional, top-down extension services must be replaced by support for farmer education, with balanced roles for the farmers and the public and private sectors.

However, privatization of extension services may have drawbacks, particularly for the environment. Early indications from Europe and the United States are that when extension is privatized, suppliers of pesticides, fertilizers, and machines quickly move to provide farmers with practical advice, but with a bias toward increasing the sale of chemical inputs.

6. Making Infrastructure Environmentally Sustainable

WORLD BANK PHOTO/CURT CARNEMARK

For the first time in history, growth in the world's urban population is outpacing that in rural areas. In rapidly expanding megacities, inadequate infrastructure for water supply, sanitation, solid waste management, roads, and public transport, as illustrated in this urban market in Ghana, impose serious constraints on environmentally sustainable development. The Bank's entire lending portfolio, including operations in the energy, transport, and urban sectors, is affected by new knowledge and concern about the environment.

Bank-supported projects devoted to meeting rising energy needs, addressing increasing transport demand, and providing essential urban infrastructure in developing countries have evolved considerably since the Rio Earth Summit. In all of these areas, much can be done to achieve sectoral objectives and improve the environment simultaneously, often at little cost. However, preserving the immediate environment and reaching other development goals in these sectors frequently imply significant tradeoffs. This chapter describes ways in which Bank energy, transport, and urban infrastructure projects have incorporated environmental and sustainable development concerns over the past several years.

Energy

The consumption of commercial energy in developing countries is rising rapidly and will soon dominate energy markets worldwide. Based on current trends, demand for energy in developing countries is likely to exceed 100 million barrels a day of oil equivalent by 2010 and perhaps 200 million barrels a day by 2030.

Over the past twenty-five years, nearly 1 billion new people in developing countries—more than the entire population of Europe, Japan, and the United States combined—have received electricity, and these countries have quintupled electricity supplies to their economies. Despite this progress, levels of per capita energy consumption in large parts of the developing world remain low (some 2 billion people still rely on dung and fuelwood for cooking), and many countries have a legacy of heavy government controls on investment decisions and prices, together with lax controls on emission of pollutants.

Responding to these challenges, the Bank has adopted a twofold approach to addressing growing energy needs while at the same time seeking to reduce the potential adverse environmental effects of energy production: (a) improving demand-side and supply-side efficiency and (b) supporting the use of cleaner energy sources and technologies.

This strategy was endorsed in two policy papers—*The World Bank's Role in the Electric Power Sector* (World Bank 1993e) and *Energy Efficiency and Conservation in the Developing World* (World Bank 1993a). The latter argues that efforts to address countrywide policy and institutional issues are the most important means by which to improve energy efficiency in developing countries.

The strategy also acknowledges that improvements in energy efficiency cannot be pursued in isolation from countrywide macroeconomic reform. Efficient use of energy requires a broad-based set of macroeconomic conditions and policies. Similarly, adequate pricing is necessary for end-use efficiency, because about half of all possible energy savings are realized from pricing measures. Combining end-use efficiency with appropriate macroeconomic conditions creates a "win-win" situation in which output is increased, energy conserved, and environmental pollution lessened. Ways in which efficiency gains can reduce undesirable environmental impacts in the power sector, for example, are illustrated in figure 6.1.

Although efficiency gains are critically important, alone they cannot meet the growing demand for energy in the developing world. The Bank therefore also supports projects that seek new, cleaner energy sources and technologies. These include using natural gas for generating power, investing in cost-effective controls for removing particulates from coal emissions, lessening the dependence on biofuels, and identifying renewable sources of energy.

Figure 6.1. Areas for Reducing Environmental Impact in the Power Sector

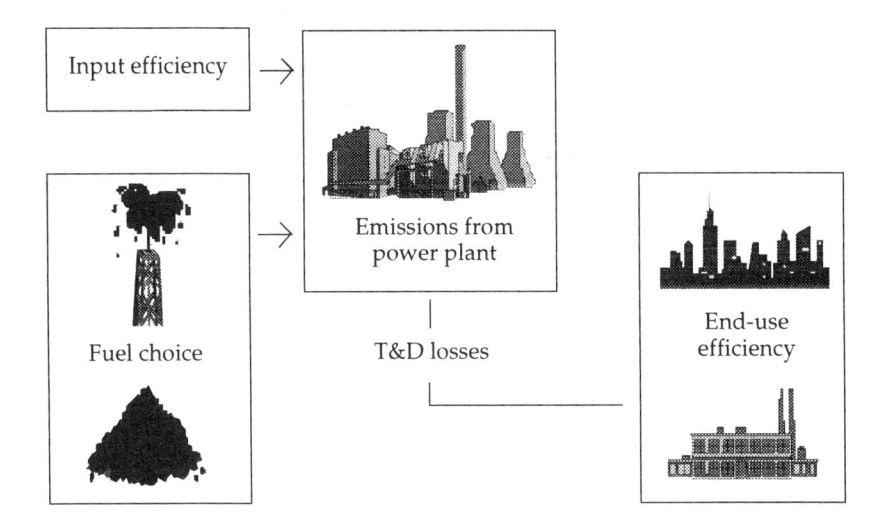

Note: Environmental impacts can be reduced at various stages of the cycle by, for example, choosing less-polluting fuels; converting fuels more efficiently to electrical energy; controlling emissions from power plants; reducing transmission and distribution (T&D) losses; and using electricity efficiently in the industrial plant or home.

Promoting Demand-Side and Supply-Side Efficiency

The Bank is promoting demand-side and supply-side efficiency in the energy sector through a variety of means, including basic institutional and pricing reforms and free-standing energy-efficiency components, as well as by helping to establish an enabling macroeconomic environment. Bank projects seek to achieve these objectives through actions ranging from stand-alone demand-side and supply-side energy-efficiency components to efforts to reform the power sector as a whole and improve supplies of energy to households and rural areas. They include measures that directly improve the environmental impact of energy projects, as well as loans to supply or upgrade existing generation, transmission, and distribution facilities where economic efficiency in the production and use of energy is the central goal.

For example, figure 6.2 shows the average carbon intensity of Bank-financed energy projects implemented over the last ten years compared with that of projects not financed by the Bank over a similar period. Both are seen against best practice in OECD countries since the turn of the century. Not only are Bank-supported energy-projects significantly less carbon-intensive than the developing-country average, but the developing-country average is less carbon intensive than that of the OECD countries at equivalent periods of development (that is, Bank-supported projects consume less carbon per unit of energy produced).

Figure 6.2. Carbon Intensity of Electricity Production, Coal-Fired Plants

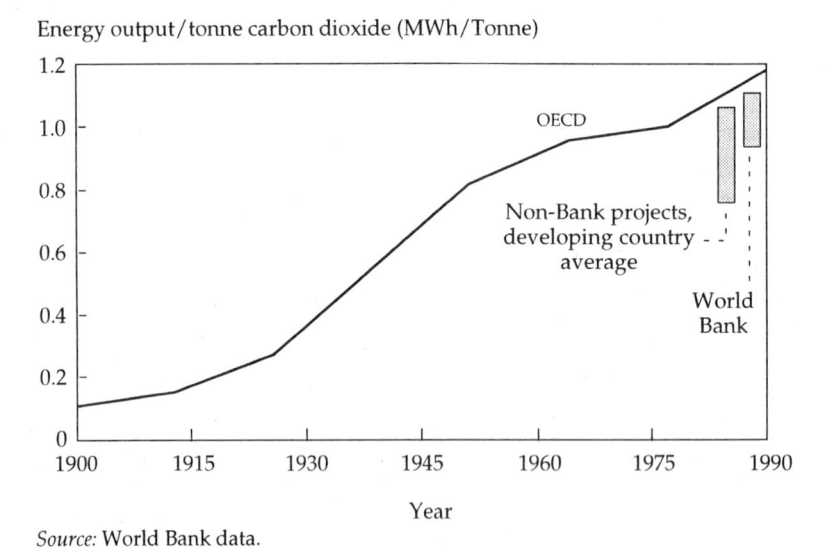

Energy output/tonne carbon dioxide (MWh/Tonne)

Source: World Bank data.

STRENGTHENING THE SECTORAL FRAMEWORK. The Bank has been promoting reform of the energy sector in a number of developing countries by supporting changes in management, structure, and ownership and development of new regulatory bodies (see table 6.1). Changes aimed at establishing autonomous and financially viable enterprises facilitate new investments and help to make energy production and transmission

Table 6.1. Approved Energy Projects with Sector Reform Components, Fiscal 1993–95

Year and country	Project name	Description of project or component
1993		
Bulgaria	Energy Project	Financial re-engineering component
Equatorial Guinea	Technical Assistance—Petroleum Project	Regulation and monitoring
Guinea	Power II Project	Performance contracts component
Honduras	Energy Sector Adjustment—Ref2 Project	Financial re-engineering, performance contracts, restructuring, and reorganization component
India	Renewable Resources Development Project	Reorganization component
	PGC Power System Project	Reorganization component and study on regulation
	Private Power Development Technical Assistance Project	Stand-alone reform project (independent power producer component)
	NRPC Power Generation I Project	Independent power producer component
Indonesia	Cirata Hydro Phase II Project	Regulation component
Iran, Islamic Rep. of	Power Sector Efficiency Project	Corporatization and commercialization component
Rwanda	Energy Sector Project	Performance contracts component
1994		
Jordan	Energy Sector Loan	Corporatization and commercialization and regulation component
Kazakhstan	Petroleum Technical Assistance Project	Management skills transfer component
Lithuania	Power Rehabilitation Project	Restructuring component

(Table continues on the following page.)

Table 6.1 *(continued)*

Year and country	Project name	Description of project or component
1994 (continued)		
Madagascar	Petroleum Sector Reform Project	Liberalization of petroleum sector
Pakistan	Power Sector Development Project	Corporatization and commercialization, privatization, regulation, and reorganization component
Papua New Guinea	Petroleum Development Technical Assistance Project	Attracting private capital exploration
1995		
China	Zhejiang Power Development Project	Corporatization and commercialization component
Colombia	Energy Sector Technical Assistance II Project	Regulation and other reform components
Côte d'Ivoire	Private Sector Energy Development Project	Privatization and regulation components
Ghana	Thermal Power (P-VII) Project	Regulation component
Pakistan	Second Private Sector Energy Development Project	Reform component
Peru	Electricity Privatization Adjustment Project	Stand-alone reform project (privatization)

more efficient. In the absence of satisfactory pricing and regulatory policies, energy producers are not induced to seek efficient means of producing and supplying energy. Effective regulatory bodies provide a forum for environmental concerns to be aired and integrated into the decisionmaking process. The resulting debate often enables national and local governments to enforce environmental standards. Helping borrowers to create the conditions under which efficiency in energy production and use is encouraged is particularly important, because external financing contributes only a minor portion of the total investments that developing countries require in the energy sector.

PRICING REFORMS. Energy price reforms are often central to gains in energy efficiency. Current worldwide fossil fuel subsidies, for example, are around $200 billion per year. Removing them—and setting prices that reflect economic costs—would not only release scarce public resources for other uses but reduce emissions of pollutants as people are induced to consume energy more sparingly. Subsidies for electricity generation account for about half of total subsidies in developing countries. As a result, they use about 20 percent more electricity than would be the case if consumers paid the true costs of supply. Moreover, by depriving producers of needed resources, underpricing electricity also discourages investment in new, cleaner technologies and more energy-efficient processes. Figure 6.3 illustrates the degree to which reforming countries are able to meet (and exceed) their costs, while nonreforming countries often must use government revenues to fill significant gaps in financing.

The Bank has promoted the use of pricing signals that convey the real costs of energy, including the costs of pollution, so that both efficient demand-side and supply-side decisions can be made, as table 6.2 illustrates.

Figure 6.3. The Impact of Reform on Electricity Prices, Selected Countries

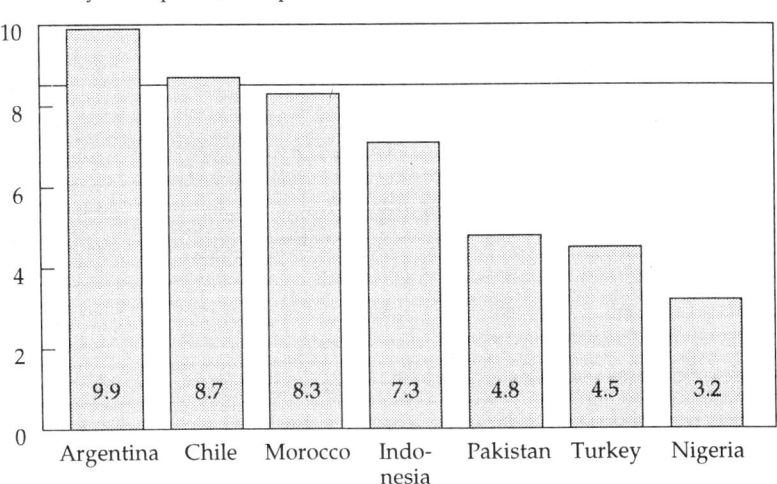

Electricity retail price (cents per kilowatt hour)

Country	Price
Argentina	9.9
Chile	8.7
Morocco	8.3
Indonesia	7.3
Pakistan	4.8
Turkey	4.5
Nigeria	3.2

Note: Numbers inside the bars represent the costs of power to customers; countries are lined up according to the degree of reform they have undertaken, Argentina having undertaken the most and Nigeria the least. A tariff level of 8.5 cents per kilowatt hour represents an efficient tariff. This number is derived from an average for OECD countries.

Source: World Bank and IFC 1994.

Table 6.2. Approved Energy Projects with Pricing Components, Fiscal 1993–95

Country and fiscal year	Project	Description of component
1993		
China	Shuikou II Project	Pricing study
Honduras	Energy Sector Adjustment—Ref2 Project	Pricing component
India	PGC Power System Project	Pricing component
Iran, Islamic Rep. of	Power Sector Efficiency Project	Pricing study
Tanzania	Power VI Project	Pricing study
1994		
Jordan	Energy Sector Loan	Pricing component
Kazakhstan	Petroleum Technical Assistance Project	Pricing component
Pakistan	Power Sector Development Project	Pricing component
1995		
Belize	Second Power Development Project	Pricing study
Côte d'Ivoire	Private Sector Energy Development Project	Pricing study
Latvia	Jelgava District Heating Rehabilitation Project	Pricing component
Thailand	Lam Takhong Pump Storage Project	Pricing component

The importance of price reform as a means of raising revenues to rehabilitate power and heating utilities—and to reduce emissions—is particularly evident in Eastern Europe and countries of the former Soviet Union. A large percentage of power generation and heat supply in these countries is based on using high-sulfur fuel oil without any form of desulfurization or particulate control. Because of low tariffs, and often low rates of bill collection, power and heat companies frequently lack the resources to rehabilitate plants, improve efficiency, switch to less-polluting fuels (notably gas), or install emissions controls. To help remedy this situation, the Bank is involved in district heating projects in Estonia, Latvia, and Poland that address the issue of adequate pricing and low rates of bill collection (see box 6.1).

STAND-ALONE ENERGY-EFFICIENCY COMPONENTS. In developing countries, potential energy savings exist on both the supply side and the

> **Box 6.1. Efficiency Improvements in District Heating in Estonia and Poland**
>
> In Estonia, energy intensity is six to seven times what would be expected for its level of gross domestic product if it were to be compared with the Scandinavian countries. The first Bank-financed project in the energy sector, the District Heating Rehabilitation Project, focuses on district heating to reduce the costs of importing heavy fuel oil by increasing the use of indigenous fuels (oil shale, peat, and wood) and the efficiency of the major systems. To improve energy efficiency, modern technologies and equipment will be introduced, and existing plants rehabilitated to reduce water loss and pumping costs. To ensure the sustainability of the district heating operations and heat supply to consumers, the heat tariff will be increased to cover operating and capital costs. This represents a major improvement from the past, when even operating costs were subsidized.
>
> In Poland, the Katowice Heat Supply and Conservation Project has similar objectives and aims to rehabilitate district heating plants that emit particulates from their low stack boilers. Despite improvements in the nation's environmental situation, the Katowice Voivodship remains an officially designated environmental disaster area. It is by far the most polluted region in Poland, accounting for about one-quarter of all atmospheric emissions in the country. The district heating project will help to reduce water loss, introduce automation and controls for the network, and eliminate small heat-only boilers or convert to gas firing, as appropriate, to abate air pollution.
>
> Prices for primary energy in Poland are now roughly the same as they would be for imported fuel, implying that subsidies have been substantially eliminated. Similarly, although in early 1994 gas, electricity, and heating prices for households were about two-thirds of their economic cost (although higher than industrial prices), district heating subsidies have now been eliminated in several major cities and are expected to be eliminated in most of the country by the end of 1995. Past increases in energy prices and the progressive phasing out of heat subsidies have already increased consumer energy awareness and improved energy conservation.

demand side. Traditionally, utilities have focused on supply-side measures to minimize losses up to the point-of-sale to consumers. Efficiency in electricity consumption, however, can also be increased by providing incentives for consumers to shift their pattern of demand from peak periods to off-peak periods or to consume electricity more efficiently, thus reducing overall demand. Increasingly, Bank energy projects have specific components to promote demand-side and supply-side efficiency (see table 6.3). In Pakistan, for example, the Bank is involved in a program in which almost all the savings in energy consumption are expected to come from supply-side measures such as improving plant efficiency and reducing transmission and distribution losses. Further savings will come from direct load control equipment, time-of-use pricing for industrial and commercial consumers, and an improved tariff structure for residential and agricultural consumers. In addition, one-third of the savings is expected from end-use efficiency measures.

CREATING AN ENABLING MACROECONOMIC ENVIRONMENT. Sound macroeconomic conditions that support long-term economic growth are essential to increasing energy production, while at the same time minimizing environmental impacts. Economywide as well as sectoral policies, particularly those that explicitly concern energy prices, can play a central role in encouraging energy efficiency.

The energy intensity of an economy tends to increase with the process of industrialization and to fall as the service sectors develop. In some countries, however, energy use is so inefficient that economic growth, accompanied by structural changes and appropriate energy policies, can result in a rapid decline in energy demand. In these cases, consumption patterns may be heavily skewed toward inefficient use of electricity, while at the same time the quality of supply is low, with frequent blackouts and wide swings in voltage and frequency. In making the transition from one stage to another, there is often a need for structural adjustment accompanied by major economic reforms. Such reforms are now under way, for example, in China, Eastern Europe, and the former Soviet Union.

In the case of China, a recent study financed by the GEF (National Environmental Protection Agency of China and others 1994) on issues and options in the control of greenhouse gas emissions shows that the country's energy intensity per unit of gross domestic product (GDP) was three to ten times higher in 1990 than that of major industrial countries. The report foresees a decline in energy intensity from 2.7 million tons of coal equivalent per $1,000 of GDP in 1990 to about 0.9 million tons of coal equivalent in 2020, with structural factors accounting for 75 to 85 percent of the total decline in energy intensity. Although tremendous scope exists for further improvement in the technical efficiency of energy use, as figure 6.4 illustrates, such improvements still amount to only 15 to 20 percent of the estimated total decline in energy intensity.

Poland, in turn, is representative of many former centrally planned economies characterized by soft budget constraints combined with very high inputs of material and energy per unit of production. In 1988, for instance, total energy intensity in Poland was 1.9 times the average for OECD. With coal as its primary energy source and lax enforcement of existing environmental statutes, Poland has suffered considerable envi-

Table 6.3. Approved Energy Projects with Stand-Alone Efficiency Components, Fiscal 1993–95

Country and year	Project	Description of project or component
1993		
China	Tianhuangping Hydro Project	Energy-efficiency component
Honduras	Energy Sector Adjustment—Ref2 Project	Study on demand-side measures and end-use fuel switching
Korea, Rep. of	Petroleum Distribution and Sector Management Project	Study on demand-side measures and conservation
Lao PDR	Provincial Grid Integration Project	Supply-side measures and loss-reduction component
Tanzania	Power VI Project	Several demand-side and supply-side measures and loss-reduction components
Thailand	Distribution System and Energy Efficiency Project	Demand-side measures component
1994		
China	Sichuan Gas Development and Conservation Project	Component to reduce production and transmission losses
Ethiopia	Calub Energy Development Project	Demand-side measures and end-use fuel-switching component
Indonesia	Sumatera and Kalimantan Project	Demand-side measures component
Madagascar	Petroleum Sector Reform Project	Demand-side measures and end-use fuel-switching component
Pakistan	Power Sector Development Project	Demand-side measures and load management component
1995		
Albania	Power Loss Reduction Project	Stand-Alone Loss Reduction Project
Armenia	Power Maintenance Project	Demand-side measures and load management component
Colombia	Energy Sector Technical Assistance II Project	Demand-side measures component
Ghana	Thermal Power VII Project	Demand-side measures component
Russian Federation	Gas Distribution Reconstruction Project	Energy-efficiency component
Thailand	Distribution System Reinforcement Project	Demand-side measures component
Viet Nam	Power Sector Rehabilitation Project	Demand-side measures study

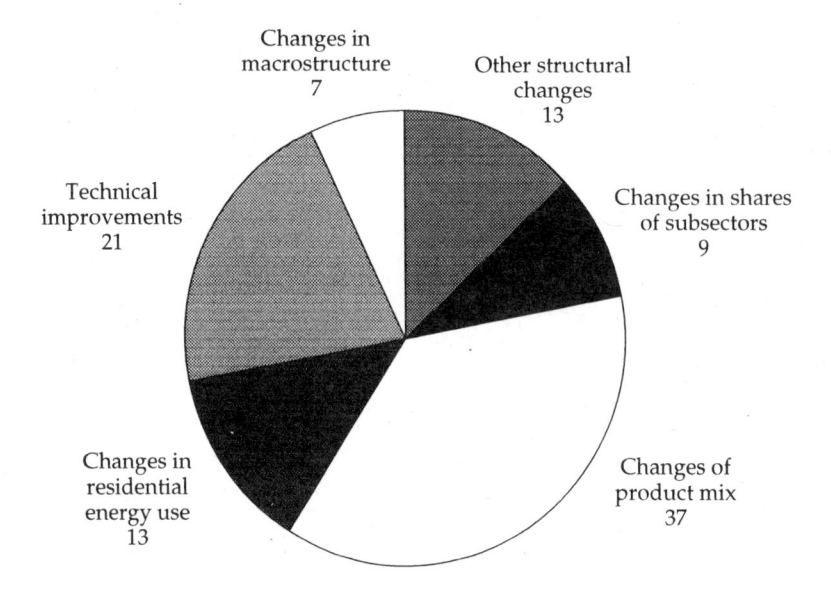

Figure 6.4. Sources of Reductions in Energy Intensity, China
(percentage of total change in energy intensity)

- Changes in macrostructure: 7
- Other structural changes: 13
- Changes in shares of subsectors: 9
- Changes of product mix: 37
- Changes in residential energy use: 13
- Technical improvements: 21

Source: National Environmental Protection Agency of China and others (1994).

ronmental degradation both from the mining and use of coal. A recent study (Bates, Gupta, and Fiedor 1994), which examined enterprise restructuring and price reform in Poland, used simulation models to project energy production and consumption and emission of pollutants. The simulations pointed to clear environmental gains from these fundamental reforms. The main lesson drawn from the study is that improvements in air quality in Poland depend simultaneously on better environmental policies and economic reform.

Supporting Cleaner Energy Sources and Technologies

The strong demand in the developing world for new energy sources has led the Bank to focus on identifying clean sources and technologies, which include using natural gas for power generation, improving the quality of automotive fuels, investing in cost-effective controls for removing particulates from coal emissions, and identifying renewable sources of energy and lessening dependence on biofuels.

SWITCHING TO GAS. The most promising cleaner energy alternative advocated by the Bank is natural gas, which is both plentiful and significantly less polluting than other sources of fuel. With new high-efficiency combined-cycle units, electricity generated through natural gas is becoming a low-cost alternative. Compared with conventional coal-fired plants, natural gas–fired combined-cycle plants avoid the need to dispose of ash, increase thermal efficiency, eliminate sulfur dioxide emissions, and halve carbon dioxide. Natural gas can also be used for thermal energy (for heating or boiler-firing in industrial plants) and for primary applications (as a component of a manufacturing process).

In recent years, the Bank has supported gas-fired power stations in Bangladesh, India, Malaysia, Tanzania, and Tunisia and has been involved in, or is currently considering, financing pipelines to provide Bangladesh, Brazil, India, Pakistan, and Thailand with access to natural gas.

ADVANCING THE APPLICATION OF RENEWABLE ENERGY SOURCES. In 1995 the Bank launched the Solar Initiative, whose objective is to accelerate the pace at which commercial and near-commercial renewable energy applications reach the marketplace. The initiative likewise works to accelerate basic research, development, and demonstration of renewable energy technologies. This means bringing into the mainstream of the Bank's lending program large-scale, grid-connected power and industrial applications for solar and renewable energy, as well as small-scale, rural-based applications that have direct effects on alleviating poverty and improving the quality of life in developing countries. Renewable energy projects in Brazil, Côte d'Ivoire, India, Indonesia, Tunisia, and several other countries have been identified and are under preparation.

The Solar Initiative also seeks to mobilize resources from the Energy Sector Management Assistance Programme (ESMAP), bilateral organizations, and other sources for project identification, market research, and definition of relevant subsector strategies. Activities using a combination of ESMAP and Bank funds have already identified appropriate solar energy investments in various countries. In addition, the Solar Initiative will be working in Asia, where a hybrid renewable energy project was launched in India in 1993, and where renewable energy projects are planned in India (solar thermal), Indonesia (mini-hydro and mini-geothermal), and Sri Lanka (hybrid). As table 6.4 indicates, the Bank has identified and prepared solar or renewable-based projects in several countries or regions.

Two projects in the Philippines demonstrate the potential for tapping into geothermal energy resources. The Leyte-Cebu Geothermal and Leyte-Luzon Geothermal projects (also supported by the GEF) add a

Table 6.4. Approved Renewable Energy Projects, Fiscal 1990–94

Country and year	Project	Description of project or component
1990		
Philippines	Energy Sector Loan	Geothermal component
1992		
Mauritius	Sugar Energy Development Project	Stand-alone biomass project
1993		
India	Renewable Energy Resources Project	Stand-alone windfarm and solar photovoltaic project
Rwanda	Energy Sector Project	Project includes a study on solar photovoltaics
1994		
Philippines	Leyte-Cebu Geothermal Project	Stand-alone geothermal project
	Leyte-Luzon Geothermal Project	Stand-alone geothermal project

combined 640 megawatts to the country's existing 1,000 megawatts of installed geothermal capacity. Geothermal energy production has much lower carbon dioxide, sulfur dioxide, and nitrogen oxide emissions than fossil fuels, and it helps to reduce the country's dependence on imported oil.

In addition to solar, wind, and geothermal power, some sources of renewable energy sometimes have significant negative effects that, where this source of energy is the most appropriate available, need to be mitigated. Normally, such alternatives are assessed and ranked at the country level as part of a sector planning process entailing the use of long-term least-cost analysis, which is increasingly taking environmental and social, as well as engineering and financial, costs into account. Sectoral environmental assessments can be used to facilitate this analysis.

One of the main alternatives for energy production is hydropower plants, which involve the construction of dams and, often, the formation of sizable reservoirs. While the construction of large hydropower-related dams worldwide has continued to be significant in recent years, World Bank financing of such projects has declined substantially from an average of eighteen dams a year between 1980 and 1985 to only six a year between 1986 and 1993. Of the more than 1,100 dams under construction in 1992, less than 7 percent were partly financed by the Bank. Most of the Bank-supported dam projects approved in recent years are in Asia, particularly China, although several such projects have also been approved in Africa and Latin America.

From an environmental and social perspective, hydropower dams raise a variety of issues, not the least of which is the frequent need to resettle large numbers of people from the area required for forming the reservoir. Some hydropower projects, however, do not require reservoirs, or at least not large reservoirs. This is the case both for mini hydro plants and run-of-river projects. Many of the alternatives to hydropower, in turn, present strong disadvantages in environmental terms, especially coal-fired power and nuclear energy plants. Even "clean coal" technologies, while reducing sulfur and particulate emissions, do not avoid carbon dioxide emissions, for example.

Many renewables, moreover, remain more expensive than conventional alternatives because the industry is still new and markets are relatively small. However, as markets expand, and as technologies progress, costs are expected to decline. The Global Environment Facility has opened up new possibilities for advancing renewable energy–based technologies since GEF grant financing can reduce the high costs of near-commercial renewable energy technologies on environmental grounds to enable projects to meet Bank investment criteria.

PROMOTING CLEAN COAL AND OTHER TECHNOLOGIES. Despite best efforts to increase energy efficiency and switch to less-polluting fuels, such as natural gas, the use of coal worldwide is projected to double by 2030. To dampen this trend, the Bank is addressing coal issues as a full energy chain, from mining to disposing of the waste, and is pushing for commercialization of appropriate technologies, such as coal washing, which is already standard practice in industrial countries, and integrated coal gasification, which is now entering commercial application in Europe and North America. It also assists countries to identify and prepare clean coal projects and facilitates technology transfer through project preparation and financing.

Because China and India are expected to double their use of coal every ten years, they are prime countries to consider for introducing clean technologies. In China, coal is expected to account for about 60 percent of all energy by 2020. In India, a study is now under way that will enable government officials and institutions to evaluate alternatives for power sector development. The study is using a least-cost power system planning model that takes explicit account of environmental impacts as well as financial and economic implications of a development scenario. Because coal is the major source of energy in India, the study will identify the environmental effects of generating more energy from coal, including environmental externalities and costs caused by the associated increase in coal production.

IMPROVING THE QUALITY OF AUTOMOTIVE FUELS. Automobile emissions can contribute significantly to local air pollution, and the Bank is involved in several projects, including one in Thailand, to improve the quality of the fuels used. Other projects seek to rehabilitate fuel oil refineries for production of better-quality fuels. For example, the Bank is financing a hydrocracker complex in Karachi, Pakistan, that will produce high-quality automotive fuel. In other cases, the Bank works toward standardizing the quality of fuel across a region to provide for more efficient end use.

Together with the Asian Development Bank, the Bank also manages the RAINS-ASIA project to study the effects of sulfur deposition in the region. The project will produce a methodology and a personal computer–based software tool to assess the consequences of emission-reduction strategies. This project is discussed further in chapter 1.

PREVENTING POLLUTION UPSTREAM AND IMPROVING TRANSMISSION INFRASTRUCTURE. In some countries, particularly the former Soviet Union, the upstream side of the oil and gas industry infrastructure has been poorly maintained. Often there has been little concern for waste and pollution mitigation at the well or along the pipeline. As a result, some of the worst environmental disasters from oil and gas pollution have taken place in these regions.

The Bank's main focus in the former Soviet Union and elsewhere is to rehabilitate existing upstream and transmission facilities and provide technical assistance to ensure that further pollution does not occur. A list of such recently approved and future projects is contained in table 6.5. These programs replace and rehabilitate worn-out infrastructure with efficient and environmentally sensitive alternatives. Over the past three years, the Bank has lent some $1.2 billion for oil rehabilitation projects in the Russian Federation alone to finance more-efficient and environmentally sound oil field operations using modern and efficient techniques and standards. The Bank has also supported projects to reduce gas flaring and, following the Usinsk oil spill in Russia, provided emergency funding and technical assistance to prevent frozen oil from moving into nearby rivers and oceans. This project is described in greater detail in chapter 1.

Table 6.5. Approved Oil and Gas Rehabilitation Projects, Fiscal 1993–95

Country and fiscal year	Project name	Loan or credit (millions of dollars)
1993		
Korea, Rep. of	Petroleum Distribution Project	120
Madagascar	Petroleum Sector Reform Project	52
Russian Federation	Oil Rehabilitation Project	610
1994		
China	Sichuan Gas Development Project	225
Kazakhstan	Petroleum Technical Assistance Project	16
Romania	Petroleum Sector Rehabilitation Project	176
Russian Federation	Oil Rehabilitation II Project	500
Zambia	Petroleum Rehabilitation Project	30
1995		
Azerbaijan	Petroleum Technical Assistance Project	21
Russian Federation	Gas Distribution Reconstruction Project	107

Rural and Household Energy

Although the largest national and international environmental problems from energy production involve industrial and urban centers, energy is often a problem for poor rural communities as well. These populations often suffer both from insufficient energy supplies and from localized environmental degradation and health problems caused by air pollution, particularly the use of fuelwood.

The Bank is addressing this problem through two groups of policies and investments. The first encourages *more sustainable forms of producing and using biofuels* based on social forestry (for which the Bank has lent approximately $1 billion since 1980), improved soil management practices, and efforts to encourage the wider adoption of improved cookstoves. Even though improved stove programs have met with mixed results over the years, one recent successful example involved a credit from the International Development Association (IDA) for better charcoal stoves in Tanzania. The stoves have raised energy efficiency 50 percent, and adoption rates have been very high: nearly half the population in Dar-es-Salaam uses the improved stove. Studies of rural energy policies are currently also under way in Sahelian countries with support from the Dutch government and the Bank.

The second group *extends modern forms of energy* to a larger share of the world's population. Efforts have been made to enable a switch to modern fuels, such as liquefied petroleum gas, which emit far less pollution. Liquefied petroleum gas is also five times more efficient as a cooking fuel than biofuels, and is more convenient to use. Electric lamps using incandescent light bulbs are ten to twenty times more efficient than kerosene lamps, which are still the most common source of light in rural areas in low-income countries. The Bank therefore continues to support expansion of electricity distribution systems. To encourage the wider distribution and use of modern fuels, the Bank encourages member countries to use pricing policies to expand the market.

Critical to improving the energy situation in rural areas are policies and institutional structures that result in more active participation on the part of the private sector and the rural population itself. In addition to encouraging countries to liberalize and commercialize their energy markets so that the availability and accessibility of household fuels is not artificially constrained, the Bank also supports credit schemes for both suppliers and consumers of energy.

Transport

Transport, which links people to local and worldwide resources and markets and gives them access to jobs, health, education, and other amenities, is crucial to development. Yet there is growing concern about how transport affects both the local and global environments, as the high economic and social costs of transport-related pollution, such as the costs of respiratory diseases and the effects of high concentrations of lead, are becoming more evident. To reduce these costs, the Bank is promoting and financing environmentally sustainable transport. In doing so, it is promoting the use of energy-efficient and low-impact modes of transport, lessening the levels and harmful effects of transport-related pollution, and developing the institutions and regulatory frameworks needed to sustain a modern, environmentally benign system.

The environmental effects of transport differ significantly by mode, and much of the Bank's effort has been concentrated on the worst problem areas. Road motor vehicles are the largest source of pollution from transport, contributing to local and continental effects (such as acid rain formation) and accounting for more than three-quarters of the transport sector's contribution to global emissions. Rail transport, in contrast, is relatively benign environmentally, although direct and indirect coal burning (to generate electricity) and rail-generated noise can have significant consequences for the local environment. For maritime transport, the operational discharging of oil at sea, while declining substantially over the past decade, still accounts for one-quarter of the oil entering the marine environment. Damage also occurs from tanker accidents and port operations and construction activities.

In response to these concerns, the Bank is undertaking a variety of initiatives to address, and in some cases redeem, the ecological degradation caused by transport. This is reflected in the Bank's review of transport policy (World Bank, TWU 1995) and lending and in an associated program of training and dissemination on critical environmental policy and operational issues in the sector. Since the 1992 United Nations Conference on Environment and Development (UNCED) meetings, Bank efforts to balance transport activities and environmental concerns have focused on (a) alleviating transport-related air pollution and water pollution and (b) reducing urban congestion. Finally, the Bank has introduced a range of innovations in its transport-related project work. These include more-frequent use of environmental assessments (EAs) at the project design stage, use of Bank economic and sector work to create a policy dialogue on critical environmental issues, and direct targeting of existing environmental problems in Bank transport projects. In some cases, funds for addressing these problems come from the GEF, enabling work to go beyond the traditional reach of Bank lending.

Developing New Policy and Training

As part of its overall strategy for helping member countries to build modern and sustainable transport systems, the Bank has recently undertaken a complete review of its transport policy and lending that will lead to a new Bank policy for the sector (World Bank, TWU 1995; see box 6.2). A major objective of this review is to place environmental considerations in the broader context of an integrated transport strategy and development program, rather than treating it as an add-on consideration. This has involved rethinking policy objectives, from mitigating existing environmental problems toward avoiding them in the first place. Linked to the policy, a program of training and research dissemination is planned for Bank transport sector staff during the next fiscal year to raise awareness of environmental concerns and ensure the practical application of these new directions.

Integrating Transport and Environmental Approaches in Bank Lending

Integrating environmental and sustainable development considerations into investment projects has led the Bank to focus on three main areas

Box 6.2. Developing an Environmentally Sustainable Transport Policy

Recognizing that transport projects, if improperly designed, can harm the environment and have adverse impacts on the poor, the Bank has begun a major effort to redefine its transport policy (World Bank, TWU 1995). In fiscal 1995 it reviewed existing projects in the sector to identify how they could be made more sustainable, both financially and environmentally, and developed a policy framework for helping governments to develop a well-functioning system of transport, which is crucial in today's competitive global environment.

The new policy identifies reducing the threats to life and health as the highest-priority areas in which Bank lending can help lead to sustainable transport. Cost-effective (rather than state-of-the-art) technology is necessary, as are better-directed land-use planning, stricter demand management, and greater incentives to use public transport through efficient pricing for congestion and pollution.

The review identifies a number of ways in which the Bank can help its member countries to develop a sustainable, well-functioning transport system. Institutional and policy reform should be the primary focus. The Bank can help governments to fulfill their enabling and supervisory role in a freer transport market through selective and focused technical assistance to build the necessary new public sector capacity and skills. Continuing the strong lending program and encouraging increased investment in the sector are also essential as investment requirements grow. New financial instruments, such as guarantees and extended on-lending arrangements, need to be explored to encourage more involvement of the private sector and the community. Partnerships are becoming more important, at the national level between stakeholders and funding agencies as well as between the financial community and the transport sector; at the international level between the development community and the government; and at the intellectual level between all persons who are addressing the challenges of improving transport. Lessons from experience must be learned more systematically from the Bank's portfolio of activities in transport. Finally, developing a strategic approach to motorization is critical (a) for finding a more appropriate pace for motorization (which requires balancing private decisions to undertake the small capital outlay to buy a car, for example, against society's ability to mobilize the very large resources needed to expand road networks), (b) for identifying a more balanced, multimodal transport network with fewer implicit or explicit subsidies, and (c) for nurturing more sustainable transport alternatives to auto-dependency.

in the transport sector: attacking vehicle-related air pollution, curbing transport-related water pollution, and reducing urban congestion.

ATTACKING AIR POLLUTION. The quality of air in the major cities of the developing world is already as bad as or worse than that in cities in industrial countries, despite lower levels of car ownership. Although road traffic is not the only—or even the most important—source of urban air pollution, it is a principal source of some of the main pollutants. In large city centers, road traffic may account for as much as 90 to 95 percent of lead and carbon monoxide, 60 to 70 percent of nitrogen and hydrocarbons, and a major share of particulate matter. Transport also harms the global environment. Pollution from motor vehicles produces about a fifth of the incremental carbon dioxide in the atmosphere from human sources (which potentially contributes to global warming), a third of the chlorofluorocarbons (which contribute to ozone depletion), and half of the nitrogen oxides (which contribute to acidification and ecological damage). The continued use of leaded fuels in developing countries poses an added cost to the environment, especially in urban areas where the buildup of lead in the soil can significantly damage the health of children.

Reducing the negative effects of automobiles on air quality requires giving attention both to the institutions that regulate transport activities and to those responsible for planning and implementing new road investments. Over the past several years, the Bank has become increasingly involved in building the technical capacity within countries to manage the environmental effects of road transport and in directly rehabilitating areas where the quality of air is already poor. Notable examples include the State Highway Management Project in Brazil, the Second Multi-State Roads Project in Nigeria, and the Highway Management Project in Venezuela, all of which build technical capacity at the state level to assess the environmental effects of road projects. Similarly, the GEF-funded Tehran Transport Emissions Reduction Project in the Islamic Republic of Iran is a comprehensive package that contains components covering emissions inventory and air quality monitoring, vehicle fleet and fuels improvement, and traffic management. Likewise, the Transport Air Quality Management Project in Mexico uses a combination of demand management, transport planning, and other emission-reduction investments to overcome existing problems largely associated with a poorly planned and managed rapid growth in transport.

In addition, the Bank has played a catalytic role in identifying and addressing the problem of lead exposure due to vehicle emissions. Removing lead from gasoline is relatively low cost, and the Bank is advocating a total phaseout. The Bank supports the design and implementation of policies that accelerate the phaseout of leaded gasoline, including the following:

- Differentiated gasoline taxation in favor of unleaded gasoline (creating a 5 to 10 percent difference in price) to increase demand for unleaded gasoline
- Public education to increase awareness of the health benefits of eliminating lead from gasoline and to address public misconceptions about the feasibility of using unleaded gasoline in cars without catalytic converters
- Incentive programs to facilitate the cost-effective phaseout of lead
- Fuel specifications to ensure that lead is not substituted by other harmful substances
- Training and education of technical staff to ensure the proper adjustment of vehicles.

Price liberalization or pricing policies should ensure a reasonable financial return, and under the right incentives and policies, financing for investments in oil refineries and for the distribution and retail sale of unleaded gasoline is available from private sources. The implementation of leaded gasoline phaseout policy, therefore, should be part of the extensive restructuring of the petroleum sector that is currently under way in many developing and transition economies. By facilitating the privatization and restructuring of the petroleum sector, the Bank can also accelerate lead phaseout policies.

In Mexico, for example, the Bank has supported the government in developing comprehensive gasoline pricing policies. In Thailand, in addition to price and market liberalization measures that have improved the environment and enhanced productivity and the participation of the private sector in the petroleum industry, the Bank is supporting restructuring of the Bangchak Petroleum Refinery to meet reformulated gasoline specifications, improve refinery operations, reduce refinery emissions, and contribute to the country's long-term strategy to abate pollution from vehicles. Projects are also under preparation in Bulgaria and Costa Rica to assist with the phasing out of leaded gasoline by refineries. In preparation for the forthcoming environment ministerial conference in Sofia, Bulgaria, the Bank is undertaking major studies on trends and projections of traffic growth and related emissions in Central and Eastern Europe, on the health impacts of leaded gasoline on urban populations (in particular, on children), and on the feasibility and costs of reducing the lead content of gasoline under various policy scenarios.

REDUCING WATER POLLUTION. Shipping and associated activities can contribute to pollution in ecologically sensitive coastal waters and rivers. The Bank has adopted the international maritime standards set by the International Convention for the Prevention of Marine Pollution from Ships as its standard for controlling environmental damage caused by shipping activities. In addition, the Bank is increasingly engaged in lending operations whose key focus is the control of transport-related water pollution. For example, marine pollution is being directly addressed by the Ship Waste Disposal Project in China and by an oil pollution prevention program in the Petroleum Sector Reform Project in Madagascar. The Oil Pollution Management Project takes a regional approach for the Mahgreb countries, funded through a grant from the GEF, and will upgrade the ability of Algeria, Morocco, and Tunisia to respond to oil spills; provide the region with pollution monitoring equipment; rehabilitate existing oil storage facilities at key ports; and provide training to staff involved in storing and managing oil. METAP provides the umbrella for dedicated pollution control projects in individual countries.

The Bank is also attempting to ensure the long-term sustainability of inland water resources and ecosystems, including the often-neglected coastal areas directly around ports and other maritime infrastructure. For example, the GEF portfolio includes pilot projects covering the management of freshwater bodies and river basins, marine pollution, and marine ecosystems (such as the Belize City Infrastructure Project and Guyana Infrastructure Rehabilitation Project), which include components to protect water quality and shorelines from damage due to port construction.

ADDRESSING URBAN CONGESTION. Cities are major engines of growth in most industrial countries. Urban populations are expanding at more than 6 percent per year, accompanied by a spiraling demand for motorized transport. Stimulated by growing per capita income in urban areas, moreover, motor vehicle ownership is expanding in developing countries at a faster rate than the proportion of urban space devoted to roads. Slow-moving vehicles combined with a poorly maintained vehicle stock are making megacities in developing countries such as Bangkok, Mexico City, and Tehran among the most polluted in the world. With the number of vehicles growing a rate of 15 to 20 percent a year, the costs of lost productivity and wasted resources due to traffic jams and congestion are becoming a serious, immediate, and growing problem in many developing countries.

The Bank has traditionally addressed urban congestion in its lending program (a) by investing in traffic management, technical assistance, and capacity building for urban transport planning and regulation and (b) by promoting the use of the most efficient forms of urban transport in the context of specific local conditions. It has also addressed urban congestion by promoting the use of demand management instruments, especially appropriate pricing (such as congestion pricing, fuel pricing, and public transport pricing). Moreover, although direct charging of road users (for instance, cordon charging and automated tolling), which was recently introduced on a pilot basis in several OECD countries, is not yet a viable alternative in most developing countries, the Bank has been at the forefront of promoting the use of appropriate proxy pricing and regulation to manage demand. For example, increased parking charges have been used to reduce on-street parking in Tunis, Tunisia, and to ration restricted off-street parking in Pusan, Korea.

The Bank is also expanding its support for nonmotorized transport, at least partly in response to the increasing congestion in city centers. Projects in Ghana (see box 6.3) and Peru aim to demonstrate that nonmotorized transport can significantly reduce air and noise pollution as well as traffic accidents, especially in densely populated areas.

The Bank is also undertaking sector research focusing on measures to reduce center-city congestion, which often has synergistic effects with broader environmental concerns such as traffic management and air pollution. Issues under consideration include how to find the appropriate balance between improvements in street design and in mass transit systems and between transport infrastructure and land development objectives. Already, these issues are finding their way into Bank operations in such projects as the Transport Air Quality Management Project in Mexico, the Transport Rehabilitation Project in Peru, the Fifth Highway Project in Thailand, and urban transport projects in Brazil (São Paulo), Chile, China, Ghana, India (Bombay), Indonesia, and Sri Lanka (see box 6.4).

Designing Better Projects

Most Bank transport projects now include at least a partial environmental assessment as part of the project design, especially when significant numbers of people are to be relocated or civil works are to be constructed in potentially environmentally sensitive areas. In addition, environmental ratings are given during project supervision, and performance is monitored as part of the general implementation process. Together, the use of environmental assessments, innovative project

Box 6.3. Promoting Bicycle Use in Ghana

Recent studies and projects pay particular attention to the transport needs of the urban poor, especially the need for nonmotorized transport, defined as any form of transport in which the primary source of energy is not mechanical or is natural. Bicycles are not only the predominant mode of nonmotorized transport, but also the world's leading vehicle for personal transport. If bicycles are adequately integrated into the transport system, they can improve the efficiency of mass transit substantially—for example, by enlarging the area served.

The Urban Transport Project in Ghana will improve traffic management, thus reducing traffic congestion and vehicle emissions. It should also mean safer conditions for nonmotorized transport, particularly for the poor, by providing footways and separate lanes for nonmotorized vehicles. Recognizing the burden of transport costs on the poor, as well as the role transport plays in providing access to jobs, the project will connect seven low-income areas in Accra identified as having the worst access to main routes.

The project is financing the construction of around 50 kilometers of dedicated cycle paths connecting low- and middle-income residential areas to commercial business districts. Cycle lanes, either parallel to or within the road pathway, are part of road rehabilitation designs for Accra. In market areas, tracks will be wide enough to accommodate manually pushed trolleys, which are used to transport goods. These bicycle tracks are only the initial phases of an integrated bike path network that will extend across the entire city.

---

design, and enhanced monitoring during implementation have improved the environmental record of Bank-financed transport projects.

Almost all transport projects are now subject to at least a partial environmental assessment, and the proportion subject to full assessments has risen from 10 percent of projects approved in fiscal 1991 to 20 percent in fiscal 1994. These full assessments have involved all modes of transport and most regions, with the rapidly developing transport activity in China attracting the most comprehensive attention.

In countries such as China, Belize, Pakistan, and Yemen, for instance, the environmental assessment process has influenced the definition of highway rights-of-way, allowing culturally sensitive sites such as burial grounds or other archaeological areas to be bypassed. Similarly, in the India Container Transport Project, final project design incorporated changes based on the findings of the environmental assessment, result-

Box 6.4. Broadening the Range of Transport Options

Part of the answer to the substantial economic and welfare losses from congestion, traffic accidents, noise, and air pollution lies in new transport infrastructure. Bank involvement in the past has favored expanding existing bus services by adding exclusive busways and improving access to roads, instead of building underground railways or elevated highways. In some megacities, however, capital-intensive investments such as rapid rail systems may be best, especially if the more-flexible busway alternatives have already reached maximum capacity. Another consideration is that bus transport often has a severe impact on the urban environment (as with the Avenida 9 de Julho busway in São Paulo). Accordingly, Bank-supported urban transport projects are now giving more consideration to intermodal options, including rail-based transit or metros.

The Integrated Urban Transport Project in São Paulo contains an infrastructure and equipment investment component for building and operating a rail connection between the suburban train systems and the subway. The environment-related objectives of the project will be achieved through an air quality and traffic safety component, with an inspection and maintenance program for vehicles emissions and noise, a traffic management and safety program, and a vehicle emissions and noise laboratory and equipment for monitoring and sampling emissions.

Another problem that calls for the development of a range of options is road safety. More than half a million people die annually in traffic accidents, and many more are injured. In developing countries, the majority of accidents involve pedestrians and cyclists, and the economic costs of such accidents are high. In Kenya in 1990, an estimated 1.3 percent of gross domestic product was lost because of traffic accidents. In many countries, the high rates of pedestrian and cyclist injuries discourage the use of nonmotorized vehicles, often in favor of less environmentally sound modes of transport.

In recognizing the difficulty of adapting industrial-country solutions to developing-world problems, the Bank has tried a variety of approaches. In Poland and Thailand, national and regional institutions have been established to improve road safety, and in India, Korea, and Peru, the Bank has invested in road design to separate motor vehicles from pedestrians and nonmotorized vehicles. The Bank has also invested in education, regulation, and enforcement of safety procedures in Bangladesh and China.

ing in less disruption to the indigenous population with minimal loss of benefits.

In addition, recent economic and sector work has strengthened Bank dialogue with borrowing member countries such as Brazil and Thailand on controlling transport-related pollution. Similar action programs are being pursued elsewhere. As part of this work, the recently published Bank handbook, "Roads and the Environment" (World Bank and SETRA 1994), provides guidance on incorporating environmental concerns into road planning and management (see box 6.5). Recent lessons are already being applied to new design approaches. In Africa, for example, innovative layouts for rural roads have proven to lessen adverse environmental effects, improve the retention of surface water in soils, and reduce soil erosion.

Urban Infrastructure

Since the Rio Earth Summit, the number of stand-alone urban environmental projects has grown significantly. UNCED underlined the fact that,

---

Box 6.5. Developing a Handbook on Roads and the Environment

The potential effects of road construction and road use on air quality, the natural environment, local communities, and undeveloped regions are an integral consideration in any road development project. The Bank has recently completed a handbook (World Bank and SETRA 1994) that helps project managers to incorporate environmental concerns into the design and construction of projects. By paying attention to both the human and the natural environments affected by road construction and maintenance, the handbook promotes continuing awareness of environmental issues, even for minor road activities and at all stages of the project cycle.

The handbook looks at the day-to-day activities of road planning, road maintenance, and traffic operations, acknowledging that negative environmental effects occur even without new construction. For example, the acquisition of land for a town bypass often receives wide public attention, while the cumulative effects of heavy road traffic through existing urban communities are less obvious. The handbook argues that it is important to avoid narrow approaches to projects by emphasizing the need for public consultation in the environmental assessment process and by encouraging institutional strengthening and enhanced training of local staff. The handbook also calls for road professionals to work more closely with experts in many areas of the environment and, to do this, to recognize the need for understanding something of each other's language, methods, and work activities.

The Bank is updating the handbook, broadening the scope to include the continually evolving issue of environmentally sustainable methods of road transportation, for example, and to provide readers with a broader range of analytical tools for taking account of the positive side of increased mobility caused by road development.

because of rapid rates of urbanization, the world's urban population is outpacing the rural population for the first time in history. In rapidly expanding urban areas, inadequate infrastructure for water supply, sanitation, solid waste management, roads, and public transport impose serious constraints on environmentally sustainable development and on the reduction of urban poverty. Bottlenecks in the provision of urban services and infrastructure often result from inefficient governance and management structures and inadequate financing mechanisms. A city's dependence on central government, for example, can undermine its incentive and capacity to operate public infrastructure and services efficiently, and can cause it to waste resources. Weak financial systems that are unable to mobilize local and private resources perpetuate the need for government services, including subsidies that induce further waste.

Until recently, however, the typically brown agenda issues most apparent in the urban environment were seen as largely distinct from those of the green agenda, requiring a different approach and different solutions. In the past few years, more and more urban planners have recognized the links between these agendas, and have taken a more integrated approach to environmental management. The second annual World Bank conference on environmentally sustainable development, held in September 1994, emphasized this approach.

The Bank's current strategy in the urban sector is built on a policy paper, *Urban Policy and Economic Development: An Agenda for the 1990s* (World Bank 1991b), that recognized urban environmental management as one of the pillars of urban and macroeconomic growth. In addition to its role in ensuring efficient delivery of essential urban environmental services, urban environmental management improves urban productivity by providing better environmental resources and services, including access to safe water and the removal of wastes, that are fundamental to ensuring the health and well-being of the urban poor. However, much work needs to be done to link the consequences of urban pollution to the health impacts on urban populations.

Incorporating the Environment in Lending for Urban Infrastructure

Recent Bank projects for urban development give increasing attention to the need to combat pollution, expand and upgrade urban sanitation services (including sewerage, drainage, and solid waste), and improve urban environmental management more generally. To do this, as in other sectors, the Bank has based its support for urban environmental infrastructure on eight key principles: (a) plan strategically, (b) choose an integrated approach to lending, (c) promote resource-based project design, (d) encourage decentralization, (e) stimulate private sector participation, (f) ensure stakeholder involvement, (g) incorporate cost recovery and demand management, and (h) build partnerships.

PLAN STRATEGICALLY. Over the past year, the Bank's operational regions have taken stock of their environmental lending and formulated strategic plans to guide future investments for urban environment and infrastructure. Similarly, national environmental action plans have helped to identify urban trends and current and future investment priorities in the countries of each region.

In Asia, for example, the Bank is confronting tremendous population growth in megacities, which is causing demand for urban infrastructure and resources, especially water, to outpace capacity and supply. Several recent projects are helping to alleviate the current backlog of demand for infrastructure and to develop new investments to meet future demand. The Changchun Water Supply and Sanitation Project in China, for example, includes infrastructure to expand access to water, together with longer-term investments in water resource development and water conservation. The Shanghai Environment Project, in turn, is designed to improve the quantity and quality of water that reaches the city's 16 million residents (see box 6.6).

Similarly in Africa, the Bank is developing medium- and long-term strategies to deal with the challenges of urbanization. Although still mainly rural, Africa is urbanizing at a faster pace than any other part of the world. Basic and outdated urban infrastructure is being strained by the growth in demand, and cities are facing the inability of physical infrastructure to keep pace with population growth, the health consequences of crowding and increased exposure to concentrated wastes, unsustainable resource consumption, and occupation of fragile lands. In response, the Bank has focused its lending on capacity building for urban environmental management, both at the local and national levels. The Urban Restructuring and Water Project in Zambia, for instance, aims at improving the quality of water supply and sanitation in the larger cities in the near term and on building capacity in local government to manage and finance urban infrastructure and services in the medium term. The National Water Development Project in Malawi and the Water Sector Project in Senegal contain strategic medium- and long-term interventions, designed to meet future urban demand for water.

In Latin America and the Caribbean, the Bank's focus has been on developing new institutional arrangements for the delivery of urban services, such as resource-based management, decentralization, public-private partnerships, and privatization (see box 6.7).

Box 6.6. Quality Water for Shanghai

Shanghai's remarkable industrial expansion in recent years has made it one of the most prosperous areas in China. But there has been a price to pay. Most of Shanghai's water comes from an intake on the Huangpu River, which runs northward through the city to join the mighty Yangtze. Heavy industrial development has steadily encroached on the intake zone, and increasing pollution threatens the quality of the river water.

Recognizing the impact this could have on future economic growth, the Shanghai municipal government started work on a major environmental program to improve water quality and control pollution. The Bank is funding the scheme through the Shanghai Environment Project, which will provide the city with a new source of water from the Huangpu River.

The project examined Shanghai's sources of industrial and municipal pollution to identify improvements to intake on the Huangpu River that are necessary to safeguard water quality. To develop control measures, a data base of pollution sources covering an area of 23,800 square kilometers was compiled, containing information on more than 600 identified sources. This made it possible to pinpoint the critical pollution sources within the upper river catchment and to evaluate various control measures. A comprehensive monitoring scheme has been designed to make sure that water quality requirements are met, and a laboratory information management system has been set up to ensure that collected information is properly processed and disseminated to the water companies and environmental protection bureaus.

A second Bank project will transfer sewage from the industrial western part of the city eastward for treated disposal. As well as improving the local environment, this vast sewerage scheme—one of the largest in the world—will provide another line of defense to safeguard the quality of river water.

CHOOSE AN INTEGRATED APPROACH TO LENDING. Current lending for urban infrastructure reflects a more integrated approach to the environment and relies on a variety of instruments and institutional arrangements. Environmental assessments have led the Bank to adopt a more intersectoral approach and to pay greater attention to the links between urban issues and environmental issues in surrounding areas.

For example, the Liaoning Environment Project in China protects and improves water, land, and air resources by strengthening institutions; improving solid waste management and wastewater collection and treatment; and alleviating industrial pollution and conserving cultural heritage in the Hun-Taizi River Basin. Similarly, the Municipal Infrastructure Rehabilitation Project in Georgia takes a multisectoral ap-

> **Box 6.7. Improving the Urban Environment in Colombia**
>
> In the 1980s, Colombia achieved one of the highest growth rates of gross national product in Latin America and one of the most stable paths of growth. It is now working to ensure that economic growth is not achieved at the expense of environmental protection and sound management of natural resources. In 1993, the government adopted an environmental framework law, Law 99, to establish a national environmental information system (SINA) and to create a new Ministry of the Environment. Under this new system, the Ministry of the Environment is the focal point for environmental policy and intersectoral coordination at the national level. In addition, thirty-two autonomous regional corporations will help to establish appropriate institutional and regulatory frameworks and will plan, implement, monitor, and enforce environmental and natural resources management programs.
>
> The objective of a Bank project currently under preparation is to support implementation of Colombia's national environmental policy by creating and strengthening environmental management institutions in the urban centers of Barranquilla, Bogotá, Cali, and Medellín; by promoting environmental planning in selected mid-size cities, industrial corridors, and urban areas of special interest; and by establishing those components of SINA that will help to improve urban environmental management. The project will provide technical assistance with the goal of establishing a sound institutional and regulatory framework at the local level and will identify priorities for environmental mitigation.

proach in addressing urban environmental priorities in energy, transport, water supply, wastewater and solid waste collection and disposal. The Northern Border Towns Environmental Project in Mexico addresses transnational environmental problems caused by air pollution from urban transport and industry, water pollution from industrial and household sources, and municipal and industrial wastes (see box 6.8). It includes protection of fragile ecosystems and strengthening of both municipal and federal environmental institutions.

Several multisectoral urban infrastructure initiatives have been funded through the creation of municipal development funds, whose proceeds are used to address urban environmental priorities. The Municipal Development Project in Colombia contains a municipal development line of credit to fund urban infrastructure subprojects in solid and hazardous waste management and transportation. In Brazil, the Minas Gerais Municipal Development Project includes a component to establish and operate a municipal development fund to improve service coverage in priority sanitation and environment-related infrastructure.

> **Box 6.8. Mexico's Northern Border Environment Project**
>
> Northern Mexico, particularly the border region with the United States, faces urgent environmental problems, including mitigation of serious environmental degradation. The Northern Border Environment Project is designed to improve environmental quality along the border by helping municipal, state, and federal authorities to strengthen their environmental planning, management, and enforcement capabilities. It will also aid in carrying out priority investments and action plans efficiently—all with a view to preserving the environment, reversing past degradation, reducing health risks, protecting biodiversity, and promoting key environmental policy objectives.
>
> The project recognizes that actions taken on one environmental problem often directly affect another. Experience has shown that when more stringent controls or fees are introduced for one medium (water, solid waste, or toxic waste), polluters divert more of their effluent to another medium. The maquiladora industries on the border, for example, include polluters with highly toxic wastes that are easily diverted from one method of disposal to another. To address this concern, the project will support about fifteen investment subprojects in five or six border cities in the areas of water treatment and sanitation, solid waste management, and air quality and urban transport. Based on master plans analyzing environmental needs and priorities (within and across subsectors), cities will present investment proposals for financing under the project. They will then be required to meet eligibility criteria concerning financial soundness, implementation arrangements, technical appropriateness, and environmental goals.

PROMOTE RESOURCE-BASED PROJECT DESIGN. More and more, the effects of urban pollution are affecting regional resources: watersheds, airsheds, fragile lands, and ecosystems, including coastal zones and drylands. A new generation of projects, especially those dealing with water resources, recognizes the need to coordinate interventions around the resource, rather than around the jurisdiction or the sector. For example, in Latvia, the Municipal Services Project will not only improve the quality of drinking water for the capital city of Riga and the city of Daugavpils but also reduce ecological damage to the river and the Gulf of Riga. Similarly, sanitation projects now comprise treatment and reuse in addition to collection and removal. Solid waste management projects include separation of hazardous wastes and appropriate disposal in addition to collection. More emphasis is also placed on intersectoral and interjurisdictional management of infrastructure in recognition of the regional and cross-media effects of urban environmental problems.

Many recent Bank initiatives, particularly in Central Asia and Europe, are centered on protecting key water resources, such as the Danube River Basin, the Aral Sea, the Black Sea, and the Caspian Sea. In some such cases, these programs are managed through interurban networks, such as the Mediterranean Coastal Cities Network (MEDCITIES). These are described in chapter 2.

Coastal zone management also requires coordination of cities both up- and downstream. In Latin America and the Caribbean, for example, the OECS Waste Management Project, partially supported by GEF, is designed to protect coastal zones through management of urban solid and liquid wastes. The Haapsalu and Matsalu Bays Project in Estonia comprises the treatment of municipal wastewater to improve beaches for tourism and protect valuable and endangered wetland habitat. The Solid Waste and Environment Project in Lebanon is designed to improve the coastal environment by improving the collection and disposal of solid wastes and by reducing industrial and transport-related air pollution as the result of better incentives and management.

ENCOURAGE DECENTRALIZATION. As countries urbanize, decentralization is becoming an effective instrument for bringing about appropriate investments in urban infrastructure. Municipal governments are more likely than national governments to understand the unique service and project design requirements of their cities. Decentralization is already playing an important role in urban projects in Latin America. For example, the Asunción Sewerage Project in Paraguay is designed to help the government to improve water and sewerage services by decentralizing activities and by promoting private sector participation. Recent initiatives in countries in the Economic Commission for Africa and in Asia are likewise focusing on decentralization as a means of delivering appropriate urban infrastructure.

In many countries, the capacity of municipal institutions needs to be strengthened before decentralization can become an effective tool. As a result, the Bank is investing in institutional development projects to promote local capacity to manage urban infrastructure investments. The Water Sector Project in Senegal, for instance, aims at improving sector and financial management in Dakar to reduce dependence on the national budget.

STIMULATE PRIVATE SECTOR PARTICIPATION. Several urban development projects in Africa, particularly in Burkina Faso and Mali, are being carried out through Agence pour l'exécution des travaux d'intérêt public (AGETIP) arrangements that essentially privatize the delivery of urban services. The Urban Works Project in Madagascar is a demonstration project to set up a private sector agency for construction and maintenance of public urban roads. Other projects, such as urban development operations in Côte d'Ivoire and Swaziland incorporate participation and labor generation as a way of involving stakeholders and reducing urban poverty.

In Latin America and the Caribbean, where countries are already highly urbanized, the focus is mainly on decentralizing and privatizing urban services. The Lima Water Privatization Project in Peru, for instance, will privatize the state-owned water authority in the interest of increasing the efficiency of operation.

ENSURE STAKEHOLDER INVOLVEMENT. Stakeholder participation is fundamental to sound environmental governance and as a means for supplementing scarce local government resources. A major component of new urban management structures is to involve stakeholders in defining investment priorities, designing projects, and providing, operating, and maintaining urban environmental infrastructure.

Stakeholder input is solicited during preparation of national environmental assessment plans and environmental assessments to incorporate their priorities into investment decisions and project design. The Village Infrastructure Project in Indonesia assists poor villages with financing for self-selected infrastructure to be implemented through self-help efforts or local contracts. Several recent Bank operations, such as the Urban Development Project in Swaziland and the Small Towns Water Project in Uganda, promote community participation in the construction and maintenance of public infrastructure. In Africa, in particular, construction of urban infrastructure is an important means of reducing urban poverty by providing employment.

INCORPORATE COST RECOVERY AND DEMAND MANAGEMENT. Because prices are often held well below costs, enormous subsidies are flowing into public infrastructure enterprises and agencies in many countries. A growing proportion of Bank urban infrastructure projects promotes the use of cost-recovery mechanisms, both to sustain the expansion of services to meet growing urban needs and to manage demand for and consumption of resources strained by rapid urban growth. Moreover, data from Africa and Latin America clearly confirm that the beneficiaries of water subsidies are almost always the rich. The poor, whose needs are frequently used to justify these subsidies, are often not served, and pay street vendors as much as ten times the public price for water, as a recent study in Onitsha, Nigeria, illustrates.

Demand management, through appropriate pricing, is increasingly being used to bring resource consumption to sustainable levels as well as to provide poor people with a safer, more reliable supply of services. Many projects incorporate willingness-to-pay surveys into project design to determine appropriate user charges, fees, and tariff schedules. For example, the Water Supply and Sewerage Project in Tunisia promotes a more efficient use of water resources by applying appropriate tariffs and cost-recovery mechanisms; the Changchun Water Supply and Sanitation Project in China links water conservation with water pricing policies; and the Emergency Recovery Project in Lebanon contains a cost-recovery component to ensure sustainability of rehabilitated infrastructure. In Brazil, the Curitiba component of the Water Quality and Pollution Control Project includes five cost-recovery mechanisms, including tariffs on water supply, sewage collection and treatment, solid waste collection and disposal, municipal property taxes, and park fees.

BUILD PARTNERSHIPS. In recent years, the Bank has joined with other international agencies in partnerships that focus on urban environmental management. The UNDP/World Bank Metropolitan Environmental Improvement Program in Asia assists Asian megacities in developing environmental management strategies and action plans, identifying and preparing priority investment projects, and involving communities in solving urban environmental problems. The Urban Management Program sponsored by the World Bank, the UNCHS (Habitat), and the UNDP contains an environmental management component that supports regional initiatives in such urban environmental areas as the disposal of solid waste and the development of citywide environmental strategies and action plans. In 1991, METAP, a partnership between the Commission of European Communities, the European Investment Bank, the UNDP, and the World Bank, launched the MEDCITIES network to share expertise and coordinate environmental action around the common resource of the Mediterranean Sea.

PART 3

Part 3 demonstrates how the private sector plays a critical role in improved environmental stewardship. This chapter explains how the International Finance Corporation (IFC) and the Multilateral Investment Guarantee Agency (MIGA) are contributing to this effort.

7. The Private Sector: IFC and MIGA

MARTYN RIDDLE

Gold mining accounts for a significant part of Ghana's economy and is critical to the future prosperity of this impoverished country. In trying to minimize environmental damage from gold mining, Ghana's government requires that mining projects submit environmental management plans, including a reclamation program, every three years. One notable example of this environmentally sound approach is the reclamation activity at the Billiton Gold Mine in Bogosu, supported by the IFC. As part of a reclamation master plan, the company has developed an outstanding nursery; by planting species (such as the vetiver grass in the photo) that are able to withstand high soil acidity, the company can control erosion and fix nitrogen in the soil, and it is now selling its plants to other mines in Ghana.

In recent years, major changes have occurred in the scope of operations of the International Finance Corporation (IFC) and the Multilateral Investment Guarantee Agency (MIGA) and in the way they do business from an environmental standpoint. The 1990s have seen a period of rapid growth for IFC, reflecting increased focus on the private sector as the engine of growth and poverty alleviation in developing countries (see figure 7.1). New countries and regions became active areas for IFC investments (Lebanon, the Occupied Territories, Peru, South Africa, the former Soviet republics, and Viet Nam), and investments in infrastructure and capital markets projects increased relative to projects in other sectors (see figure 7.2).

The private sector in both industrial and developing countries has become more aware of the environment as a business concern affecting products, markets, technologies, and long-term sustainability. Forward-thinking companies anticipate environmental trends and adjust their product mix and operations to capitalize on them. As IFC's corporate emphasis on environmental issues grew, the IFC increasingly applied its strengths in working with the private sector to address environmental issues, and fortified its organizational and procedural capability to address environmental matters.

Figure 7.1. Growth in IFC Operations

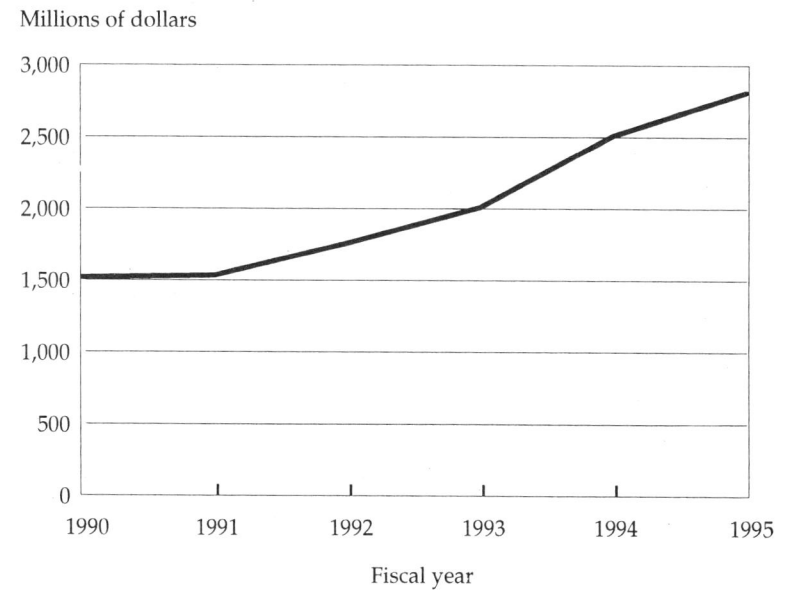

Millions of dollars

Source: IFC data.

Figure 7.2. Project Approvals by Sector, Fiscal Years 1992 and 1995
(millions of dollars)

Fiscal year 1992
(Total, $3,226)

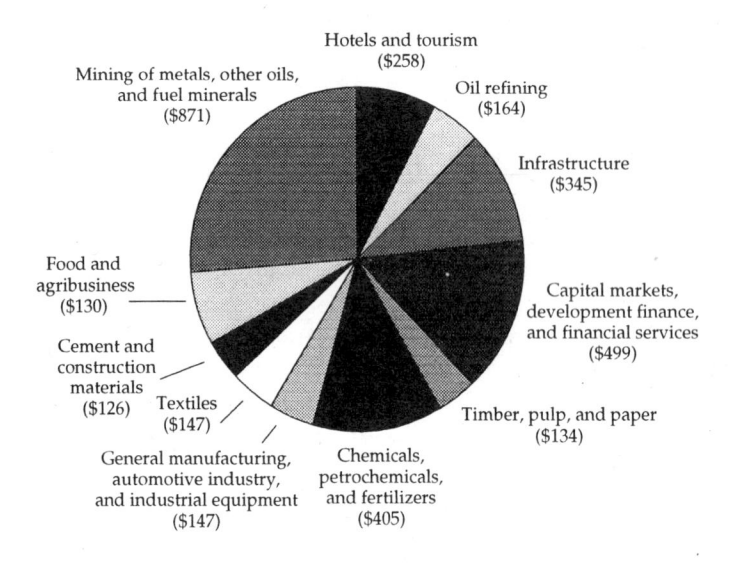

- Hotels and tourism ($258)
- Mining of metals, other oils, and fuel minerals ($871)
- Oil refining ($164)
- Infrastructure ($345)
- Food and agribusiness ($130)
- Capital markets, development finance, and financial services ($499)
- Cement and construction materials ($126)
- Textiles ($147)
- Timber, pulp, and paper ($134)
- General manufacturing, automotive industry, and industrial equipment ($147)
- Chemicals, petrochemicals, and fertilizers ($405)

Fiscal year 1995
(Total, $5,467)

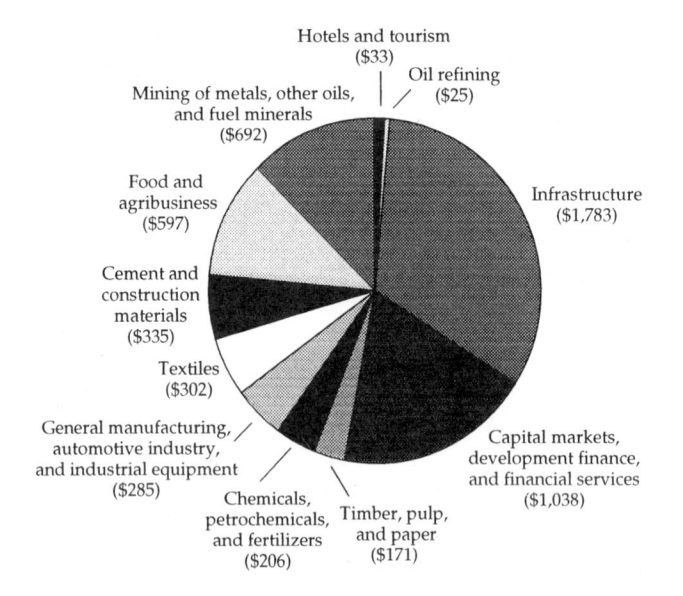

- Hotels and tourism ($33)
- Oil refining ($25)
- Mining of metals, other oils, and fuel minerals ($692)
- Infrastructure ($1,783)
- Food and agribusiness ($597)
- Cement and construction materials ($335)
- Capital markets, development finance, and financial services ($1,038)
- Textiles ($302)
- General manufacturing, automotive industry, and industrial equipment ($285)
- Chemicals, petrochemicals, and fertilizers ($206)
- Timber, pulp, and paper ($171)

Source: IFC Controller's and Budgeting Department, Data Management Unit.

Among the multilateral development banks, IFC occupies a special niche as the only institution that invests exclusively in the private sector of developing countries on a commercial-risk basis, without government guarantees. Its impact on development results from the activities of the private sector and from its own role in stimulating and enhancing the flow, composition, and efficiency of private capital.

Despite its rapid growth, IFC is still relatively small in terms of overall private investment, and its effectiveness lies in acting as a catalyst and creating a demonstration effect that encourages replication by other investors. The need to ensure replicability means that IFC has to function within a framework (or incentive structure) that the private sector can clearly understand. Long-term profitability and economic sustainability are thus necessary conditions of all its investment and mobilization activities. IFC's technical assistance and advisory work are also guided by this private sector framework, which strongly influences its corporate culture and approach to environmental matters.

In the past, the private sector tended to perceive environmental requirements as costs that reduce profitability. During the 1990s, this perception has shifted gradually toward viewing environmental management as an efficiency measure. For example, environmental improvements by Fundición Refimet S.A., a copper smelter in Chile, to resolve air emission problems are expected to generate more than $11 million in new revenues from the recovery of sulfur dioxide and the production of sulfuric acid. Reducing waste and pollution is increasingly considered essential to the long-term growth and sustainability of an enterprise.

IFC has come to view environmental issues as opportunities for adding value to the investment, as business risks requiring proper management to protect the value of assets, and as opportunities for making profitable investments in companies that solve environmental problems.

This evolving perspective is related to many factors. Among them are the growing awareness that sustainable development and environmental performance are linked, increasing recognition by industrial clients of ecoefficiency as a criterion for long-term success and profitability, the environmental training of staff, and experience with project-related problems linked to environmental issues. There is also greater awareness that global environmental problems addressed by the various conventions will not be solved unless the private sector contributes its vast technical, managerial, and financial resources and expertise. Moreover, investments in environmental sector projects such as the Aguas Argentinas water and wastewater privatization project have demonstrated that such investments can both be profitable and have a very significant impact on development (see box 7.1).

Box 7.1. Environmental Sector Projects

An investment in Aguas Argentinas, a private sector consortium that is operating, improving, and expanding water and wastewater services in metropolitan Buenos Aires, Argentina, was originally approved in fiscal 1994, and a second investment was approved in fiscal 1995. In its two years of implementation, Aguas Argentinas has achieved impressive results. An additional 500,000 Buenos Aires residents received water service, and 300,000 received sewerage collection service. An average of 8,000 water leaks and 13,000 sewer blockages were corrected monthly, and 38,000 water meters were installed or changed. Water production capacity increased from 3.5 million cubic meters per day to 4.4 million, resulting in the first summer in fifteen years without a water shortage in Buenos Aires. As a result of improved efficiency, staff were reduced from 7,450 to 3,600. The level of nonpayment also fell, from 15 to 7 percent, net revenues increased 70 percent, and profitability moved from a loss to a net income of $25 million. In addition, a 120,000 cubic meters per day wastewater treatment plant was rebuilt, and three new regional plants are under construction. By 1988, these plants will provide 2 million cubic meters per day of wastewater treatment, representing wastes from two-thirds of the region's population.

Another project is an investment approved in fiscal 1994 in Compañía Tratadora de Aguas Negras de Puerto Vallarta, S.A. de C.V., in Mexico. The project is sponsored by Biwater, Ltd., United Kingdom, and consists of the construction and operation of a 750 liter per second wastewater treatment plant to serve the city and environs of Puerto Vallarta. Under its build-own-operate-transfer (BOOT) contract, the plant will provide sewage treatment services over the next fifteen years, after which the facilities will be transferred to the municipal water authority, SEAPAL. The plant is producing very high-quality effluent that exceeds the requirements of SEAPAL and World Bank guidelines. For example, biochemical oxygen demand, suspended solids, and fecal coliform levels are about one-tenth or less of maximum values established by the contract. The plant also removes ammonia from the sewage, although this is not required. Operational efficiency is high as well, with operation and maintenance costs at about one-third the level expected for well-operated plants. This BOOT project has become a model for similar projects.

Proactive Programs

IFC has been taking an increasingly proactive approach in working with private sector sponsors to address environmental issues. This emphasis is apparent in the focus since 1992 on development of environmental projects (for example, water supply and wastewater management, solid and hazardous waste management, and ecotourism) and on projects addressing global environmental issues. It is also manifested in efforts to guide small and medium-size sponsors on environmental matters, advise financial institutions on environmental risk management, and explore innovative financing mechanisms to address environmental issues, such as targeted investment funds. In all these activities, IFC focuses on "win-win" situations in which the private sector can achieve profitability commensurate with risk, while addressing environmental problems.

Environmental Business Development

In 1992 IFC undertook a study of the market for environmental goods and services in nine developing countries to determine whether the environmental business sector could be a promising new area for IFC investment.[1] While the study's estimate of market size and IFC's potential share was cautious, it concluded that a large, viable market was developing. As a result, IFC initiated a new program to identify and promote investments in the environmental sector. Shortly thereafter, in July 1992, IFC was reorganized and established in the process an investment department focused exclusively on infrastructure projects. Environmental infrastructure projects (water and waste management) were housed in the Infrastructure Department, further underscoring IFC's commitment to explore opportunities in this area.

IFC has found that expanding its environmental project portfolio is more challenging than originally anticipated. Initially, IFC announced through conferences, publications, and other media that it was willing to finance environmental projects. Later, it pursued a more direct approach as well, contacting major players in the environmental industry regarding potential investments in developing countries.

After three years of active encouragement, IFC's board approved four environmental projects (two in fiscal 1994 and two in 1995), although several more are in process, and some are approaching final approval. The two projects now being implemented are significantly exceeding expectations and requirements (box 7.1).

Progress in environmental sector investments has been slower than anticipated for a number of reasons. Not least is the involvement of both the private and public sectors in many, if not all, phases of these projects. The need to integrate private sector approaches with public sector goals is particularly challenging under these circumstances. Often government policy must first change to allow the private sector to provide such services, and pricing and subsidy issues must be addressed before the private sector is willing or able to invest. To facilitate this process, IFC has been coordinating project development activities more closely with counterparts in the World Bank who are working with governments to address the relevant policy issues.

The demonstration effect of the above projects in Argentina and Mexico is already evident. As the success of these and other projects has become more widely known, and as awareness of IFC's interest in financing such projects has grown, so too has the number of inquiries and proposals to IFC for similar initiatives.

IFC is also exploring the feasibility of venture and investment funds with environmental objectives, including an investment fund targeted at projects in the water sector and two investment funds targeted at global environmental issues. In 1995, a study was begun to consider the feasibility of establishing a private sector fund for renewable energy and energy efficiency projects.[2] The feasibility of a fund to invest in businesses linked to the sustainable use or preservation of biodiversity in Latin America (for example, sustainable agriculture or forestry, ecotourism, nontimber forest products, or biodiversity prospecting) is also under consideration.[3] IFC will continue to pursue its environmental portfolio with vigor, regarding this sector as an important part of its environmental mandate for the future.

Global Environmental Initiatives

The private sector is a major user of natural resources and has an interest in protecting the global environment, including the worldwide climate, biological diversity, and international water resources. Moreover, the private sector's role as an economic actor in developing countries has grown in recent years, bringing with it technology, expertise, and financial leverage. Flows of private capital to developing countries now exceed traditional flows of official development assistance as the key source of economic development.

The challenge is to encourage private enterprises to make investments that benefit the global environment within the incentive framework in which the private sector operates. In 1992, grants from the Global Environment Facility (GEF) and the Multilateral Fund of the Montreal Protocol (MFMP) were expected to serve as incentives for a variety of innovative private sector approaches to global environmental issues. The World Bank Group's MFMP activities are now focused mainly at the enterprise level, and IFC's program complements that of the Bank.

The executive bodies of the GEF and MFMP have endorsed five projects under development by IFC and its clients (see box 7.2). To date, the Poland Efficient Lighting and the MISR Compressor Manufacturing Company projects have been approved by IFC management. Donor and recipient countries and NGOs have expressed a desire to expand the role of the private sector in the GEF and MFMP, and the GEF Secretariat has invited broader private sector participation. Moreover, the various en-

> **Box 7.2. IFC Projects Endorsed by GEF/MFMP Executive Bodies**
>
> - A GEF grant for the Poland Efficient Lighting Project, a cooperative effort among IFC, GEF, private utilities, and Polish lighting manufacturers, will potentially replace 1.15 million incandescent lights with energy-efficient compact fluorescent lamps over a two-year period.
> - An MFMP grant would help MISR Compressor Manufacturing Company (Egypt) convert its production process for compressors in order to use alternatives to chlorofluorocarbons (CFCs).
> - An MFMP grant would assist Assan Demir ve Sac Sanayi (Turkey) to eliminate the use of CFCs in its production of insulated sandwich panels.
> - A GEF grant would assist two refrigerator manufacturers in the Slovak Republic to change their production processes in order to stop using CFCs.
> - A GEF grant would finance a pilot project to channel funds through financial intermediaries to small and medium-size companies for work in climate change or biodiversity.

vironmental conventions are seeking additional financial resources and innovative mechanisms to implement their objectives.

Although the private sector is substantially involved in MFMP activities, private sector involvement in GEF has remained limited for various reasons, including the difficulty of defining eligible incremental costs in a private sector context. IFC has been working with the GEF programs to address these and other issues critical to enlisting private sector partnership.

IFC is working to find practical, innovative solutions. For example, small and medium-size enterprises can help to address global environmental problems, but there has been no convenient GEF mechanism to support them. A pilot program is under development to channel GEF funds to such firms through financial intermediaries. These intermediaries—including banks, venture capital companies, and business foundations oriented to small and medium-size enterprises—would use the funds to provide financing to clients for work in climate change or biodiversity.

Capital Markets

IFC emphasis on the development of capital markets has been increasing for several years as the financial sector in many developing countries has become more open to private sector investment. The variety and complexity of capital markets projects pose interesting challenges from an environmental standpoint. Many projects have no environmental impact, such as hedging facilities, stock brokerage houses, and stock registry companies. In other cases, IFC invests in a financial institution that funds a variety of subprojects that potentially have environmental impacts (category FI projects).

During the past three years, IFC has strengthened its environmental scrutiny of capital markets transactions. As a result, more types of transactions are now categorized as FI, and conditions are imposed regarding environmental review of subprojects. However, few financial institutions in developing countries assess environmental aspects of investments, and they often need assistance in establishing review mechanisms to meet IFC's requirements. To address this problem, IFC developed an innovative training program on environmental risk management for financial institutions, targeted at senior managers and credit officers in current as well as prospective client institutions. By the end of fiscal 1995, workshops had been conducted with participants from 198 financial institutions across 22 emerging markets. Financial intermediaries are now required to submit annual environmental performance reports.

IFC is working closely with its counterparts in the World Bank and the European Bank for Reconstruction and Development to develop a consistent, pragmatic approach to managing environmental risk in financial intermediary investments. This is a rapidly evolving area, in which there is little precedent or guidance in the commercial financial sector. Thus, IFC is seeking to take the lead in assisting financial institutions worldwide to incorporate environmental issues into their investment decisions.

Assistance for Project Sponsors

Although many project sponsors are multinational corporations or large companies that are environmentally aware and financially capable of hiring environmental experts, many IFC clients are smaller, with fewer resources and specialists to address environmental issues. During the past three years, IFC has sought ways to assist such companies to improve their environmental performance, often with the support of bilaterally funded trust funds administered by IFC.

For example, with support from the Norwegian Agency for Development Cooperation, IFC and Norwegian consultants produced materials to help these sponsors to understand the nature and purpose of IFC's environmental requirements and to introduce them to environmental management systems and techniques to avoid and minimize waste and pollution. An energy audit of the dyeing, printing, and finishing operations of a leading Indian textile company was undertaken with the support of the United Kingdoms Overseas Development Administration.

IFC and the Business Council for Sustainable Development (BCSD) have cooperated to identify ways to increase the private sector's contribution to sustainable development.[4] A training program on ecoefficiency for small- and medium-size enterprises conceived by IFC and the BCSD is now under development with support from the European Commission through the European Community/IFC Technical Assistance Facility for Economic Cooperation with Asia. IFC has also provided support to the World Business Council for Sustainable Development task force on joint implementation under the Framework Convention on Climate Change (for a discussion of joint implementation, see chapter 2).

Organization and Procedures

There have been significant changes in how IFC organizes its operations to address environmental matters. IFC investment departments are supported on environmental matters by an Environment Division within the Technical and Environment Department. Under a mutually agreed arrangement with MIGA, IFC also acts as environmental adviser on all MIGA projects. At MIGA's request, Environment Division staff review MIGA projects and provide comments and guidance on environmental matters.

The Environment Division has grown from two higher-level staff in 1992 to the equivalent of eighteen higher-level staff in 1995 (eight regular staff members and ten consultants), and this growth occurred during a period in which growth of corporatewide administrative expenses was generally restrained. In addition, the director of the Technical and Environment Department now reports directly to IFC's executive vice-president. Furthermore, to achieve a better integration of environmental activities within IFC operations, a Vice-President of Operations has assumed corporate oversight for environmental matters.

In September 1993, after consultation with staff, shareholders, clients, and NGOs, IFC implemented a revised environmental review procedure that clearly defined the roles and responsibilities of staff and project sponsors and strengthened requirements for public disclosure of environmental information about proposed projects. Under the new procedure, project information became available worldwide through the Bank's Public Information Center. To improve staff capability, IFC launched an intensive internal training program on environmental risk management and the new procedure.

Table 7.1. Number of Approved Projects, by Environmental Review Category, Fiscal 1992–95

Fiscal year	Category A	Category B	Category C	Category FI	Total
1992[a]	14	72	48	91	225
1993	10	103	60	12	185
1994	8	123	69	31	231
1995	14	104	54	41	213

a. Excludes Africa Enterprise Fund projects, which were not categorized in fiscal 1992.

Proposed projects are screened into category A, B, or C according to potential environmental impact. IFC also has a separate category, FI, for investments in financial intermediaries, which may fund a variety of subprojects with potential environmental impacts (see table 7.1). Typical category A and B projects are described in boxes 7.3 and 7.4. Although most category A projects are large, some are small, as the One Earth Diving Lodge Project, a forty-bed tourist lodge located in a sensitive ecological area in Tanzania (see box 7.5).

Environmental disclosure requirements were incorporated into a general disclosure policy adopted by IFC in 1994. The disclosure policy attempts to balance the private sector's need for confidentiality with the public's right to know about issues affecting it and involving the use of public funds. Under the new policy, IFC releases the following environmental information through the Public Information Center:

- For all IFC projects, a "Summary of Project Information" document is prepared that includes the environmental category of the proposed investment and an overview of environmental issues. These summaries are issued a minimum of thirty days prior to consideration by the IFC board.
- For category A projects, an environmental assessment (EA) for each category A project is issued no later than sixty days prior to the decision of the IFC board.
- For category B projects: an Environmental Review Summary of IFC's environmental review of each category B project is issued no later than submission of project documents to the board.

These deadlines are minimum requirements. In practice, during fiscal 1995 the average release before approval by the board was 69 days for "Summaries of Project Information," 209 days for EAs, and 59 days for "Environmental Review Summaries."

In addition to disclosure of environmental information, IFC requires sponsors of category A projects to consult with affected local groups and

> **Box 7.3. La Société d'Exploitation des Mines d'Or de Sadiola (Mali)**
>
> A typical category A project is La Société d'Exploitation des Mines d'Or de Sadiola, where a gold mine will be developed through open-pit technology, and a treatment plant and infrastructure facilities will be built. Early in project development and before seeking IFC financing, the sponsor completed a socioeconomic impact study, archaeological surveys, and extensive consultations with affected villagers. IFC then helped the sponsor to integrate this information into an environmental assessment detailing a comprehensive program to mitigate the project's environmental impacts.
>
> Villagers from three local villages have indicated a desire not to relocate, despite the proximity of the mine. Groundwater wells drilled for project development will be turned over to the villages to provide a sustainable water supply. As noise and dust from the mine increase over time, it may become necessary to move the villages, and present households will be assisted in relocation. At IFC's suggestion, the project sponsor established a trust fund to provide general compensation for lifestyle and environmental disruptions, as well as to initiate community-driven programs. This fund will be administered by project representatives, local villagers, and regional officials.

interested parties during preparation of the environmental assessment, which is subsequently released to the public. Consultation is carried out in a culturally and socially acceptable way. Local laws and regulations affect the forum used for the consultation process as well as the method of notifying local groups of the availability of environmental information. These methods have included newspaper announcements, public hearings, and direct contact. Consultation techniques include official review committees established by local regulatory requirements, social acceptance surveys, and meetings with village elders. Meetings with elders are particularly common in areas where local communities are primarily illiterate. In the Philippines, for example, social acceptance surveys in the affected community are mandatory during preparation of the environmental impact statement and are the basis for public hearings on major projects such as the Sual Thermal Power Plant.

In another case, during planning for construction of a toll highway in Argentina the sponsor held meetings with local officials and nongovernmental organizations, and a sample survey of the families to be relocated was conducted to determine the social impact of the resettlement. At IFC's suggestion, a nongovernmental organization was created in cooperation with the municipality to facilitate relocation of families and to

> **Box 7.4. Liteksas Ir Calw A.B. (Lithuania) and SOCMA Americana (Argentina)**
>
> Typical category B projects are Liteksas in Lithuania and SOCMA Americana S.A. (SOCMA) in Argentina. Liteksas will expand and modernize a woolen textile mill comprising of spinning, weaving, and finishing plants. The project consists of upgrading and expanding the woolen production facility. The plant is currently in compliance with local laws and regulations. The expanded facility will include a pretreatment system for liquid effluents to ensure that discharges continue to meet local requirements and World Bank guidelines. A spill prevention plan will be developed and leakage detection systems installed. Employees' work areas will be monitored for noise and dust to control exposure levels, and employees will be trained in fire prevention, safety procedures, and emergency response.
>
> SOCMA Americana, one of the principal holding companies of the SOCMA Group, focuses on four business sectors: infrastructure, environmental services, food, and information services. A corporate loan to modernize and expand SOCMA's operations included an evaluation of the company's environmental management system, which is a systematic approach to managing environmental issues based on well-defined policy and procedures, with clear responsibilities and feedback mechanisms to facilitate continuous improvement. With IFC's help, the company expanded its environmental management system to eighteen company holdings that were beneficiaries of the IFC loan.

act as an intermediary between affected families and local and national authorities.

IFC has also placed more emphasis on monitoring and supervision. Staff of the Environment Division and other IFC technical specialists are making more site visits to projects under implementation to determine the progress and effectiveness of mitigation measures.

For example, in 1994, IFC audited thirty-nine Africa Enterprise Fund projects in Benin, Côte d'Ivoire, Ghana, Kenya, Mauritius, Swaziland, Uganda, and Zimbabwe.[5] The purpose of the audits was to ensure compliance with the World Bank's guidelines, assess the guidance given to sponsors on environmental issues, advise on measures to improve performance in these areas, recommend changes to the project review system to ensure compliance with requirements, and identify additional assistance needed from the Corporation. Most projects were found to be in compliance, and in other cases action plans to correct problems were developed. Problems in occupational health and safety were found to be the most common shortcoming but often were also the easiest to resolve at minimal or no cost, such as enforcing requirements for workers to use protective gear.

Supervision can afford an opportunity to improve on the original project design. For example, a supervisory visit to a kaolin mine in Brazil during early construction resulted in a more cost-effective method for controlling erosion and vehicular access along a pipeline right-of-way associated with the project. Instead of using terracing to control erosion and brush pile barriers to control access as previously planned, the sponsor will now use logs cleared during pipeline construction as water barriers across the right-of-way, minimizing erosion while blocking access.

Box 7.5. One Earth Diving Lodge (Tanzania)

IFC is supporting a project to build a small ecotourism lodge on the beach of Panga ya Watoro, north of a national forest on a peninsula of Pemba Island. The project is supported by a loan of $700,000 from the Africa Enterprise Fund.

Five villages with a total population of 1,200 are located within 6 kilometers of the uninhabited project site. The lodge will employ the villagers and provide a ready market for local agricultural produce. The sponsor intends to provide treated wastewater free of charge to farmers for irrigation. The lodge is expected to have a positive impact on the fishery resources of the peninsula and Pemba Island in general. Benefits include providing permanent boat mooring sites to reduce damage to coral reefs, producing jobs to lessen reliance on fishing as a livelihood, and policing coastal waters to prevent illegal fishing and dynamiting by mainland and foreign vessels.

Because the lodge is close to the forest, turtle nesting sites, and coral reefs, and because of the general environmental sensitivity of the area, IFC categorized the project as having potential for diverse and significant environmental effects (category A). To protect endangered species and sensitive habitats, project sponsors will shield turtle nesting sites from construction and other activities, use directional sodium vapor lighting in all public areas to avoid disorienting nesting turtles and hatchlings, and restore a coastal evergreen thicket that serves as a corridor for animals such as the duiker, civet, and Pemba flying fox (an endangered species of bat).

The sponsors, committed to making the lodge a world-class center for diving and marine research, plan to establish an environmental research station. They also are negotiating with local communities and authorities to declare reefs off Panga ya Watoro an exclusion zone, which could serve as a control area for ecological surveys of neighboring coral reefs.

A recent supervisory mission to the Empresa Eléctrica Pangue S.A. hydroelectric power plant (Chile), a category A project approved in fiscal 1993 and now under construction, found that environmental mitigation programs appear to be functioning well. For example, the Pehuen Foundation, an organization established to support development initiatives by local Pehuenche communities affected by the project, is fully operational, and the number of projects and level of community participation are increasing. A resettlement program and watershed protection and management plan are being implemented satisfactorily. Additional study of the downstream impact of the project and development of operational guidelines are progressing according to the agreed schedule. An ecological station, established by the project to monitor ecological impacts, conducts regular environmental inspections, as well as a significant number of research projects.

During 1995, IFC developed a strategy to improve supervision of projects under implementation. Measures include more site visits by environmental specialists during project appraisal and implementation, increased vigilance on the submission of annual monitoring reports by project sponsors, and stronger legal documentation of environmental requirements. IFC has increased the number of supervision visits to improve understanding of the quality of implementation and effectiveness of required measures. In fiscal 1995, Environment Division staff visited forty-two projects for appraisal purposes and thirty-five projects for supervision.

Lessons Learned and Future Directions

IFC's development mandate is played out in the challenging interface between the policy framework established by the public sector and the capabilities and incentives of the private sector. Environmental issues are, potentially, among the most controversial and sensitive issues considered in investment decisions. The increasing transparency of the project review process tends to heighten awareness of the issues outside the Corporation. Creative and innovative solutions are expected, and IFC is committed to situating itself at the leading edge in resolving these issues.

Challenges arise in all aspects of IFC's environmental program. Environmental management of projects clearly requires both a serious commitment from project sponsors and vigilance by IFC during project implementation.

An appreciation by project sponsors of the benefits of identifying and managing environmental issues as early as possible is beginning to emerge. More and more private sector enterprises in developing countries and their financiers understand that environmental issues can directly affect project success, affording opportunities for efficiency gains and minimizing risk. Project review is proceeding through approvals and into the implementation phase more efficiently and with fewer delays, as environmental issues are increasingly addressed and, to the extent possible, resolved early in the process.

Recent experience in developing environmental projects has given IFC a more realistic appreciation for their slower pace. Modest successes have provided IFC with experience on how to be more effective in advancing such projects in the future—both in structuring the investments and in enlisting the support of the World Bank and others in establishing the policy and regulatory framework that enables the private sector to act. Economic trends and the shifting social and political climate worldwide continue to drive such initiatives and are expected to increase the demand for IFC support in the future.

IFC is committed to becoming more proactive in the environmental arena. Investment decisions will continue to incorporate environmental factors, with the goal of improving the quality of both the environmental analyses prepared by project sponsors and their environmental performance during project implementation. Refining IFC's own project review process to retain a high standard of excellence while avoiding unnecessary bureaucracy is also an objective.

IFC will explore ways in which the private sector can assist in solving environmental problems. It will continue to assist financial institutions to build environmental risk management capability through training, follow-up assistance, and supervision, with a focus on developing practical methods for various types of institutions to address environmental issues in a cost-effective manner. Opportunities will also be sought to provide increased support to small and medium-size companies on environmental matters.

IFC's GEF activities will focus on ways to engage the private sector in innovative projects and financing approaches. The priorities are to streamline the review process to provide ease and speed of processing consistent with private sector needs and expectations and to clarify a practical definition of incremental costs for private sector projects.

In summary, the last three years brought a new reality to the commitments made at the Rio Earth Summit. The issues are of considerable complexity and have many dimensions: social, technical, scientific, and economic. IFC's transaction-oriented approach is helping to translate important improvements in the overall policy approach to private sector development being implemented by many developing countries into actual private sector investment. In all of its activities, IFC will continue to ensure that environmental issues and opportunities are fully addressed and that the lessons of experience are applied.

Notes

1. The study was supported by the European Union, Finland, the Netherlands, and Sweden through trust funds administered by IFC.

2. The study is funded by the governments of France, Germany, Norway, the Netherlands, the United States, and IFC.

3. The study is partially funded by the Heinz Endowments.

4. BCSD merged with the World Industry Council on Environment in 1995 to form the World Business Council for Sustainable Development (WBCSD).

5. The Africa Enterprise Fund, established in 1989, is a vehicle for financing small and medium-size projects with costs between $250,000 and $5 million.

Annex A. Environment- and Social-Related Operational Policies and Bank Procedures

Beginning in fiscal 1993, existing Operational Directives (ODs) began to be converted into a new system of operational policies and Bank procedures. The new system consists of three categories: Operational Policies (OPs), Bank Procedures (BPs), and Good Practices (GPs). Where the policies listed below have already been converted and reissued, the new citations are given. Where conversions are under way, the new citations are annotated in parentheses as "to be issued."

The following list summarizes current environment- and social-related statements. Primary statements on environment and social issues are listed, as well as many policies that support the environment or make environmental references.

Primary Statements on Environment and Social Issues

OD 4.01   Environmental Assessment (to be issued as OP/BP/GP 4.01)

This document outlines Bank policy and procedures for the environmental assessment of Bank lending operations. All environmental consequences are recognized early in the project cycle and are taken into account in the selection, siting, planning, and design of a project.

OP/BP/GP 4.02   Environmental Action Plans

These documents outline Bank policy on the preparation of country environmental action plans by IBRD and IDA borrowing governments. The Bank encourages and supports efforts of governments to prepare and implement environmental action plans and to revise them periodically as necessary. The plans identify environmental problems, set priorities, lead to national environmental policy, guide investment programs, and should be reflected in Bank operational work.

OD 4.03/GP4.03 Operational Note 11.01 Agricultural Pest Management (to be issued as OP 4.09 Pesticides)

The Bank promotes effective and environmentally sound pest management practices in Bank-supported agricultural development. Any Bank loan that provides substantial funding for pesticide procurement or increases the use of pesticides in the project must include specific measures to promote environmentally sound pest management, as well as safety in pesticide handling and use.

OP 4.07 Water Resources Management

The policy promotes economically viable, environmentally sustainable, and socially equitable management of water resources. It includes the provision of potable water, sanitation facilities, flood control, and water for productive activities. Among priority areas for Bank assistance and involvement are the development of a comprehensive framework for designing water resource investments, policies, and institutions; adoption of appropriate pricing and incentive policies for water resources; decentralization of water service delivery; restoration and preservation of aquatic ecosystems against overexploitation of groundwater resources; avoidance of water quality problems associated with irrigation investments; and establishment of strong legal and regulatory frameworks to enforce policies. In cases where the borrower has made inadequate progress in priority areas of water resources management, Bank lending is limited to operations that do not draw additionally on water resources.

OD 4.20 Indigenous Peoples (to be issued as OP/BP/GP 4.10)

This policy ensures that indigenous peoples, defined as social groups whose social and cultural identity is distinct from that of the dominant society and makes them vulnerable to being disadvantaged in the development process, benefit from development projects. It also ensures that potentially adverse effects of Bank projects on indigenous people are avoided or mitigated. An indigenous people development plan is prepared, as appropriate, in tandem with the main investment project.

OD 4.30 Involuntary Resettlement (to be issued as OP/BP/GP 4.12)

This document outlines the Bank policy and procedures covering Bank staff and borrower responsibilities in operations involving involuntary resettlement. Any operation that involves land acquisition or is screened as a category A or B project for environmental assessment purposes is reviewed for potential resettlement requirements early in the project cycle to protect the livelihood of people who lose their land, their houses, or both. The objective of the Bank's resettlement policy is to assist displaced persons in their efforts to restore or improve former living standards and earning capacity. To achieve this objective, the borrower is required to prepare and carry out resettlement plans or development programs.

OP/GP 4.36 Forestry

Bank lending in the forest sector aims to reduce deforestation, enhance the environmental contribution of forested areas, promote afforestation, reduce poverty, and encourage economic development. Sector work should examine the legal and institutional basis for ensuring environmentally sustainable development of the forest sector. The Bank expects governments to have adequate provisions in place for conserving protected areas and critical watersheds, as well as for establishing environmental guidelines and monitoring procedures. The Bank does not provide financing for logging in primary tropical moist forests.

OD 4.00 Annexes B-B4 Environmental Policy for Dam and Reservoir Projects (to be issued as OP/BP/GP 4.05)

The Bank's environmental policy for dam and reservoir projects aims to avoid, minimize, or compensate for adverse environmental impacts wherever possible, using design features (for example, modifying the dam's location or height) and measures implemented as part of the project. The potential project impact is determined at an early stage with the advice of environmental specialists.

OD 9.01 Procedures for Investment Operations under the Global Environment Facility (to be issued as OP/BP 10.20)

This policy describes the steps, in addition to standard Bank investment lending procedures, required to process Global Environment Facility (GEF) operations. Other GEF operational procedures, including those for environmental assessment, generally follow standard Bank procedures for investment lending.

OP/BP 10.21 Investment Operations Financed by the Multilateral Fund of the Montreal Protocol

This policy describes the identification process, eligible activities, and the steps required to receive grants from the Multilateral Fund for the

Implementation of the Montreal Protocol. The processing of operations and procedures for appraisal under the Ozone Projects Trust Fund of the Montreal Protocol follow the Bank's general procedures.

Operational Policy Note 11.02 Wildlands: Their Protection and Management in Economic Development (to be issued as OP/BP/GP 4.04 under the title Natural Habitats)

The Bank supports the protection, maintenance, and rehabilitation of natural habitats. The Bank does not finance projects that involve the conversion of designated critical natural habitats. Where no feasible alternatives exist for projects that convert natural habitats, mitigation and restoration are included in the project to minimize habitat loss. In addition, the Bank may require that the project include the establishment and maintenance of an ecologically similar compensatory area.

Operational Policy Note 11.03 Management of Cultural Property in Bank-Financed Projects (to be issued as OP/BP/GP 4.11 under the title Cultural Property)

The Bank's general policy regarding cultural properties is to assist in their preservation and avoid their elimination. Normally, the Bank declines to finance projects that will significantly damage nonreplicable cultural property, and it assists only projects that are sited or designed so as to prevent such damage.

Statements Supportive of the Environment

OP/BP/GP 8.41 Institutional Development Fund (IDF)

The Institutional Development Fund is a grant facility designed to fill gaps in the Bank's set of instruments for financing technical assistance for institutional development work associated with policy reform, country management of technical assistance, and areas of special operational emphasis, particularly poverty reduction, public sector management, private sector development, and environmental management.

OD 14.70 Involving Nongovernmental Organizations in Bank-supported Activities (to be issued as OP/BP/GP 14.70)

This policy sets out a framework for involving NGOs in Bank-supported activities and provides staff with guidance on working with NGOs, bearing in mind their potential contribution to sustainable development and poverty reduction. NGOs heighten awareness and influence policy concerning environmental degradation, involuntary resettlement, and tribal people.

Statements with Environmental References

OD 2.00 Country Economic and Sector Work

Country economic and sector work analyzes the macroeconomic and sector development problems of borrower countries. Because long-term quality and sustainability of development depend on factors in addition to economic ones, country economic work may also focus on questions of the environmental effects of alternative policy options.

BP 2.11 Country Assistance Strategies

The country assistance strategy (CAS) is the central vehicle for review by the Bank's Executive Directors of the Bank Group's assistance strategy for IDA and IBRD borrowers. It is a concise, analytic, and issue-oriented statement that provides information on the historical perspective and recent economic and portfolio performance; the country's external environment in terms of external trade, investment, and financial policies; and the Bank Group's country assistance strategy. The CAS presents the main objectives of the Bank's program of assistance for the country, including efforts to reduce poverty and sustain the environment.

OD 2.20 Policy Framework Papers (to be issued as OP/BP 2.20)

Policy framework papers are vehicles for governments to reach agreements with the Bank and the International Monetary Fund on the broad outline of medium-term programs to overcome balance of payments problems and foster growth. The papers should maintain an adequate balance in the coverage of macroeconomic, sectoral, social, environmental, and institutional aspects. In the diagnoses of the current situation, any long-term constraints on development, including the environment, should be covered briefly.

OD 4.15 Poverty Reduction (to be issued as OP/BP/GP 4.15)

Sustainable poverty reduction is the Bank's overarching objective. Maintaining the environment is critical if gains in poverty reduction are to be sustained and if future increases in poverty are to be avoided. In sector work, particular attention is paid to the impact of sector policies on the links between environmental issues and poverty.

OP/BP/GP 7.50 Projects on International Waterways

The Bank recognizes that projects involving the use of international waterways for development purposes may affect relations between the Bank and its borrowers and also between states, whether members of the Bank or not. The international aspects of Bank-supported projects on international waterways are dealt with at the earliest possible opportunity and, where appropriate, other riparians are notified of the proposed project and its project details. Any proposed project's potential to harm the interests of other riparians through deprivation of water, pollution, or otherwise is determined and affected riparians are notified. The Bank attaches great importance to riparians making appropriate agreements or arrangements for the use and protection of the waterway; where differences exist, prior to financing, the Bank urges states to negotiate to reach appropriate agreements or arrangements.

OP/BP/GP 8.40 Technical Assistance

Technical assistance (TA) for policy and project preparation includes support for environmental action plans, project preparation, and environmental assessment. Institutional development TA addresses the need to strengthen capacity for environmental analysis and enforcement.

OD 8.60 Adjustment Lending Policy (to be issued as BP 8.60 under the title Adjustment Lending)

Analysis of adjustment programs considers implications for the environment. Bank staff review the environmental policies and practices in the country. The design of adjustment programs takes into account the findings and recommendations of such reviews.

OP/BP 10.00 Investment Lending: Identification to Board Presentation

During project identification, Bank staff decide on the environmental category assigned to a project, the type and timing of any environmental assessment, and the environmental and natural resource management issues to be examined. The project identification document (PID) and staff appraisal report (SAR) address or track these same points. The memorandum and recommendation of the Bank's president discuss the project's environmental impact, the main findings of the environmental assessment, consultation with affected groups, and feedback to these groups on the findings of the assessment.

OP/BP 10.04   Economic Evaluation of Investment Operations

The economic evaluation of Bank-financed projects takes into account any domestic and cross-border externalities. A project's global externalities—normally identified in the Bank's sector work or in the environmental assessment process—are considered in the economic analysis when (a) payments related to the project are made under an international agreement, or (b) projects or project components are financed by the Global Environment Facility.

OD 13.05   Project Supervision (to be issued as OP/BP 13.05)

A supervision plan is prepared and discussed for each project with the borrower during project appraisal. The plan covers the entire supervision period and includes aspects of the project, such as the environment, that require special Bank attention during supervision. In addition, in the project implementation summary, the project is rated in terms of both implementation of any environmental component included and any unforeseen environmental deterioration resulting or threatening to result from implementation of the project.

OP/BP/GP 13.55   Implementation Completion Reporting

This policy requires an implementation completion report (ICR) for each lending operation the Bank finances. The ICR assesses the degree of achievement of the project's major objectives (including environmental objectives), prospects for the project's sustainability, Bank and borrower performance, project outcome, and the plan for the project's future operation. Special attention is given to evaluation of environmental and other objectives, in order to improve project performance in these areas and build a store of information for expanded evaluation. For projects requiring an environmental assessment, the ICR evaluates specific concerns raised in the environmental assessment process, including environmental impacts anticipated in the environmental assessment report, the effectiveness of the mitigation measures taken, and institutional development and training regarding the environment.

BP 17.50   Disclosure of Operational Information (OP/GP 17.50 to be issued along with the reissue of BP 17.50)

This statement describes the Bank's policies and procedures with respect to the disclosure of project information documents, staff appraisal reports, gray cover economic and sector work reports, sectoral policy papers, and environment-related documents. Copies of environmental assessments (EAs) required for Category A projects must be made available in the borrowing country at some public place accessible to affected groups and local NGOs and must be submitted to the Bank; once locally released and officially received by the Bank, country departments send a copy to the Public Information Center. Copies of environmental action plans are also sent to the Public Information Center once the Bank has officially received the plan and obtained the government's consent. This policy applies also to documents prepared for projects financed or cofinanced from trust funds under the Global Environment Facility, including the Montreal Protocol project financed through the Ozone Projects Trust Fund.

Annex B. Guidance on Identification of World Bank Environmental Projects and Components

This annex indicates the criteria used to identify Bank projects and project components having primarily environmental objectives. For the most part, it is organized according to the traditional areas and sectors of Bank lending (urban development, transport, industry, agriculture, health, and so on). However, certain specific types of environmental interventions, such as watershed management or conservation and those involving cross-cutting environmental activities, are also distinguished. This is a working list that will be periodically reviewed and updated as Bank initiatives in support of country environmental management continue to evolve.

Table B.1. Guidance on Identification of World Bank Environmental Projects and Components

Project sector	Examples of environmental project objectives or components
Infrastructure and urban development	
Urban (planning, sites and services, housing)	Urban institutions and planning for pollution control, monitoring, regulation, and enforcement; environment-based land-use planning; slum upgrading; wastewater and solid waste treatment, management, and disposal; reduced urban air, water, and noise pollution
Transport (roads, airports, traffic engineering)	Traffic management for reduced congestion; vehicle fuel efficiency and modification; reduced vehicle emissions; emissions standards; incentives for higher occupancy vehicles; mass transit; reduced marine pollution and ships' waste and spills; port environmental safety and cleanup; noise pollution reduction; institutional strengthening
Water supply and sanitation	Water quality management (ground and surface); water pollution abatement; wastewater and sewage treatment, management, and disposal; water pricing and conservation incentives; setting, regulation, monitoring, and enforcement of standards; institutional strengthening

(Table continues on the following page.)

Table B.1 *(continued)*

Project sector	Examples of environmental project objectives or components
Disaster relief and reconstruction	None
Telecommunications	None
Industry and finance	
Industry	Increased plant efficiency; reduced waste and emissions; clean technologies; end-of-pipe pollution abatement; recycling; control and prevention of air and water pollution; hazardous waste treatment, management, storage, and disposal; standards setting, regulation, monitoring, and enforcement for quality management; institutional strengthening
Industrial development finance	Lending for pollution abatement; support to financial intermediaries to conduct environmental assessment
Natural resources management	
Agriculture and livestock	Soil management, conservation, and restoration; extension for environmentally sound land management; surface and groundwater management; pasture and grazing management; pesticide management such as integrated pest management; multisectoral water allocation; input pricing for water and agrochemicals; institutional strengthening; research extension
Forestry	Natural forest management, plantation development, and reforestation; management and afforestation for noncommercial uses (for example, social forestry, extractive reserves); conservation management, including biodiversity; institutional strengthening
Watershed management	Watershed and river basin protection, management, and rehabilitation; multisectoral planning and allocation; institutional strengthening
Land management	Land mapping, titling and tenure, and transfers; land restoration and reclamation; institutional strengthening
Fisheries and marine resource management	Management of marine and freshwater resources; coastal zone management; biodiversity conservation; marine and riverine fisheries management; institutional strengthening

Project sector	Examples of environmental project objectives or components
Conservation, including biodiversity	Terrestrial and aquatic biodiversity conservation; protected areas; ex-situ conservation; financing mechanisms; training and institutional strengthening
Energy Energy and power sectors	Supply-side energy efficiency; demand-side management and conservation; reduced emissions; alternative and renewable energy technologies; removal of energy subsidies; institutional strengthening; standards setting, regulation, monitoring, and enforcement
Population and human resources Population	None
Public health and nutrition	Environmental health components
Education	Environmental awareness and education; environmental extension services; environmental research, science, and technology
Social	Resettlement associated with biodiversity projects; preservation of cultural property
Cross-cutting environmental activities	Environmental assessment; National Environmental Action Plans; institutional development for environmental policy, regulation, monitoring and enforcement, and research; natural resource accounting, environmental indicators, environmental valuation; transfer of clean technology; environmental technical assistance and training (Bank and borrower); environmental information systems, including natural resource monitoring and geographic information systems
Structural adjustment loans (monetary, fiscal, exchange rate, trade policies)	Reduction of subsidies for natural resource use

Annex C. Projects with Primarily Environmental Objectives Approved in Fiscal 1995

This annex provides details on projects approved by the Bank's Board of Directors between July 1, 1994, and June 30, 1995, that have primarily environmental objectives. Table C.1 illustrates the broad range of environmental concerns addressed by Bank projects. The dollar figures provided for projects with environmental objectives represent the Bank share (IBRD loan or IDA credit), as well as the total project cost.

Table C.1. Projects with Environmental Objectives Approved in Fiscal 1995

Country	Project	Project description
Africa		
Benin	Environmental Management ($8 million, IDA; $9 million, total project cost)	Allows the government to develop the national environmental management capacity required to implement and monitor effectively the priority actions identified in the National Environmental Action Plan (June 1993). Supports planning and implementation of policies and programs, monitoring and enforcement of legislation, strengthening of coordination mechanisms, development of information systems, and promotion of the integration of environmental concerns in socioeconomic development plans. Improves the awareness and understanding of environmental issues for various segments of the population and fosters the integration of environmental considerations in the education system.

Country	Project	Project description
Burkina Faso	Urban Environment ($37 million, IDA; $50 million, total project cost)	Assists with the rehabilitation or improvement of priority primary drainage networks, the development of piped sewerage and on-site sanitation, the closing or upgrading of existing landfills and construction of new landfills, and the improvement of current toxic and industrial solid waste management systems. Aims to strengthen the central government's capacity for urban management.
Asia		
China	Liaoning Environment ($110 million, IBRD; $351 million, total project cost)	Assists the government in reducing pollution and improving operational efficiency through upgrading of technology, minimization of waste, and reuse. Strengthens local capabilities in monitoring and enforcement of environmental regulations, corporatization of the sewerage utilities, and establishment of a sound cost-recovery policy for pollution abatement services. Includes an environmental protection fund for eligible pollution control subprojects of industrial enterprises and enhances institutional development through technical assistance and training. Also includes a component to rehabilitate and conserve cultural heritage sites.
India	Industrial Pollution Prevention ($168 million, IBRD/IDA; $330 million, total project cost)	Promotes cost-effective abatement of industrial pollution through components that support institutional strengthening of state pollution control boards as well as investments by individual firms for pollution abatement with a focus on minimization of waste and cleaner production methods. Renews financing for common effluent treatment plants for treating wastewater and solid materials at industrial and other sites with a concentration of industries, particularly those of small size. A technical assistance component supports the development, diffusion, and transfer of technologies with environmental benefits.

(Table continues on the following page.)

Table C.1 *(continued)*

Country	Project	Project description
India *(continued)*	Madhya Pradesh Forestry ($58 million, IDA; $67 million, total project cost)	Supports improvements for the Madhya Pradesh forestry sector, including innovative programs for participatory forest management. Involves forest regeneration and improved silvicultural practices; improved implementation, monitoring, and evaluation; a village resource development program based on participatory planning and the integration of forest management and protection with activities to generate alternative incomes to reduce pressures on the forest; forestry research, extension, and technology improvements; and biodiversity conservation through improved management of twelve protected areas while supporting the development of alternative resources or incomes for local communities.
Korea, Rep. of	Waste Disposal ($75 million, IBRD; $305 million, total project cost)	Assists the governments in Pusan and Chunbak Province in addressing environmental, institutional, and technological concerns regarding wastewater and specified waste disposal, the health hazards of surface and groundwater contamination, and the reuse of treated effluent. The Kusan waste disposal plant will ensure satisfactory management of most hazardous waste substances generated in industries.
	Ports Development and Environmental Improvement ($100 million, IBRD; $1,107 million, total project cost)	Provides comprehensive support for addressing environmental issues in port and harbor development. Includes facilities to collect, manage, and treat ship waste and to remove timber- and fish-processing plants that cause air, noise, and traffic pollution. Provides training and technical assistance to strengthen the environmental capability of the Korea Maritime and Port Authority and a program to monitor pollution, ecosystem productivity, biodiversity, and changes in the yields of living marine resources in the Yellow Sea.

Country	Project	Project description
Pakistan	Punjab Forest Sector Development ($25 million, IDA; $34 million, total project cost)	Strengthens the Punjab Forestry Department's capabilities to assist local communities and the private sector in the development and conservation of forest and rangelands through natural, financial, and human resource management. Helps to disseminate technology and information required to promote farmers' involvement in nursery and timber production; develop and strengthen community organizations to manage scrub forests and rangelands jointly with public sector institutions; and implement a pilot component for the reorganization of timber plantations to enhance their environmental value.
Sri Lanka	Colombo Environmental Improvement ($39 million, IDA; $49 million, total project cost)	Focuses on improving solid waste services, controlling surface and groundwater contamination from wastewater discharge, and building up the capabilities of the local governments in municipal waste management. Promotes private sector participation in environment-related operations. Finances the construction of a sanitary landfill and compost facilities to replace open dumps and equipment for the collection, transport, and disposal of hospital wastes; wastewater collection systems in industrial zones; wastewater pollution abatement measures in the Beira Lake catchment area; and technical assistance.
Thailand	Clean Fuels and Environmental Improvement ($90 million, IBRD; $370 million, total project cost)	Supports the reduction of air pollutants attributable to petroleum fuels in Thailand by assisting the government in meeting reformulated gasoline and diesel oil specifications, improving its refinery operations through the installation of appropriate facilities and equipment to reduce refinery emissions and ensure safety.

(Table continues on the following page.)

Table C.1 *(continued)*

Country	Project	Project description
Eastern Europe and Central Asia		
Estonia	Haapsalu and Matsalu Bays Environment ($2 million, IBRD; $8 million, total project cost)	Includes improvements in water and wastewater treatment in Haapsalu and promotes management of point and nonpoint source pollution in the catchment areas of Haapsalu and Matsalu Bays, with a view to reducing pollution in the Baltic Sea. Supports the planning and management of ecotourism and implementation of the management plan for the Matsalu State Nature Reserve. This project is part of the Bank's support for the Baltic Sea Environment Program.
Latvia	Liepaja Environment ($4 million, IBRD; $21 million, total project cost)	Includes water and wastewater investment components, which are complemented by an environmental management component. Restores and enhances water quality in the city of Liepaja and the northern portion of Lake Liepaja and promotes environmentally sustainable development, including tourist development, of the coastal zone and protected areas in and around Liepaja, Ventspils, and Talsi regions. This project is part of the Bank's support for the Baltic Sea Environment Program.
Lithuania	Klaipeda Environment ($7 million, IBRD; $23 million, total project cost)	Focuses on the city of Klaipeda. Seeks to improve water supply and sanitation services in the city as well as the operational efficiency and management of the Klaipeda State Water Supply Enterprise and to promote environmentally sustainable management and development of the Kursiu Lagoon and adjacent coastal areas. This project is part of the Bank's support for the Baltic Sea Environment Program.

Country	Project	Project description
Poland	Katowice Heat Supply and Conservation ($45 million, IBRD; $93 million, total project cost)	Addresses the environmental, health, and economic problems caused by soot and dust particulates generated by energy production. Enhances energy conservation and efficiency in the district heating sector by extending the life of existing district heating assets through rehabilitation and introduction of modern technologies and by reducing environmental pollution through investments in energy-efficient equipment and systems as well as by supporting a program to eliminate coal-fired, heat-only boilers.
Russian Federation	Environmental Management ($110 million, IBRD; $195 million, total project cost)	Provides support to the Russian Federation's Environmental Framework Program, which addresses environmental and natural resource management issues at federal, regional, and local levels and mainstreams them into the economic, social, and political adjustment process. Includes policy and regulatory support and environmental epidemiology; water quality management; hazardous waste management; the creation and capitalization of a National Pollution Abatement Facility for the funding of economically and financially viable pollution abatement projects; and the creation of a Center for Project Preparation and Implementation under the Ministry of Environmental Protection and Natural Resources.

(Table continues on the following page.)

Table C.1 *(continued)*

Country	Project	Project description
Russian Federation *(continued)*	Emergency Oil Spill Recovery ($99 million, IBRD; $140 million, total project cost)	During 1994, one of the world's largest oil spills occurred in the Usinsk region of the Komi Republic as a result of leaks from the regional oil pipeline. The project assists the Russian Federation and the pipeline operator in stabilizing the oil in the spill area and preventing ecological damage in the Pechora River Basin; continues cleanup in an environmentally appropriate way; supports safe pipeline operations in the near term and evaluates the need for a replacement pipeline; and identifies and implements other measures to mitigate against possible oil spills in the future.

Latin America and the Caribbean

Country	Project	Project description
Honduras	Environmental Development ($11 million, IDA; $13 million, total project cost)	Strengthens the governmental agencies' capacity in environmental and natural resource planning; policy, legal, and regulatory framework development; environmental monitoring; and the enforcement of environmental laws and regulations. Assists with the strengthening and implementation of a national system of environmental impact assessment that engages NGOs, communities, and the private sector in the review process. Develops the environmental management capacity of selected municipalities in a manner that will increase the involvement of affected organizations and individuals.
OECS countries	Solid Waste Management ($12 million, IDA and IBRD; $51 million, total project cost)	Improves existing national systems of solid waste storage, collection, and disposal; provides for investments in port reception facilities to address the problems of ship-generated solid waste and the rationalization of the existing institutional framework through the creation of solid waste management entities. At the regional level, provides technical assistance for sewerage master plans, sewerage and sewage treatment projects, and the preparation of an institutional framework for regional coordination.

Country	Project	Project description
Trinidad and Tobago	Environmental Management ($6 million, IBRD; $11 million, total project cost)	Establishes an environmental management agency that is responsible for the legal and regulatory framework covering all aspects of the environment in the country. Through technical assistance and training, helps to bring the newly created Environmental Management Authority to full operational capacity.
Venezuela	INPARQUES ($55 million, IBRD; $96 million, total project cost)	Strengthens the government's capability to manage Venezuela's national and urban parks, natural monuments, and wildlife refuges and reserves. In particular, the project strengthens conservation and protection of vulnerable areas; intensifies public environmental research, training, and education efforts, and improves the economic sustainability of the national parks and other protected areas.

Middle East and North Africa

Country	Project	Project description
Lebanon	Solid Waste/ Environmental Management ($55 million, IBRD; $135 million, total project cost)	Completes the rehabilitation of the solid waste collection and disposal systems as envisaged under the National Emergency Reconstruction Program, improves the collection and disposal of hospital waste, strengthens the government's and the private sector's capabilities for solid waste management, and helps to develop a coastal zone management plan that will protect the Lebanese coast from further degradation.

Annex D. Projects with Major Environmental Components Approved in Fiscal 1995

This annex provides details on projects approved by the World Bank's Board of Directors between July 1, 1994, and June 30, 1995, that have major environmental components.

Table D.1. Projects with Major Environmental Components Approved in Fiscal 1995

Country	Project	Environmental component
Africa		
Central African Republic	Livestock Development and Rangeland Management	Supports activities focused on rangeland management; grassroots capacity development, and the establishment of agropastoral areas or buffer zones that help to conserve the savanna ecosystems.
Côte d'Ivoire	Private Sector Energy	Reduces environmental impacts of energy production by supporting efficient gas-fired capacity and the use of indigenous natural gas.
	Municipal Support	Contributes to sustainable development through improvement and protection of the urban environment.
Ethiopia	National Fertilizer Sector	Supports the training of farmers and extension personnel in efficient and balanced use of nutrients so that losses of nutrients and other polluting elements into the environment are minimized; establishes arrangements to compile and maintain a data base on the impact of fertilizers and other materials on the environment; and establishes monitoring and testing activities at strategic locations for environmental protection.

Country	Project	Environmental component
Gabon	Transport Sector Technical Assistance	Provides training and seminars to sensitize actors in the transport and urban sectors to environmental considerations in the design, implementation, and monitoring of transport and urban projects, plans, and policies.
Ghana	Fisheries Subsector Capacity Building	Provides for the establishment of a monitoring, control, and surveillance system for marine and inland fisheries, as well as the long-term conservation, protection, and sustainability of the fishery resource.
	Mining Sector Development and Environment	Provides support to the Mining Commission to review existing monitoring and enforcement practices (including an assessment of jurisdictional responsibilities of sectoral agencies and the Environmental Protection Agency with regard to environmental monitoring); to develop guidelines and standards for implementing sectoral and environmental regulations; and to establish an environmental information system.
Madagascar	Second Irrigation Rehabilitation	Improves environmental management through the development of techniques for environmental assessment of irrigation rehabilitation and the reinforcement of local capacity for such assessment; improves the drainage of stagnant waters, which will have a beneficial effect on the accumulation of salinity and mineral deposits in the soils.
Malawi	National Water Development	Ensures the protection and management of water resources and of aquatic and riparian environments through institutional and capacity building, as well as studies on alternative sources of water, hydrogeological and hydrological assessments and mapping, water quality, and sediment loads.

(Table continues on the following page.)

Table D.1 *(continued)*

Country	Project	Environmental component
Mauritius	Port Development and Environment Protection	Provides for a study to define the requirements and to design facilities for collection and disposal of land- and ship-based oily waste and to draft regulations to enforce safety in port operations and control vessels' seaworthiness; constructs facilities for the collection and pretreatment of oily waste; and supervises contracts for civil works and equipment and training to fight oil spills.
Niger	Pilot Private Irrigation Promotion	Finances the materials and part of the operating costs for the monitoring of replenishable shallow aquifers and erosion control works.
Senegal	Water Sector	Supports institutional capacity building, which will formulate a national strategy for sanitation in urban and periurban areas, and provides for the treatment and reuse of periurban municipal sewage for irrigation; prepares sewerage master plans for nineteen secondary cities and riparian areas, implements a rainwater sanitation project, and implements the Rufisque sewerage and urban drainage subproject.
Swaziland	Urban Development	Provides for the construction, rehabilitation, or expansion of existing wastewater treatment plants.

Country	Project	Environmental component
Tanzania	Mineral Sector Development	Helps artisans and small-scale miners to mitigate the environmental hazards of present mining methods through specific project interventions, including education and training, the promotion of simple and environmentally sensitive technologies, and improved mining and work safety measures; the monitoring of environmental aspects of mining operations and the introduction of effective regulatory measures; and support to the Regional Miners' Association to address the environmental and social problems on a self-help and self-policing basis. For medium- and large-scale industrial mining operations, develops and implements appropriate environmental policies, regulatory standards, and monitoring mechanisms. This project also provides necessary manpower, and logistical and institutional capacity to enable the government of Tanzania to implement a new environmental framework. |//

Asia

Bangladesh	Gas Infrastructure Development	Supports the development of the energy sector's institutional capabilities, particularly in the areas of safety and environmental protection.
China	Shenyang Industrial Reform	Finances the implementation of hazardous waste collection and treatment facilities, an automatic wastewater monitoring network to improve enforcement of discharge standards, and technical assistance for the environmental protection bureaus to enhance their capabilities to monitor and enforce pollution control standards.

(Table continues on the following page.)

Table D.1 *(continued)*

Country	Project	Environmental component
China (continued)	Seventh Railway	Supports the conversion from diesel to electric railcars, strengthening capabilities of the Ministry of Railways environmental staff, developing a solid waste management strategy for the Shenyang station, assessing techniques for cleaning up contaminated soil at the Taopu freight yard, treating oily wastewater at a locomotive depot, training railway environmental staff in environmental impact assessment techniques, developing a fuel additive for diesel locomotives to boost combustion and reduce emissions, preparing an environmentally sound strategy to dispose of more than 1 million Styrofoam lunch boxes per day.
	Yangtze Basin Water Resources	Improves environmental monitoring in the water sector and introduces comprehensive river basin management and nonwater subprojects on forestry, grassland development, and soil improvement.
India	Second Madras Water Supply	Supports improvements of environmental monitoring in the water sector and introduces comprehensive river basin management and nonwater subprojects in forestry, grassland development, and soil improvement.
	Tamil Nadu Water Resources Consolidation	Includes capacity building in water planning, environmental management, and research to introduce multisectoral water planning, to incorporate environmental management in all aspects of water planning, investment, and management, and to enhance research in the water sector.

Country	Project	Environmental component
Indonesia	Kalimantan Urban Development	Provides for investment in urban infrastructure in five cities (Banjarmasin, Balikpapan, Palangkaraya, Pontianak, and Samarinda), including drainage, human waste management, and solid waste management infrastructure. Also provides for assistance in program management and monitoring, municipal management, improved environmental and resettlement practices, institutional capacity-building for relevant agencies.
Korea, Rep. of	Pusan Urban Transport Management	Provides for transport system management actions for a bus priority corridor, as well as a congestion management component.
Pakistan	Second Private Sector Energy Development	Provides consulting services to develop environmental and resettlement assessment guidelines, as well as strengthen capabilities for monitoring compliance with these guidelines.
Thailand	Lam Takhong Pump Storage	Provides funding for computer hardware, software, and training for strengthening the environmental capabilities of the Electricity Generating Authority of Thailand.
Eastern Europe and Central Asia		
Albania	Irrigation Rehabilitation	Provides technical assistance to update the Waste Master Plan and ensure against water loss.
Armenia	Irrigation Rehabilitation	Contributes to improvements in water management by establishing pilot projects with water users' associations and assistance to update the Water Master Plan.

(Table continues on the following page.)

Table D.1 *(continued)*

Country	Project	Environmental component
Azerbaijan	Greater Baku Water Supply Rehabilitation	Assists with a water demand management plan to help conserve water at the household level through a program of consumer awareness initiatives, pipe maintenance, and rationalizing of water use through meter installations and implementation of a progressive water tariff.
Estonia	Financial Institutions Development	Provides technical assistance to train financial advisers of participating commercial banks in environmental screening and assessments.
Georgia	Municipal Infrastructure Rehabilitation	Provides for infrastructure rehabilitation investment for wastewater and solid waste collection and disposal; institutional development aimed at initiating a process to develop local capabilities in environmental assessment and management; and development of strategies and action programs to control or alleviate pollution problems along the Black Sea coast.
Hungary	Budapest Urban Transport	Provides for the replacement of fifty worn-out buses with low-polluting and energy-efficient substitutes and the support of an automatic vehicle monitoring system.
Latvia	Jelgava District Heating Rehabilitation	Aims to improve environmental conditions by improving the efficiency of fuel use, facilitating the elimination of low-stack coal-fired boilers in residential areas, and reducing water wastage.
Russian Federation	Gas Distribution Rehabilitation and Energy Efficiency	Increases the efficiency of gas use by upgrading and increasing the use of customer metering and by supporting investments in more efficient equipment; provides assistance and disseminates information to industrial enterprises to evaluate and access commercial funding for energy efficiency measures.

Country	Project	Environmental component
Turkey	Antalya Water Supply and Sanitation	Finances a new sewerage network and preliminary wastewater treatment plant.
Uzbekistan	Cotton Sub-Sector Improvement	Supports integrated pest management through equipment and technical assistance. Also supports the development of improved pesticide spraying equipment to allow the integration of biological and chemical control of pests with proper cropping practices. Provides for equipment and training to demonstrate effective ways to reduce water use in cotton production while improving land productivity and avoiding water-based damage to the environment.

Latin America and the Caribbean

Belize	Second Power Development	Carries out environmental audits and offers cleanup loans designed for seven thermal power plants.
Bolivia	National Land Administration	Includes components that clarify and systemize the land tenure situation in Colombia by identifying overlapping land titles, alleviate land conflicts, continuing the land-titling process for small-holders, organize land tenure information, and carry out territorial planning. These activities would consistently improve the management of land resources in Bolivia.
Brazil	Recife Metropolitan Transport Decentralization	Supports the development of an integrated urban transport system as well as the design of an inspection and maintenance program for vehicle emissions; the preparation of an integrated transport policy, land use, and air quality management strategy to meet both transport and air quality targets; and the strengthening of air quality planning and monitoring of vehicle-based emissions.

(Table continues on the following page.)

Table D.1 *(continued)*

Country	Project	Environmental component
Brazil *(continued)*	Ceara Urban Development and Water Resource Management	Endorses a state water resources plan, the approval of a state water law, and the creation of an integrated water resource management system.
	Belo Horizonte Metropolitan Transport Decentralization	Supports the development of an integrated urban transport system as well as the design of an inspection and maintenance program for vehicle emissions; the preparation of an integrated transport policy, land use, and air quality management strategy to meet both transport and air quality targets; and the strengthening of air quality planning and monitoring of vehicle-based emissions.
Chile	Third Road Sector	Strengthens the capacity of the Ministerio de Obras Públicas (Ministry of Public Works) for environmental impact assessment and monitoring in the road sector.
Colombia	Energy Sector Technical Assistance	Provides assistance in executing sectoral environmental assessments, formulating energy sector environmental regulations and guidelines, and promoting user awareness and participation in the definition of energy sector projects. Also provides for the development of a demand-side management strategy for efficient energy use.
Mexico	Rainfed Areas Development	Provides for rural investment in soil conservation works, the transfer of agricultural technology for soil and water conservation practices and equipment, and institutional development and training to strengthen the expertise in areas of soil conservation and the monitoring and evaluation of environmental impacts.

Country	Project	Environmental component
Paraguay	Asunción Sewerage	Provides for the design of a control and monitoring program for sewage disposal into the Paraguay River as well as the design of a monitoring system to control hazardous and toxic chemicals from future industrial wastes.
Peru	Lima Water Rehabilitation and Management	Aims to improve the efficiency of water and sanitation delivery in the Lima-Callao metropolitan area. Initiates conjunctive use of surface and groundwater in three districts where groundwater is depleted and the risk of saline contamination is serious. Rehabilitates damaged water supply and sewerage systems and supports reforms in the legal and institutional framework of the water and sanitation sector.
Trinidad and Tobago	Water Sector Institutional Strengthening	Strengthens existing and new institutions, develops an integrated approach to water resources management, and strengthens and complements environmental planning and management. Provides funding for hydrological and hydrometeorological telemetering equipment and geographic information systems needed to improve data collection and analysis for improved water resource management.
Venezuela	Agricultural Extension	Provides for training in environmental impact of traditional and emerging agricultural production techniques and integrated pest management and other practices designed to permit more effective incorporation of ecological factors into overall farm management. Also provides for the inclusion of a specialist in environmental issues in agriculture among staff of the Foundation for Training and Applied Research for Agrarian Reform.

(Table continues on the following page.)

Table D.1 *(continued)*

Country	Project	Environmental component
Middle East and North Africa		
Jordan	Agriculture Sector Adjustment	Supports efficient natural resource use by supporting reforms to restructure water sector institutions to maximize efficiency and unify planning and management, promote efficient use of existing water resources through demand management, establish control over overexploited groundwater resources, and prioritize public investments in water.
	Agriculture Sector Technical Support	Supports initiatives for measuring and managing water in the Jordan Valley, monitoring and controlling groundwater in the basin; and strengthening research and monitoring and evaluating the impacts of the country's agricultural policy adjustments.
Tunisia	Water Supply and Sewerage	Includes the construction of sewage treatment facilities in three towns and supports institutional development with a view to enhancing water resources management.

Annex E. Active Environmental Projects under Implementation

This annex lists projects with primarily environmental objectives that were approved by the Bank's Board of Executive Directors prior to July 1, 1995. Those approved prior to July 1, 1994, were under implementation throughout fiscal 1995. The annex identifies active projects for urban environmental management and pollution control (table E.1), natural resource management (table E.2), and environmental institution building (table E.3), as well as all committed projects categorized according to year in which they were approved (table E.4) and those closed or canceled (table E.5). Each table specifies whether the project is being financed through an IBRD loan, an IDA credit, or both; the fiscal year in which the project was approved; the Bank's financial contribution; and total estimated project cost.

Table E.1. Active Projects for Urban Environmental Management and Pollution Control, Fiscal 1986–95 (55 Projects)
(millions of dollars)

Country	Project	Fiscal year approved	Loan or credit	World Bank Group contribution	Total project cost
Algeria	Water Supply and Sewerage Rehabilitation	1994	L	110	170
Angola	Lobito-Benguela Urban Environment Rehabilitation	1992	C	46	59
Brazil	Espirito Santo Water Supply and Coastal Pollution Management	1994	L	154	308
	Water Quality and Pollution Control—São Paulo/Paraná	1993	L	245	494
	National Industrial Pollution Control	1992	L	50	100
	Minas Gerais Water Quality and Pollution Control	1993	L	145	308
	Second Industrial Pollution Control	1988	L	50	100
Burkina Faso	Urban Environment	1995	C	37	50
Burundi	Energy Sector Rehabilitation	1991	C	23	23
Chile	Second Valparaiso Water Supply and Sewerage	1991	L	50	142
China	Liaoning Environment	1995	L	110	351
	Shanghai Environment	1994	L	160	457
	Ship Waste Disposal	1992	C	15	64
	Beijing Environment	1992	L + C	125	299
	Tianjin Urban Development and Environment	1992	C	100	195
	South Jiangsu Environment Protection	1993	L	250	584
Côte d'Ivoire	Abidjan Environmental Protection	1990	L	22	50
Cyprus	Limassol Amathus Sewerage and Drainage	1990	L	25	69
	Southeast Coast Sewerage and Drainage	1992	L	32	103

Czech Republic	Power and Environmental Improvement	1992	L	246	246
Ecuador	Mining Development and Environmental Control—Technical Assistance	1994	L	14	24
Egypt	Private Sector Tourism	1993	L	130	784
Estonia	Haapsalu and Matsalu Bays Environment	1995	L	2	8
	District Heating Rehabilitation	1994	L	38	65
India	Industrial Pollution Prevention	1995	C + L	168	330
	Industrial Pollution Control	1991	L + C	156	236
	Renewable Resources Development	1993	L + C	190	440
Indonesia	Surabaya Urban Development	1994	L	175	618
Korea, Rep. of	Ports Development and Environmental Improvement	1995	L	100	1,107
	Waste Disposal	1995	L	75	305
	Pusan and Taejon Sewerage	1992	L	40	130
	Kuangju and Seoul Sewerage	1993	L	110	530
Latvia	Liepaja Environment	1995	L	4	21
Lebanon	Solid Waste/Environmental Management	1995	L	55	135
Lithuania	Klaipeda Environment	1995	L	7	23
Mauritania	Water Supply	1992	C	11	15
Mexico	Northern Border Environment	1994	L	368	762
	Second Solid Waste Management	1994	L	200	416
	Water and Sanitation II	1994	L	350	770
	Transport Air Quality Management	1993	L	220	1,087
	Solid Waste Management	1986	L	25	50
Niger	Energy	1988	C	32	79

(Table continues on the following page.)

239

Table E.1 *(continued)*

Country	Project	Fiscal year approved	Loan or credit	World Bank Group contribution	Total project cost
OECS countries	Solid Waste Management	1995	L + C	12	51
Poland	Katowice Heat Supply and Conservation	1995	L	45	93
	Heat Supply Restructuring and Conservation	1991	L	340	739
	Energy Resource Development	1990	L	250	590
Russian Federation	Emergency Oil Spill Recovery	1995	L	99	140
Sri Lanka	Colombo Environmental Improvement	1995	C	39	49
Thailand	Clean Fuels and Environmental Improvement	1995	L	90	370
Togo	Lomé Urban Development	1994	L	26	29
Tunisia	Energy Conservation Demonstration	1987	L	4	4
Turkey	Bursa Water Supply and Sanitation	1993	L	130	258
	Izmir Water Supply and Sewerage	1987	L	184	522
	Istanbul Water Supply and Sewerage	1988	L	218	570
	Ankara Sewerage	1990	L	173	557
Portfolio total				6,075	16,079

Table E.2. Active Projects for Natural Resource Management, Fiscal 1986–95 (62 Projects)
(millions of dollars)

Country	Project	Fiscal year approved	Loan or credit	World Bank Group contribution	Total project cost
Algeria	Pilot Forestry and Watershed Management	1992	L	25	37
Bangladesh	Forest Resources Management	1992	C	50	59
Benin	Natural Resources Management	1992	C	14	24
Bhutan	Third Forest Development	1994	C	5	9
Bolivia	Eastern Lowlands	1990	C	35	55
Brazil	Rondônia Natural Resource Management	1992	L	167	228
	Mato Grosso Natural Resource Management	1992	L	205	286
	Minas Gerais Forestry Development	1988	L	49	100
	Land Management I—Paraná	1989	L	63	138
	Land Management II	1990	L	33	72
Burkina Faso	Environmental Management	1991	C	17	25
Central African Republic	Natural Resource Management	1990	C	19	34
China	Forest Resource Development and Protection	1994	C	200	356
	Loess Plateau Watershed Rehabilitation	1994	C	150	259
Colombia	Natural Resource Management Program	1994	L	39	65
Côte d'Ivoire	Forestry Sector	1990	L	80	147
Ecuador	Lower Guayas Flood Control	1991	L	59	98

(Table continues on the following page.)

Table E.2 (*continued*)

Country	Project	Fiscal year approved	Loan or credit	World Bank Group contribution	Total project cost
Egypt	Matruh Resource Management	1993	C	22	31
Gabon	Forestry and Environment	1993	L	23	38
Ghana	Forest Resource Management	1989	C	39	65
Guinea	Forestry and Fisheries Management	1990	C	8	23
India	Andhra Pradesh Forestry	1994	C	77	89
	Forestry Research Education and Extension	1994	C	47	56
	Uttar Pradesh Sodic Lands Reclamation	1993	C	55	80
	Madhya Pradesh Forestry	1995	C	58	67
	Maharashtra Forestry	1992	C	124	142
	Integrated Watershed Development—Hills	1990	C	75	75
	Integrated Watershed Development—Plains	1990	C	55	55
Indonesia	National Watershed Management and Conservation	1994	L	57	488
	Second Forestry Institutions and Conservation	1990	L	20	33
	Integrated Pest Management	1993	L	32	53
	Yogyakarta Upland Area Development	1991	L	16	25
	Forestry Institutions and Conservation	1988	L	30	63
Kenya	Forestry Development	1991	C	20	65
	Protected Areas and Wildlife Services	1992	C	61	143
Lao PDR	Forest Management and Conservation	1994	C	9	20
Madagascar	Antananarivo Plain Development	1990	C	31	69
	Forests Management and Protection	1988	C	7	23

Malawi	Fisheries Development	1991	C	9	16
Malaysia	Sabah Land Settlement and Environmental Management	1989	L	72	203
Mali	Natural Resource Management	1992	C	20	32
Morocco	Second Forestry Development	1990	L	49	100
Nepal	Hill Community Forestry	1989	C	9.2	45
Pakistan	Balochistan Natural Resource Management	1994	C	15	18
	Northern Resource Management	1993	C	29	40
	Fordwah E. Sadiquia Irrigation and Drainage	1993	C	54	71
	Second Scarp Transition	1991	C	20	49
	Punjab Forest Sector Development	1995	C	25	34
Paraguay	Natural Resources Management	1994	L	50	79
	Land Use Rationalization	1992	L	29	41
Philippines	Environment and Natural Resource Management	1991	L + C	224	369
Poland	Forest Development Support	1994	L	146	335
Seychelles	Environment and Transport	1993	L	5	7
Sri Lanka	Forest Sector Development	1989	C	20	31
Sudan	Southern Kassala Agriculture	1989	C	20	35
Tanzania	Forest Resources Management	1992	C	18	26
Tunisia	Northwest Mountainous Areas Development	1994	L	28	50
	Second Forestry Development	1993	L	69	148
Turkey	Eastern Anatolia Watershed Rehabilitation	1993	L	77	121
Uruguay	Natural Resources Management and Irrigation Development	1994	L	41	74

(Table continues on the following page.)

Table E.2 *(continued)*

Country	Project	Fiscal year approved	Loan or credit	World Bank Group contribution	Total project cost
Venezuela	INPARQUES	1995	L	55	96
Yemen	Land and Water Conservation	1992	C	33	48
Portfolio total				3,193	5,763

Table E.3. Active Projects for Environmental Institution Building, Fiscal 1986–95 (20 Projects)
(millions of dollars)

Country	Project	Fiscal year approved	Loan or credit	World Bank Group contribution	Total project cost
Benin	Environmental Management	1995	C	8	9
Bolivia	Environmental Technical Assistance	1993	C	5	5
Brazil	National Environment	1990	L	117	166
Chile	Environment Institutions Development	1993	L	12	33
China	Environment Technical Assistance	1993	C	50	70
Gambia, The	Capacity Building for Environmental Management—Technical Assistance	1994	C	3	5
Ghana	Environment Resource Management	1993	C	18	36
Honduras	Environmental Development	1995	C	11	13
Indonesia	BAPEDAL Development Technical Assistance	1992	L	12	15
Korea, Rep. of	Environmental Technology Development	1994	L	90	156
	Environmental Research and Education	1993	L	60	97
Madagascar	Environment Program	1990	C	26	86
Mauritius	Environmental Monitoring and Development	1991	L	12	21
Mexico	Environment/Natural Resources	1992	L	50	127
Morocco	Environmental Management	1994	L	6	11
Nigeria	Environmental Management	1992	C	25	38

(Table continues on the following page.)

Table E.3 (*continued*)

Country	Project	Fiscal year approved	Loan or credit	World Bank Group contribution	Total project cost
Pakistan	Environmental Protection and Resource Conservation	1992	C	29	57
Poland	Environment Management	1990	L	18	27
Russian Federation	Environmental Management	1995	L	110	195
Trinidad and Tobago	Environmental Management	1995	L	6	11
Portfolio total				668	1,178

Table E.4. Environmental Projects Approved, by Year, Fiscal 1986–95 (140 Projects)
(millions of dollars)

Fiscal year approved and country	Project approved	Loan or credit	IBRD/IDA (rounded)	Total project cost
1986				
Mexico	Solid Waste Management	L	25	50
Total			25	50
1987				
Rwanda	Second Integrated Forestry	C	14	20
Tunisia	Energy Conservation Demonstration	L	4	4
Turkey	Izmir Water Supply and Sewerage	L	184	522
Total			202	546
1988				
Brazil	Minas Gerais Forestry Development	L	49	100
Brazil	Second Industrial Pollution Control	L	50	100
Indonesia	Forestry Institutions and Conservation	L	30	63
Madagascar	Forests Management and Protection	C	7	23
Niger	Energy	C	32	79
Turkey	Istanbul Water Supply and Sewerage	L	218	570
Total			386	935
1989				
Brazil	Land Management I Paraná	L	63	138
Ghana	Forest Resource Management	C	39	65
Malaysia	Sabah Land Settlement and Environmental Management	L	72	203

(Table continues on the following page.)

Table E.4 (*continued*)

Fiscal year approved and country	Project approved	Loan or credit	IBRD/IDA (rounded)	Total project cost
Nepal	Hill Community Forestry	C	31	45
Sri Lanka	Forest Sector Development	C	20	31
Sudan	Southern Kassala Agriculture	C	20	35
Total			245	517
1990				
Bolivia	Eastern Lowlands	C	35	55
Brazil	National Environment	L	117	166
	Land Management II	L	33	72
Central African Republic	Natural Resource Management	C	19	34
Côte d'Ivoire	Forestry Sector	L	80	147
	Abidjan Environmental Protection	L	22	50
Cyprus	Limassol Amathus Sewerage and Drainage	L	25	69
Guinea	Forestry and Fisheries Management	C	8	23
India	Integrated Watershed Development—Hills	C	75	75
	Integrated Watershed Development—Plains	C	55	55
Indonesia	Second Forestry Institutions and Conservation	L	20	33
Madagascar	Environment Program	C	26	86
	Antananarivo Plain Development	C	31	69
Morocco	Second Forestry Development	L	49	100
Poland	Environment Management	L	18	27
	Energy Resource Development	L	250	590
Turkey	Ankara Sewerage	L	173	557
Total			1,036	2,208

1991

Burkina Faso	Environmental Management	C	17	25
Burundi	Energy Sector Rehabilitation	C	23	23
Chile	Second Valparaiso Water Supply and Sewerage	L	50	142
Ecuador	Lower Guayas Flood Control	L	59	98
India	Industrial Pollution Control	L + C	156	236
Indonesia	Yogyakarta Upland Area Development	L	16	25
Kenya	Forestry Development	C	20	65
Malawi	Fisheries Development	C	9	16
Mauritius	Environmental Monitoring and Development	L	12	21
Pakistan	Second Scarp Transition	C	20	49
Philippines	Environment and Natural Resource Management	L + C	224	369
Poland	Heat Supply Restructuring and Conservation	L	340	739
Total			946	1,808

1992

Algeria	Pilot Forestry and Watershed Management	L	25	37
Angola	Lobito-Benguela Urban Environment Rehabilitation	C	46	59
Bangladesh	Forest Resources Management	C	50	59
Benin	Natural Resources Management	C	14	24
Brazil	Rondônia Natural Resource Management	L	167	228
	Mato Grosso Natural Resource Management	L	205	286
	National Industrial Pollution Control	L	50	100
China	Ship Waste Disposal	C	15	64
	Beijing Environment	L + C	125	299
	Tianjin Urban Development and Environment	C	100	195
Cyprus	Southeast Coast Sewerage and Drainage	L	32	103
Czech Republic	Power and Environmental Improvement	L	246	246

(Table continues on the following page.)

Table E.4 *(continued)*

Fiscal year approved and country	*Project approved*	*Loan or credit*	*IBRD/IDA (rounded)*	*Total project cost*
Haiti	Forestry and Environmental Protection	C	26	29
India	Maharashtra Forestry	C	124	142
Indonesia	BAPEDAL Development Technical Assistance	L	12	15
Kenya	Protected Areas and Wildlife Services	C	61	143
Korea, Rep. of	Pusan and Taejon Sewerage	L	40	130
Mali	Natural Resource Management	C	20	32
Mauritania	Water Supply	C	11	15
Mexico	Environment/Natural Resources	L	50	127
Nigeria	Environmental Management	C	25	38
Pakistan	Environmental Protection and Resource Conservation	C	29	57
Paraguay	Land Use Rationalization	L	29	41
Tanzania	Forest Resources Management	C	18	26
Yemen	Land and Water Conservation	C	33	48
Total			1,553	2,543
1993			
Bolivia	Environmental Technical Assistance	C	5	5
Brazil	Water Quality and Pollution Control—São Paulo/Paraná	L	245	494
	Minas Gerais Water Quality and Pollution Control	L	145	308
Chile	Environment Institutions Development	L	12	33
	Environment Technical Assistance	C	50	70
	South Jiangsu Environment Protection	L	250	584
Egypt	Matruh Resource Management	C	22	31
	Private Sector Tourism	L	130	784
Gabon	Forestry and Environment	L	23	38
Ghana	Environment Resource Management	C	18	36

India	Uttar Pradesh Sodic Lands Reclamation	C	55	80
	Renewable Resources Development	L + C	190	440
Indonesia	Integrated Pest Management	L	32	53
Korea, Rep. of	Environmental Research and Education	L	60	97
	Kuangju and Seoul Sewerage	L	110	530
Mexico	Transport Air Quality Management	L	220	1087
Pakistan	Northern Resource Management	C	29	40
	Fordwah E. Sadiquia Irrigation and Drainage	C	54	71
Seychelles	Environment and Transport	L	5	7
Tunisia	Second Forestry Development	L	69	148
Turkey	Eastern Anatolia Watershed Rehabilitation	L	77	121
	Bursa Water Supply and Sanitation	L	130	258
Venezuela	National Parks Management	L	55	96
Total			1,986	5,411
1994				
Algeria	Water Supply and Sewerage Rehabilitation	L	110	170
Bhutan	Third Forest Development	C	5	9
Brazil	Espirito Santo Water Supply and Coastal Pollution	L	154	308
China	Forest Resource Development and Protection	C	200	356
	Loess Plateau Watershed Rehabilitation	C	150	259
	Shanghai Environment	L	160	457
Colombia	Natural Resource Management Program	L	39	65
Ecuador	Mining Development and Environmental Control—			
	Technical Assistance	L	14	24
Estonia	District Heating Rehabilitation	L	38	65
Gambia, The	Capacity Building for Environmental Management—			
	Technical Assistance	C	3	5
India	Andhra Pradesh Forestry	C	77	89
	Forestry Research Education and Extension Project	C	47	56

(Table continues on the following page.)

Table E.4 (continued)

Fiscal year approved and country	Project approved	Loan or credit	IBRD/IDA (rounded)	Total project cost
Indonesia	National Watershed Management and Conservation	L	57	488
	Surabaya Urban Development	L	175	618
Korea, Rep. of	Environmental Technology Development	L	90	156
Lao PDR	Forest Management and Conservation	C	9	20
Mexico	Northern Border Environment	L	368	762
	Second Solid Waste Management	L	200	416
	Water and Sanitation II	L	350	770
Morocco	Environmental Management	L	6	11
Pakistan	Balochistan Natural Resource Management	C	15	18
Paraguay	Natural Resources Management	L	50	79
Poland	Forest Development Support	L	146	335
Togo	Lomé Urban Development	L	26	29
Tunisia	Northwest Mountainous Areas Development	L	28	50
Uruguay	Natural Resources Management and Irrigation Development	L	41	74
Total			2,558	5,689
1995				
Benin	Environmental Management	C	8	9
Burkina Faso	Urban Environment	C	37	50
China	Liaoning Environment	L	110	351
Estonia	Haapsalu and Matsalu Bays Environment	L	2	8
Honduras	Environmental Development	C	11	13

India	Industrial Pollution Prevention	L + C	168	330
	Madhya Pradesh Forestry	C	58	67
Korea, Rep. of	Ports Development and Environmental Improvement	L	100	1,107
	Waste Disposal	L	75	305
Latvia	Liepaja Environment	L	4	21
Lebanon	Solid Waste/Environmental Management	L	55	135
Lithuania	Klaipeda Environment	L	7	23
OECS countries	Solid Waste Management	L + C	12	51
Pakistan	Punjab Forest Sector Development	C	25	34
Poland	Katowice Heat Supply and Conservation	L	45	93
Russian Federation	Emergency Oil Spill Recovery	L	99	140
	Environmental Management	L	110	195
Sri Lanka	Colombo Environmental Improvement	C	39	49
Thailand	Clean Fuels and Environmental Improvement	L	90	370
Trinidad and Tobago	Environmental Management	L	6	11
Venezuela	INPARQUES	L	55	96
Total			1,116	3,458
Total, 1986–95			10,053	23,165
Total number of projects approved, 140				

253

Table E.5. Closed or Canceled Environment Projects, Fiscal 1986–95
(millions of dollars)

Fiscal year approved and country	Project	Fiscal year closed or canceled	Loan or credit	IBRD/IDA (rounded)	Total project cost
1987 Rwanda	Second Integrated Forestry	Closed 1994	C	14	20
1992 Haiti	Forestry and Environmental Protection	Canceled 1994	C	26	29
1993 Venezuela	National Parks Management	Canceled 1995	L	55	96

Annex F. Projects with Full Environmental Assessment Approved in Fiscal 1995, Category A Projects

Since October 1989, Bank staff have been required to screen all proposed new investment projects with respect to their potential environmental impacts and to classify them accordingly. Category A projects are those considered likely to have significant environmental impacts that may be sensitive, irreversible, and diverse. Such projects require a full environmental assessment (EA). This annex lists all category A projects for both IBRD (table F.1) and IFC (table F.2) that were approved in fiscal 1995. For each, the annex indicates the estimated total cost and the amount of IBRD financing or IDA investment and provides a brief description of the project and the contribution of the environmental assessment.

Table F.1. IBRD and IDA Projects with Full Environmental Assessment, Fiscal 1995

Country	Project and cost	EA description
Africa		
Central African Republic	Livestock Development and Rangeland Management ($17 million, IDA; $32 million, total project cost)	Aims to raise livestock productivity, to alleviate poverty among herders, and to ensure sustainable management of their natural resources. The EA addresses the negative environmental risks through measures designed to provide special assistance to the poorest herders so as to avoid overgrazing and to train them in environmentally suitable techniques in alternative farming activities, provide training for the staff of the livestock sectors in environmental management techniques, to ensure that alignments adopted for the ZAGROP (agropastoral action area) do not promote a rush to occupy zones that have been isolated, and to ensure appropriate management of the brushfire timetable, accompanied by deferment measures to reduce possible adverse consequences of uncontrolled fires.

(Table continues on the following page.)

Table F.1 *(continued)*

Country	Project and cost	EA description
Côte d'Ivoire	Private Sector Energy ($70.7 million, IDA; $76.7 million, total project cost)	Aims to improve the efficiency and reliability of the power supply and to reduce the environmental impacts through the transition from the use of liquid fuels and biomass to natural gas. Positive global environmental impacts are expected from the project as a result of the decrease in air pollution (reduction of NO_x, SO_x, and CO_2) from the use of gas and the decrease in deforestation through the use of butane in place of fuelwood and charcoal. A full EA, acceptable to IDA, was carried out. The main environmental risks are noise level, oil spills, waste disposal, fire and explosions, and possible pollution during drilling of the production wells, for which an appropriate mitigation plan has been adopted. Skills development training for the staff in the areas of environmental safety and monitoring will be also be conducted. |//
Asia		
Bangladesh	Gas Infrastructure Development ($141.7 million, IDA; $194.8 million, total project cost)	Aims to alleviate the worsening gas supply shortages through partially financing the sector's priority investments. The project is expected to have significant environmental benefits as increased gas supply and use reduces the consumption of liquid petroleum products and fuelwood, which in turn reduces sulfur dioxide and carbon dioxide emissions and deforestation. The gas produced from known fields produces no sulfur and emits only half as much carbon dioxide as an oil-fired power plant. The potential significant negative effects are (a) surface and groundwater contamination that may be caused by improper handling of wastes from well drilling sites, processing facilities, and pipeline construction and operation and (b) soil erosion that may arise during construction. The environmental and safety aspects fully address these potential impacts and recommend appropriate mitigation measures. The pipeline route has been selected based on the criterion of minimizing involuntary resettlement. Directional drilling underneath the riverbeds will be used for river crossing in order to eliminate the impact on river flow regimes

Country	Project and cost	EA description
Bangladesh *(continued)*		and fish habitat. Drilling well sites and surface facilities will be located to minimize land requirement and degradation. The entire project design and construction will conform with international engineering and safety standards as well as environmental management practices.
China	Liaoning Environment ($110 million, IDA; $338.1 million, total project cost)	Provides physical works and technical assistance for institutional development in water supply, wastewater treatment, air pollution control, waste management, industrial water conservation, and process improvements, as well as rehabilitation and reconstruction of the Liaoning Provincial Museum, the Great Wall, and Jieshi Gong. The environmental assessment identified the following potential negative impacts of the project: loss of land for construction of four wastewater treatment facilities, loss of significant water from the Yunliang and Taizi, resettlement of people in the area of the Benzi treatment plant, and spoil and sludge generated by the construction of facilities and from the flow of wastewater. The principal adverse impact of construction activities will be on the urban air quality and noise levels. Appropriate mitigating and monitoring measures were identified by the EA.
	Inland Waterways ($210 million, IBRD; $508.5 million, total project cost)	Seeks to (a) improve and expand the inland waterways by widening and deepening channels to improve navigation, which requires constructing dams to increase the water level and (b) generate hydroelectric power by using the differential heads at the dams. EAs for the four channels and three ports under the Zhejiang project component have been completed. On the basis of their findings, environmental action plans and environmental monitoring plans were prepared. The potential impacts that were identified are land acquisition, dredging, water pollution, ship wastes, and noise. In addition, wastewater and solid wastes from ships and port activities, drinking water in-take, wastewater, dust from coal yards, and noise and air pollution could be problematic. With regard to dam construction in Hunan and

(Table continues on the following page.)

Table F.1 *(continued)*

Country	Project and cost	EA description
China *(continued)*		Guangxi, impacts on the ecology and cultural relics, water quality in reservoir areas, danger to fish migration, and changes in the hydrological regimes are potential problems. Appropriate mitigation and monitoring measures for treatment, protection, design, construction, and operational phases have been prepared for all components of the projects. Administrative arrangements will also be established to ensure that measures are enforced. This project requires some relocation and resettlement of 12,101 people, including about 700 households to be physically relocated. Resettlement action plans have been prepared and found satisfactory by the Bank. The affected groups and people subject to resettlement, in particular, have been consulted. The process of environmental review involved inputs from provincial and local environmental protection bureaus, research institutions, and universities.
	Yangtze Basin Water Resources ($100 million, IBRD; $110 million, IDA; $551 million, total project cost)	Aims to raise agricultural production and incomes, reduce the risk and impact of floods, and introduce a more sustainable and cost-effective system for irrigation and drainage systems. The project has been classified as a category A project as a result of the Jiangya Dam and reservoir component. The potential problems of the project are (a) the loss of endangered flora species (which are well represented outside this area), (b) impacts on irrigation subprojects, (c) increased risks of malaria and schistosomiasis, and (d) threat to the local water quality. A comprehensive mitigation and monitoring plan has been developed to reduce the environmental risks of the project. The Jiangya Dam will require resettlement of 12,587 people, and an additional 3,196 people will lose their land but not their houses. Resettlement will be conducted in five stages. Economic compensation will be received by all the resettled people. A resettlement action plan has been prepared.

Country	Project and cost	EA description
China *(continued)*	Zhejiang Power Development ($400 million, IBRD; $150 million, cofinancing under IBRD guarantee; $1,789.3 million, total project cost)	Aims to help meet the rapidly expanding electricity demand in the Zhejiang Province in a least-cost manner and to reduce the environmental impacts of new generation of electricity. EAs were conducted for all the construction components. The main environmental impacts are due to atmospheric emissions, thermal discharges, ash disposal, and noise emission. The main impact on the aquatic environment will result from warm cooling-water discharge. The EAs underwent considerable refinement in response to the Bank's comments and are now of a high standard. Environmental mitigation plans are included within the EAs. This project will involve resettlement of 4,675 persons. A resettlement action plan has been prepared that is satisfactory to the Bank.
	Xinjian Provincial Highway ($150 million, IBRD; $317.5 million, total project cost)	Aims to support continued development of the road infrastructure, support the regions highway agencies for transport planning and investment prioritization, and improve highway maintenance operations. The EA identified noise and air and water pollution, along with impacts on cultural relics, as the major potential impacts. Supplementary studies were conducted on migration patterns of Kazakh herders and other livestock migration routes, detailed cultural relics survey, impact of construction traffic, and social survey of people affected by resettlement or compensation for land allocation as an input into the environmental assessment of the project. The EA specified organization measures and monitoring arrangements required to mitigate potential adverse impacts on the environment during the construction and operation of the highway. The engineering design and technical specifications for the highway incorporated the appropriate measures required for environmental protection. Equipment for environmental monitoring will be provided by the project.

(Table continues on the following page.)

Table F.1 *(continued)*

Country	Project and cost	EA description
India	Second Madras Water Supply ($257.8 million, IBRD; $421 million, total project cost)	Aims to provide water to Madras on an urgent basis in order to provide health, economic efficiency, and environmental benefits; to improve the distribution of water within Madras; and to strengthen conservation of water through the introduction of revised water tariffs and other measures. The EA led to environmental mitigation and monitoring plans to address the potential adverse impacts. The positive aspects of the program are the improvement in public health through the increased quantity, quality, and reliability of the water supply. The potential negative impacts are soil erosion due to the excavation of trenches for transmission pipelines and dust and noise pollution during the construction activities. Appropriate mitigation measures to minimize the impacts will be carried out. Construction of bunds at the Veeranam tank, transmission mains, and related infrastructure will result in the loss of agricultural land, for which there will be appropriate compensation and rehabilitation and resettlement of project-affected persons. Three public meetings were organized along with continued public consultation on the project.
	Tamil Nadu Water Resources Consolidation ($282.9 million, IDA; $315.6 million, total project cost)	Seeks to (a) improve agricultural productivity through improved water management and modernization of existing irrigation systems, including scheme completion works as needed, (b) assure sustainability of infrastructure and the environment, (c) improve institutional and technical capability for irrigation, and (d) introduce water resources planning across all uses of water. A sectoral EA has been carried out for the project. The EA provided a detailed review of water-related environmental issues in the state, assessed the investment components of the project, and reviewed state capacity to handle environmental issues. The improved water management was expected to mitigate against the potential problems of waterlogging, salinization, depletion of groundwater

Country	Project and cost	EA description
India (continued)		levels, and disease risks caused by stagnant water. The EA did, however, recommend a comprehensive set of actions to improve the Water Resources Organization's environmental capability to monitor, plan, develop, and manage the state's water resources. An environmental action plan has also been incorporated in the project to enhance the environmental management capabilities. These measures, which incorporate institutional and procedural improvements, major strengthening of technical capabilities, and field action and studies, have been incorporated in an environmental action plan to be funded under the project. A baseline survey has found that acquisition of some 570 hectares of farmed land involving about 1,460 people in 710 households would be affected. The needs of all affected persons would be catered to on the basis of detailed socioeconomic surveys, action plans, and consultations.
Korea, Rep. of	Ports Development and Environmental Improvement ($100 million, IBRD; $1,107 million, total project cost)	Involves the construction of two new port facilities and an industrial complex, all of which require dredging and reclamation. The industrial facility at Dadaepo will generate some noise, air pollution, and wastewater. An environmental impact statement was prepared for the new Port of Dadaepo after an analysis of alternative sites. This report includes an environmental analysis for the industrial facility. An environmental impact statement was also prepared for the construction of a new container terminal in Pusan. A management and monitoring plan will be developed to control the above environmental issues. As part of the review of the EAs, the local population and nongovernmental organizations had access to the reports and provided comments to the Ministry of Environment.

(Table continues on the following page.)

Table F.1 *(continued)*

Country	Project and cost	EA description
Korea, Rep. of *(continued)*	Waste Disposal ($75 million, IBRD; $237 million, total project cost)	Aims to address, in Pusan City and Chunbuk Province, environmental, institutional, and technological concerns regarding wastewater and specified waste disposal; reduce the health hazards of surface and groundwater contamination; and promote the reuse of treated effluents on a major scale. The Pusan and Kunsan component will treat and dispose of municipal and industrial waste and thus have a positive impact on the environment and public health. This project aims to mitigate the negative impacts during construction with provision of adequate drainage with retention ponds and protection against dust, noise, vibration, and odor. Adequate supervision and monitoring measures have been incorporated in the project. Plant performance and environmental impact will be monitored and corrective measures applied if the performance is found to be unsatisfactory.
Sri Lanka	Colombo Environmental Improvement ($39 million, IDA; $49 million, total project cost)	Aims to support the achievement of a sustainable environment for the long-term economic and social development of Colombo. The specific objectives of the project are to improve municipal and solid waste management and services in the participating municipal authorities, reduce wastewater pollution in the Beira Lake catchment area and selected industrialized zones, develop local institutional capabilities to plan and manage municipal services, and assist in mobilizing private participation in the development and operation of urban infrastructure services. A full EA of the proposed sanitary landfill of the project was prepared. This landfill site was chosen after detailed evaluation. The potential significant negative environmental impacts pertain to surface and groundwater contamination, which may be caused by improper handling of waste, construction materials during construction of the landfill site, or escape of leachate during operation, and changes to the flood storage capacity of the catchment of the Kalu Oya River, which may lead to increased

Country	Project and cost	EA description
Sri Lanka *(continued)*		flooding upstream and downstream of the landfill site. The EA fully addresses these potential impacts and recommends appropriate mitigation measures. To minimize negative impacts due to siting and operation of the two wastewater treatment plants, separate environmental assessments will be carried out.
Thailand	Clean Fuels and Environmental Improvement ($90 million, IBRD; $370 million, total project cost)	Aims to provide the additional refinery facilities required to meet Thailand's new clean fuels standards, in addition to upgrading safety and environmental operations in order to meet expected standards. The project will include additional emissions and effluent control and treatment processing equipment required to handle additional loadings from the added refinery process equipment, as well as upgrading of current pollution control facilities, mainly in the wastewater treatment area. Adequate monitoring measures have been established to measure air and water quality. The potential negative impacts of the project are air pollution (mainly SO_x and NO_x) and water pollution through effluents and treatment system upsets and industrial hazards due to fires or oil spills. Appropriate mitigation measures have been prepared. In addition, an emergency plan for the refinery, covering fire fighting, oil spill cleanup, and evacuation, has also been prepared.
	Lam Takhong Pump Storage ($100 million, IBRD; $586 million, total project cost)	Aims to provide the following: an upper reservoir bounded by a rockfill dam, two morning-glory intakes leading to steel-lined inclined shafts, an underground power house containing four reversible Francis-type generating and pumping units, and two concrete-lined tailrace tunnels. The main impact of the project will be caused by the construction of the upper reservoir and will include (a) displacement of 59 hectares of established forest plantations, (b) loss of access to a 218 hectare area during the construction stage, (c) permanent loss of access to 65 hectares that will become the upper reservoir and ancillary areas, (d) changes in soil characteristics due to excavation, spoil disposal, and regrading, and (e)

(Table continues on the following page.)

Table F.1 *(continued)*

Country	Project and cost	EA description
Thailand *(continued)*		associated losses of agricultural produce and income. The main impact on fisheries will be increased mortality of fish through exposure to high pressure in the penstocks during pumping. There is potential concern that downstream users may suffer losses of water. Other potential environmental impacts are the impacts of a large labor force, truck traffic, erosion, air and water pollution, noise, and other public health problems. Environmental impact mitigation and monitoring and evaluation plans have been developed. A detailed rehabilitation policy has been framed by the government for the Lam Takhong project. This policy was designed with the active participation of the affected people.
	Second Gas Transmission ($155 million, IBRD; $675 million, total project cost)	Aims to promote greater energy efficiency and increase the use of domestic natural gas resources. This project will have minimal negative environmental impacts because natural gas will be less harmful than either oil or coal. However, the EA identified the following negative impacts: disruption to marine life, which could take place because of changes in seabed conditions near the pipeline during construction; the discharge of liquids such as mercury; and noise pollution caused by equipment used on the production platforms. The EA proposed mitigation measures such as pretreatment of liquid effluent, safe disposal of solid wastes to approved land sites, and safe mercury. The design of equipment will be according to international standards for maximum safety and allowable levels of noise and vibration. Principles for payment of compensation and relocation of affected persons were defined in this project.

Country	Project and cost	EA description
Viet Nam	Irrigation Rehabilitation ($100 million, IDA; $138 million, total project cost)	Aims to restore or establish sustainable irrigation by rehabilitation and completion of infrastructure and improvement of operation and maintenance in selected irrigation schemes. The objectives of the project are to increase agricultural production and farmers' income and reduce poverty in selected rural areas of Viet Nam. The potential environmental problems are (a) its proximity to Ho Chi Minh City and the existence of plans for extending urban developments over part of the area, (b) the extensive disposal of industrial liquid effluent and domestic garbage in the area, and (c) potential impacts due to the release of acids and, possibly, increased levels of aluminum and iron, due to disturbance of acid sulfate soils during drainage operations. The Hoc Mon North Binh Chanh subproject was classified as category A. During the course of the subproject preparation, several of the environmental concerns were addressed through changes in project design. Environmental action plans have been prepared to provide for the mitigation of any significant impacts identified as a result of the environmental investigations. The procedures recommended to mitigate the construction impacts will form part of the construction specifications. The locations of any sites of cultural or historical value will be identified together with the actions proposed for the protection of these sites. Approximately 633 households will have to be resettled. The inventories and surveys have been completed, and the resettlement action plans are being drafted.

(Table continues on the following page.)

Table F.1 *(continued)*

Country	Project and cost	EA description
Viet Nam *(continued)*	Power Sector Rehabilitation ($165 million, IDA; $258 million, total project cost)	Aims to improve the efficiency of power supply systems by (a) rehabilitating and reinforcing transmission and distribution systems, (b) converting generating plants from open to combined-cycle operation, and (c) installing modern load dispatch centers. The proposed project will finance priority investments in the power systems of southern and central Viet Nam. The rehabilitation of old, cluttered distribution networks will improve safety. The Krongbuk-Nhatrang transmission line route traversing through agricultural and tree cropland does not encroach on any environmentally sensitive areas. However, eighty houses have to be relocated along these areas. This transmission line traverses through areas inhabited by ethnic minorities, and care has been taken in routing to protect their rights. A detailed resettlement action plan has been prepared. A detailed EA concluded that with proper design and mitigation measures, atmospheric impacts (NO_x and noise levels) and aquatic impacts (cooling water temperature, chlorine concentration, and impact on shrimp farming and mangroves) will be within acceptable limits. However, an alternative cooling system is being studied. If this option is chosen, there will be no need to create a cooling water lagoon in the river estuary, and the corresponding impact on the marine environment will disappear. Appropriate mitigation and monitoring measures have been established. In addition, an environmental unit with an environmental coordinator will become part of the management structure of the power station.

Country	Project and cost	EA description

Europe and Central Asia

Croatia — Highway Sector ($80 million, IBRD; $568 million, total project cost) — Aims to support and speed up the modernization and transformation of the transport sector, with special emphasis on the main road network. EAs were prepared for the project. The major environmental issues anticipated are water pollution due to carriageway runoff, land acquisition and resettlement, protection of historical monuments, and noise pollution due to proximity to urban areas. Croatia is preparing legislation on regulating air pollution, specially targeting traffic pollution. The government of Croatia has also agreed to reduce the use of leaded gasoline by taxing leaded gasoline more than unleaded gasoline.

Middle East and North Africa Region

Lebanon — Solid Waste/Environmental Management ($55 million, IBRD; $135 million, total project cost) — Aims to (a) eliminate hazardous and unsightly dumping of solid waste, (b) improve methods of waste collection and disposal, (c) improve cost recovery and modernize municipal accounting systems, and (d) strengthen the Ministry of Municipal and Rural Affairs and participating municipalities. The proposed project is expected to have positive environmental impacts by elimination of indiscriminate dumping of solid wastes. The potential negative environmental impacts are the risks associated with treatment plants, including the change in land use at the selected site from agricultural use to a waste disposal site and the nuisance to the local population, including noise from plant operations, generation of odors, and deterioration of roads due to heavy trucks. Mitigation measures to minimize these negative impacts were developed, and a management plan for applying them has been established.

(Table continues on the following page.)

Table F.1 *(continued)*

Country	Project and cost	EA description
Latin America and the Caribbean		
Brazil	Ceara Urban Development and Water Resources Management ($110 million, IBRD; $240 million, total project cost)	Aims to support institutional development and urban infrastructure investments, as well as water supply and sewerage investments; water resource management infrastructure investments including construction of medium-size water storage reservoirs and conveyance facilities to bring bulk water to urban areas and rehabilitate existing storage facilities. An EA was prepared for one of the reservoirs to be financed under the project. EAs will also be prepared for the other thirty to fifty dams and reservoirs, prior to disbursement of financing. In addition, a sectoral EA is being prepared for the water development sector in the state of Ceara, looking at cumulative impacts of the subprojects. Detailed resettlement plans have been prepared for the first four reservoirs and will be prepared for each of the dam and reservoir subprojects to be implemented within this project.
OECS countries	OECS Solid Waste Management ($6.8 million, IBRD; $4.7 million, IDA; $50.5 million, total project cost)	Aims to improve domestic solid waste management facilities and facilitate compliance with the "special area" designation of the Caribbean Sea under the MARPOL convention. This project is the first in a series of environmentally oriented activities that will ensure the future maintenance of environmental quality in the OECS countries. Environmental impact assessments have been prepared, and hydrogeological surveys have been undertaken, for each project site in all the countries. These assessments have focused on the proposed sanitary landfill disposal sites. The EAs generally confirmed the appropriateness of site choice. The potential environmental problems are odor, fly and rodent nuisance, and leachate and gas movement. The design of the landfill disposal sites has incorporated measures to mitigate these negative impacts.

Country	Project and cost	EA description
Paraguay	Asunción Sewerage ($47 million, IBRD; $72 million, total project cost)	Aims to improve the provision of urban water and sewerage services in the country and to improve the health conditions for 250,000 inhabitants in Greater Asunción by increasing the current coverage of sewerage services by 60 percent. The project is expected to have an overall positive impact. The main environmental concern is the discharge of sewerage into the Paraguay River. As a result of the EA, several actions have been identified as necessary to mitigate the environmental impact of the project during project design, construction, and operation of the installed system.

Table F.2. IFC Projects with Full Environmental Assessment, Fiscal 1995

Country	Project sponsor and cost	EA description
Africa Congo	Elf Congo ($50 million, IFC; $1,600.2 million, total project cost)	Develops the Nkossa offshore oil field in partnership with other oil companies. Key environmental issues include the effects of a major spill on marine and coastal resources, discharge of liquids and solids and emergency response plans. The project sponsor proposes to operate the project in accordance with international guidelines in line with environmental requirements applicable in the Gulf of Mexico (U.S. waters). Oil spill sensitivity studies of the coasts of Gabon and Congo will be used in preparing oil spill contingency plans.
	Engen Congo ($46.4 million, IFC investment; $45.0 million, syndication; $99.8 million, total project cost)	Finances a share of the Nkossa offshore oil field development. (This is the same project as Elf Congo, described above; financing was provided to an additional project sponsor. It is included as two projects in the total number of 1995 approvals.)
Côte d'Ivoire	United Meridian Corporation ($57.3 million, IFC investment; $40 million, syndication; $161 million, total project cost)	Seeks to produce up to 24,000 barrels a day and supply up to 90 million cubic feet of gas from an offshore facility to supply local power and other users. Key environmental issues include discharge of produced water, air emissions, locations of pipelines and other onshore facilities, and oil spill contingency plans. The EA examined several alternatives for transporting oil and gas from the offshore platforms to an existing oil refinery and power station in Abidjan. The preferred route was determined to be an onshore pipeline following the coastline. Extensive discussions were also held with local village elders regarding optimum route selection, use of existing rights-of-way where feasible, and minimal disruption of village activities. (Included as two projects in the number of fiscal 1995 approvals in table 7.1.)

Country	Project sponsor and cost	EA description
Mali	La Société d'Exploitation des Mines d'Or de Sadiola ($39.8 million, IFC investment; $25.0 million, syndication; $246.2 million, total project cost)	Develops the Sadiola gold mine to produce about 270,000 ounces of gold a year. The EA demonstrates that infrastructure facilities were sited to take up the least amount of land, with the least impact on the natural and social environment. Modern open-pit mining techniques, a carbon-in-pulp cyanide treatment plant, and a state of the art tailings dam will ensure minimal impact on the environment. Extensive consultations were undertaken with potentially impacted villages to identify socially acceptable mitigation measures. A trust fund financed by profits from the project will finance mitigation and social adjustment programs.
Tanzania	One Earth Diving Lodge (African Enterprise Fund Project) ($0.7 million, IFC investment; $2.9 million, total project cost)	Constructs a small ecotourism lodge on the island of Pemba. Key environmental issues include impacts on coastal ecosystems and endangered species, socioeconomic impacts on neighboring communities, water supply, supply of construction materials, solid and liquid waste treatment and disposal, and fire safety. The lodge and associated structures will be built and operated so as to avoid the disturbance of sea turtle nesting sites. The sponsors are committed to making the lodge a world-class center for diving and marine research and plan to establish an environmental research station on site. In addition, the lodge will use rainwater for its water supply and supply treated wastewater free of charge to adjoining villages for irrigation.

(Table continues on the following page.)

Table F.2 *(continued)*

Country	Project sponsor and cost	EA description
Zambia	Kaila Lodge Limited (Africa Enterprise Fund Project) ($0.2 million, IFC investment; $0.4 million total project cost)	Completes a ten-bed safari lodge on a private farm in the Chiawa Game Management Area. Key environmental issues include impacts on wildlife habitat and game movement, water supply, fuelwood use, sewage and solid waste disposal, impacts associated with secondary development, and general health and safety issues. The EA addresses the importance of proper management of the farm property from a wildlife perspective because it forms a buffer zone between village communities in the Chiawa area and the Lower Zambezi National Park. The sponsors are exploring the possibility of burning solid and flammable waste generated from the operation to be used as fuel. In addition, solar-powered systems and efficient wood-fired boilers will be installed. The farm has been used for tourism since 1991, and there has been extensive public consultation both prior to and during IFC's involvement in the project. This includes numerous consultations with the local community, the Department of National Parks and Wildlife, the Lower Zambezi Conservancy, and the international team responsible for development of the Lower Zambezi National Park Plan (1992).
Asia India	Ib Valley Power Private Limited ($70 million, IFC investment; $80 million, syndication; $720.6 million, total project cost)	Builds a 420-megawatt coal-fired power plant under a thirty-year build-own-operate agreement with the state electricity board. The EA demonstrates that the use of low sulfur coal, low NO_x burners, and baghouses will minimize the projects impacts on local and regional air quality. Extensive consultations were conducted with affected landowners to arrive at equitable compensation packages. The project is to be built adjacent to a 420-megawatt plant now being constructed by the Orissa Power Generation Corporation (OPGC). Project planning has had a noticeable positive effect on the environmental performance of the OPGC plant, in particular, the design and operation of its ash disposal ponds.

Country	Project sponsor and cost	EA description
Philippines	Sual Thermal Power ($47.5 million, IFC investment; $200 million, syndication; $1,400 million, total project cost)	Builds and operates a 1,200-megawatt coal-fired power plant north of Manila to sell power to the National Power Corporation under a twenty-five-year agreement. Key environmental issues include air emissions, ash disposal, cooling water discharge, modification of existing land use, and related socioeconomic impacts. Air emissions will be controlled with high-efficiency electrostatic precipitators and flue gas desulfurization equipment. The site was selected to minimize adverse impacts on marine habitats and to reduce to eighty-seven families the number of people who must be relocated.
Thailand	Bangkok Mass Transit System (BTS) ($50 million, IFC investment; $1,648 million, total project cost)	Installs an elevated mass transit rail system to help alleviate traffic problems in the central business district of Bangkok. The EA considered system alignment and design measures to mitigate air quality, ambient noise, and visual and cultural impacts. The BTS alignment is above existing highways and will not require acquisition of property or resettlement of persons. During project design, the main maintenance depot was relocated from a site in the city's major park to an existing bus terminal complex. During construction, the use of silenced equipment and bored pilings and the employment of best management practices will minimize air quality and noise impacts. Design measures, including ventilation systems and noise barriers, will minimize such impacts during project operation. Visual impacts at sites of cultural and historical importance are being minimized in a cooperative effort with the affected communities through alignment adjustment, landscaping, and attractive design features.

(Table continues on the following page.)

Table F.2 *(continued)*

Country	Project sponsor and cost	EA description
Central Asia, the Middle East, and North Africa		
Kyrgyz Republic	Kumtor Gold Company ($40 million, IFC investment; $335 million; total project cost)	Develops a gold mine to produce 480,000 ounces per year. Environmental issues dealth with include erosion control, effluent discharge, reclamation planning, provision of adequate health and safety training, hazardous substance handling and storage, work place air quality, and provision and use of personal protection equipment. Effluent discharges from the tailings impoundment and sanitary sewage treatment will be strictly controlled to meet Canadian environmental standards. Wildlife that may migrate through the project area are expected to benefit from prohibition of hunting on mine property. Reclamation planning has taken into consideration the harsh permafrost conditions.
Pakistan	AES Lal Pir (Pakistan) Ltd. ($49.5 million, IFC investment; $343 million; total project cost)	Builds and operates a 362-megawatt thermal power plant and sells power to the national power utility under a thirty-year contract. The EA outlines a comprehensive environmental mitigation and monitoring program. Extensive consultations were done with interested parties, including the fifty owners of the 190 acres required for the project. As part of the mitigation plan, the sponsor has committed to planting ten acres of trees for every megawatt of generating capacity. While the existing Pakistan State Oil (PSO) Company fuel oil decanting facility is not part of the project, the project sponsor has developed a plan with PSO to improve the environmental performance of the fuel oil decanting facilities, as well as to clean up fuel oil contamination of soils and water in the vicinity.

Country	Project sponsor and cost	EA description
Latin America		
Argentina	Acceso Ezieza Canuelas S.A. ($20 million, IFC investment; $61 million, syndication; $161 million, total project cost)	Privatizes and upgrades, in conjunction with two similar projects, the major toll highways radiating from the Metropolitan Area of Buenos Aires (MABA). The EA identified air pollution, ambient noise, land acquisition, and resettlement as potential impacts to be addressed. The proposed highway alignment was modified to minimize the need for land expropriation. Affected property owners and residents are being equitably compensated consistent with IFC and government policies. An NGO, the Asociación Pro-Vivienda del Acceso, has been created in cooperation with the municipality to facilitate the relocation of families and to act as an intermediary between affected families and local and national authorities. The project design and cooperative efforts between the project sponsor and governmental authorities will minimize air pollution and ambient noise during construction and operation.
Dominican Republic	Smith-Enron Cogeneration ($32.3 million, IFC investment; $100 million, syndication; $204.3 million, total project cost)	Builds and operates a 185-megawatt combined cycle power plant. The EA demonstrates that three sites were considered for the project, with the preferred site selected on the basis of its remoteness from built-up areas and population. The outfall of the thermal discharge pipeline was sited to avoid impacting seagrass and coral reef ecological communities in the vicinity of Puerto Plata Harbor. Use of low NO_x burners, water injection, stack clustering and numerous noise mitigation measures will be employed to minimize impacts to air quality and to reduce noise. The sponsors have engaged in extensive consultations with regulatory authorities and potentially affected parties. The project's environmental components will serve as a demonstration project for the Corporación Dominicana de Electricidad.

Annex G. Global Environment Facility (GEF) and Multilateral Fund for the Implementation of the Montreal Protocol (MFMP) Investments Approved in Fiscal 1995

This annex provides brief descriptions of all GEF Pilot Phase, GEF1, and MFMP investment projects managed by the Bank Group that were approved between July 1, 1994, and June 30, 1995 (tables G.1 and G.2). All Bank-approved GEF Pilot Phase, GEF1, and MFMP projects are listed in tables G.3 and G.4. In the case of GEF projects, dollar figures represent grant financing from the Global Environment Trust Fund, the core fund of the GEF. In most cases, figures represent only a portion of the total project cost. In the case of projects funded by the MFMP, figures represent grant financing from the Multilateral Fund and will pay full eligible incremental costs of phaseout activities for ozone-depleting substances (ODS). In this case, the amounts that the client and the Bank have agreed to under an umbrella grant agreement and the overall amount committed by the MFMP Executive Committee are both shown.

Table G.1. GEF Projects Approved in Fiscal 1995

Country and grant amount	Project
Cameroon $6m grant	Biodiversity Conservation and Management: Participatory biodiversity conservation plans will be developed and implemented for eight sites in the species-rich lowland forests of southeast Cameroon and parts of the northern savanna ecosystem. The capacity of natural resource management institutions will be strengthened through financing zoological and biological inventories, by providing equipment, training, and technical assistance, and through "twinning" between the National Herbarium and the Kew Botanical Gardens and the National Herbarium of France.

Country and grant amount	Project
China $17.9m grant	Nature Reserves Management: In accordance with China's NEAP and Biodiversity Action Plan priorities, this project will prepare and implement management plans in five priority protected areas, train staff, fund physical investments, and work with communities adjacent to and within protected area boundaries to create incentives for sustainable use of resources. A second component will restructure a major timber industry in Changqing to promote sustainable forestry and create a core protected area of giant panda habitat, surrounded by a limited-use production-buffer zone. The project will build technical and managerial capacity of the Division of Nature Reserves through developing a national training team for biodiversity. It will fund a national nature reserve plan, equipment, and policy studies and research and will set up an information management system.
Czech Republic $2.3m grant	Phaseout of Ozone-Depleting Substances: The project will eliminate production of chlorofluorocarbons (CFCs) in the Czech Republic. It will establish a national refrigerant recovery-reclamation-recycling program. It will phase out CFCs in certain commercial, industrial, and transport refrigeration systems and introduce low- and nonozone-depleting foam technologies.
Malawi $5.0m grant	SADC Lake Malawi/Nyasa Biodiversity Conservation: Lake Malawi, Africa's third-largest lake, is a unique freshwater ecosystem, home to over 500 endemic species of fish. The project will conduct faunal surveys, identify biodiversity hot spots, prepare a conservation and management plan for the lake, recommend revisions to national environmental legislation, and fund environmental training and education activities. A parallel Canadian project (C$4.2 million) will finance research capacity-building through twinning with a Canadian institution, limnology and water quality monitoring, laboratory equipment, and public education.
Mali $2.5m grant	Household Energy: The project addresses both the demand for and supply of household energy in a country where people depend heavily on environmentally damaging woodfuels. Consumption of these fuels will be reduced by promoting the use of more efficient stoves and by substituting woodfuels with kerosene and bottled gas through technical assistance and credit to manufacturers and marketers. In parallel, forest planning and management will be strengthened through training and technical assistance.

(Table continues on the following page.)

Table G.1 *(continued)*

Country and grant amount	Project
Morocco $6m grant	Repowering of Power Plant: Repowering an existing plant with a second-generation advanced combustion turbine, together with improving the quality of the materials and enhancing the scheme's performance in the power generating system of Morocco. Close monitoring of the project's impact and careful analysis of the findings will help to determine its wider applicability for use throughout the country.
OECS countries $12.5m grant	Ship-Generated Waste Management: Project will assist OECS governments in reducing pollution of international and territorial waters caused by the discharge of ship-generated solid wastes by supporting appropriate actions aimed at improving collection, treatment, and disposal of these wastes. Project includes national components consisting of the establishment of port waste-reception facilities and incremental expansion of landfill sites to handle ship-generated wastes, together with a regional component comprised of support activities and technical assistance for project management, training and education, establishment of common legal framework for ship waste management, recycling possibilities, and public awareness programs. Project activities will also protect critical habitat for the endangered Grenada dove.
Peru $5m grant	National Trust Fund for Protected Areas: The GEF will provide seed money for the Trust Fund for Conservation of Peru's Protected Areas. Annual revenue from the trust will finance management activities—including training, management plans, operational costs, salaries, awareness programs, and buffer zone alternative livelihood activities—for three key protected areas: Manu National Park and Biosphere Reserve, Noroeste Biosphere Reserve, and Rio Abiseo National Park. As the fund grows through outside contributions, additional protected areas will receive support. The Deutsche Gesellschaft für Technische Zusammenarbeit GmbH (GTZ) is providing parallel financing to support the National Institute of Natural Resources and recurrent expenses of the fund's administrative agency during 1995. The GTZ parallel grant also finances development of a master plan for all Peruvian protected areas and a two-year NGO small grants program for sustainable, integrated conservation and development projects.

Country and grant amount	Project
Poland $5m grant	Efficient Lighting: Through the IFC, direct subsidies will be given to manufacturers of compact fluorescent lighting. Manufacturers and wholesalers will be required to pass on full savings on to retailers, who will apply a standard percentage-based mark-up, passing savings on to consumers. This will spark demand for compact fluorescent lighting in Poland and demonstrate the financial and commercial benefits of energy-efficient lighting. The results will be large power savings and reduced emissions from coal-fired generation plants.
$25m grant	Coal-to-Gas Conversion: The project expects to demonstrate interfuel substitution and technological innovation as a means of reducing carbon dioxide emissions. GEF funds will be used to extend coal-to-gas conversions to medium-size boilers whose owners could not achieve acceptable financial rates of return without concessional financing.
Romania $4.5m grant	Danube Delta Biodiversity: The project aims to protect the Romanian delta ecosystem and contribute to the conservation of biodiversity within the delta. It will strengthen institutional capacity to monitor and manage protected areas effectively, work with local community groups to ensure sustainable use of resources, and restore some wetlands to their natural condition by testing various approaches and monitoring their impact.
Tunisia $4m grant	Solar Water Heating: The project will promote the commercialization of solar water-heating technology in the residential and tertiary sectors by conditioning the market for sustained penetration of the technology as a least-cost alternative under competitive market conditions.
Uganda $4m grant	Conservation of the Bwindi Impenetrable National Park and the Mgahinga Gorilla National Park: The project will establish a trust fund, the income from which will provide a sustainable source of funds for the management of the Bwindi Impenetrable National Park and Mgahinga Gorilla National Parks and the conservation of their biodiversity. A Trust Management Board, which represents local communities, NGOs, and the government will allocate the fund's net income to selected park management, research, and community development projects.

Table G.2. MFMP Investments Approved in Fiscal 1995

Country and grant and commitment amounts	Project
China $90m Grant Agreement $29m commitment	ODS Project III: The project will support from thirty to forty subprojects (about ten in each tranche) in all five ODS-user industries aimed at adoption of Grant Agreement on non-ODS technology through technical and financial assistance to enterprises for technology transfer, design, training, and implementation; assist in closures of CFCs production and halon plants; and provide technical assistance to the National Environment Protection Agency and China Investment Bank in the areas of procurement, disbursement, ODS technology, and project development and implementation. The projected average subproject size is about $1.5 million.
Egypt $2m Grant Agreement $2m commitment	IFC-MCMC Compressor: A grant of $2.1 million has been approved by the MFMP to assist the MISR compressor manufacturing company (MCMC) in converting its compressor production facility from CFC-12 compressors to HFC-134a. Originally a grant was approved for $2.8 million; however, Zanussi (Italy) will purchase 25 percent of the company as part of a financial and technical restructuring. This foreign ownership reduced the eligible funding to $2.1 million. With the financial restructuring of MCMC in Egypt, it is likely to be approved by IFC's Board—the grant agreement was signed in May 1995—and is expected to be disbursed quickly because a substantial part of the capital investments required for the conversion have already been made. After conversion is complete, it is expected that about 385 tons of CFCs will be eliminated per year.
India $50m Grant Agreement $8m commitment	ODS Project II: Two-part project: (a) supports about forty subprojects in all ODS-user and -production industries including refrigeration, air conditioning, foam, aerosols, and solvents and halons, and (b) supports non-ODS production and ODS closure projects. Each subproject will support participating enterprises in technology transfer, design, training, and implementation. Subprojects are being selected on the basis of cost-effective ODS-reduction impact. In addition, UNDP is preparing foam projects that complement the proposed Bank project.

Country and grant and commitment amounts	Project
India $1.25m Grant Agreement $1.25m commitment	ODS Project I: The project has two components: Shriram Refrigeration Industries, Ltd., to provide assistance for conversion of compressor manufacture from CFC-12 to HFC-134a designs and Blue Star, Ltd., to support funding for substitution of CFC-11 refrigerant with HCFC-123 in centrifugal chillers. Both components are designed to assist the participating enterprises in switching from use of ODS to non-ODS materials and technology. The subprojects represent measures that must be taken early to enable India to develop a cost-effective program to phase out ODS consumption, and they require no policy actions to be taken by the Montreal Protocol Executive Committee. Each subproject includes technology (from established technology supply relationships), design, training, equipment, and implementation of product and engineering development activities to enable each enterprise to convert to non-ODS technology.
Indonesia $17m Grant Agreement $9m commitment	ODS Project I: The project is composed of three elements: subproject preparation, subproject investments, and technical assistance. Under an Ozone Trust Fund–Project Preparation Advance, a consulting firm has been selected to prepare twenty subproject concepts and to finalize twelve for preappraisal. Additional project preparation advance funds will be requested from the Montreal Protocol Executive Committee as required. The project will support from twenty-five to thirty subprojects in several tranches and will cover all major ODS-use sectors in Indonesia, including refrigeration, air-conditioning, foams, fire protection (halons), aerosols, and solvents. Subprojects will assist beneficiaries with technology transfer, design, safety, training, and implementation. The project also includes $50,000 of technical assistance for the strengthening of UPPINDO Bank's technical capabilities in project review and supervision.

(Table continues on the following page.)

Table G.2 *(continued)*

Country and grant and commitment amounts	Project
Philippines $30m Grant Agreement $12m commitment	ODS Project I: The project includes an investment component and a technical assistance (TA) component. The TA component includes an Institutional Strengthening Project to strengthen the Department of Environment and Natural Resources' capability to implement the country's ODS Phaseout Program and Technical Assistance to the Financial Agent (the Land Bank of the Philippines) to strengthen its capability to appraise and supervise subprojects in ODS refrigerant recycling and conversion to non-ODS technology in solvents, refrigeration, foam blowing, and tobacco puffing. Of the sixteen identified subprojects, ten subprojects, representing about 85 percent of the total project investment cost and about 75 percent of the total grant amount, have been preappraised. The project is expected to be complete by December 31, 1997.
Thailand $140m Grant Agreement $13m commitment	ODS Project I: The project will support a total of forty-five to fifty-five subprojects in solvents, refrigeration, air conditioning, foams, and recycling. Each subproject includes technical assistance to support participating enterprises with technology transfer, design, training, and implementation. About twenty subprojects have been identified thus far, out of which twelve subprojects have been preappraised, representing about 30 percent of the total project investment cost and about 30 percent of total project amount. Another twenty-five to thirty-five proposals will be developed during the next two years.

Country and grant and commitment amounts	Project
Uruguay $5m Grant Agreement $1.2m commitment	ODS Project I Investment: The project has two components. First, the investment component will provide subgrants to private firms to assist them in switching to nonozone-depleting materials and technology. This component consists of approximately ten subprojects, four of which have been already appraised by the Bank and approved by the Montreal Protocol Executive Committee. The subproject will address production process conversions, mechanical equipment and installations, recovery and recycling equipment, and retrofitting of existing facilities. Second, a TA component will strengthen the Comisión Tecnica Gubernamental de Ozono as the executing unit in supporting the Ministerio de Vivienda, Ordenamiento Territorial y Medio Ambiente to provide assistance to the beneficiaries in the identification, preparation, evaluation, and administration of subprojects. This TA component will provide funds for specialized training, office equipment, and consulting services. The project's expected completion and closing dates are December 31, 1997, and June 30, 1998, respectively.
Venezuela $3m Grant Agreement $3m commitment	ODS Project III—FAACA: The proposed project consists of retooling a heat exchanger fabrication and assembly line and related training and technical assistance costs. The assembly line conversion will permit production of mobile air conditioning systems that permit use of HFC-134a rather than CFC-12 as the refrigeration agent. A Calorimeter test laboratory for which funding was originally requested was not found to be an incremental cost and has been deleted from the project scope. Certain categories of recurrent annual investments related to model changes were also considered to be nonincremental and, likewise, are not included in the project scope.

(Table continues on the following page.)

Table G.2 *(continued)*

Country and grant and commitment amounts	Project
Venezuela *(continued)* $.25m Grant Agreement $.25m commitment	ODS Project II Conversion of CFC-12 to HCFC-134a: The project involves the retrofitting of twenty-five existing chiller units with ten or more years of expected useful life and the installation of four new HFC-134a chillers to replace CFC-12 chillers whose useful life has expired. The retrofits are equipment-specific and have been engineered and specified by the Snyder General McQuay Co. (SGMQ), current owner of the former Westinghouse compressor technology. The four new SGMQ chillers will also replace Westinghouse chillers on a sole-supplier basis. The refitting is mechanical, involving changing of gears, seals, and gaskets.

Table G.3. GEF Pilot Phase and GEF 1 Investments Approved through Fiscal 1995

Country	Project name (fiscal year of Bank approval)	Grant amount (millions of dollars)
GEF 1 investment		
China	Nature Reserves Management (1995)	17.9
Total GEF 1 investments		17.9
GEF Pilot Phase investments		
Algeria	El Kala National Park and Wetlands Management (1994)	9.2
Algeria, Morocco, Tunisia	Oil Pollution Management Project for the Southwest Mediterranean Sea (1994)	18.3
Belarus	Biodiversity Protection (1992)	1.0
Bhutan	Trust Fund for Environmental Conservation (1992)	10.0
Bolivia	Biodiversity Conservation (1993)	4.5
Cameroon	Biodiversity Conservation and Management (1995)	6.0
China	Ship Waste Disposal (1992)	30.0
	Sichuan Gas Transmission and Distribution Rehabilitation (1994)	10.0
Congo	Wildlands Protection and Management (1993)	10.0
Costa Rica	Tejona Wind Power (1994)	3.3
Czech Republic	Phaseout of Ozone-Depleting Substances (1995)	2.3
	Biodiversity Protection (1994)	2.0
Ecuador	Biodiversity Protection (1994)	7.2
Egypt	Red Sea Coastal and Marine Resource Management (1993)	4.8
Ghana	Coastal Wetlands Management (1993)	7.2
India	Alternate Energy (1993)	26.0
Indonesia	Biodiversity Collections (1994)	7.2
Iran, Islamic Rep. of	Teheran Transport Emissions Reduction (1994)	2.0
Jamaica	Demand Side Management Demonstration (1994)	3.8
Lao PDR	Wildlife and Protected Areas Conservation (1994)	5.0
Malawi	SADC Lake Malawi/Nyasa Biodiversity Conservation (1995)	5.0
Mali	Household Energy (1995)	2.5
Mauritius	Sugar Bio-Energy Technology (1992)	3.3
Mexico	Protected Areas Program (1992)	25.0
Mexico	High Efficiency Lighting Pilot (1994)	10.0
Morocco	Repowering of Power Plant (1995)	6.0

(Table continues on the following page.)

Table G.3 *(continued)*

Country	Project name (fiscal year of Bank approval)	Grant amount (millions of dollars)
OECD countries	Ship-Generated Waste Management (1995)	12.5
Peru	Trust Fund for Parks and Protected Areas (1995)	5.0
Philippines	Conservation of Priority Protected Areas (1994)	20.0
	Leyte-Luzon Geothermal (1994)	30.0
Poland	Forest Biodiversity Protection (1992)	4.5
	Efficient Lighting (1995)	5.0
	Coal-to-Gas Conversion (1995)	25.0
Romania	Danube Delta Biodiversity (1995)	4.5
Seychelles	Biodiversity Conservation and Marine Pollution Abatement (1993)	1.8
Slovak Republic	Biodiversity Protection (1994)	2.3
Thailand	Promotion of Electricity Energy Efficiency (1993)	9.5
Tunisia	Solar Water Heating (1995)	4.0
Turkey	In-Situ Conservation of Genetic Biodiversity (1993)	5.1
Uganda	Conservation of the Bwindi Impenetrable National Park and the Mgahinga Gorilla National Park (1995)	4.0
Ukraine	Transcarpathian Biodiversity Protection (1994)	0.5
	Danube Delta Biodiversity (1994)	1.5
Wider Caribbean	Wider Caribbean Initiative for Ship-Generated Waste (1994)	5.5
Total GEF 1 investments		17.9
Total GEF Pilot Phase investments		362.3
Total Fiscal 1992–95		380.2

Table G.4. Montreal Protocol Investment Operations Approved by the World Bank, Fiscal 1992–95
(millions of dollars)

Fiscal year	Country	Project	Umbrella	Committed
1992	Mexico	MAC Recycling and Aerosols		0.18
1992	Malaysia	Halons and MAC Recycling		1.63
1992	Philippines	ODS Phaseout Engineering		0.39
1992	Thailand	ODS Phaseout Engineering		0.39
Total				2.59
1993	Chile	ODS Phaseout		1.21
1993	Mexico	Ozone Protection Policy		4.00
1993	Venezuela	ODS Phaseout I–Plasticos Molanca		1.30
Total				6.51
1994	Brazil	ODS Phaseout I	10.90	5.14
1994	China	ODS Phaseout I		6.93
1994		ODS Phaseout II		4.47
1994	Ecuador	ODS Phaseout I		1.57
1994	Jordan	TA and Investment Project		1.50
1994	Turkey	ODS Phaseout I		6.17
1994	Tunisia	ODS I		1.79
Total			10.90	27.57
1995	China	ODS III	90.00	29.45
1995	Egypt	MCMC Compressor (IFC)		2.10
1995	India	ODS I		1.25
1995		ODS II	50.00	8.12
1995	Indonesia	ODS I	17.00	8.68
1995	Philippines	ODS I	30.00	11.73
1995	Thailand	ODS Phaseout I	40.00	12.50
1995	Uruguay	ODS I	5.00	1.23
1995	Venezuela	Chiller Retrofits		0.25
1995		FAACA		3.10
Total			232.00	78.41
Total			242.90	115.08

Bibliography

Titles published by the World Bank can be obtained from the bookstores at the World Bank offices in Washington, D.C., and Paris or through the World Bank's authorized commercial distributors and depository libraries throughout the world. Abbreviations used are as follows: EDI, Economic Development Institute (of the World Bank); GEF, Global Environment Facility; and World Bank Environment Department divisions (ENVGC, Global Environment Coordination; ENVLW, Land, Water and Natural Habitats Division; ENVSP, Social Policy and Resettlement Division; ENVPE, Pollution and Environmental Economics Division). Titles preceded by an asterisk are available by writing directly to the department named.

Ahmed, Kulsum. 1994. *Technological Development and Pollution Abatement: A Study of How Enterprises Are Finding Alternatives to Chlorofluorocarbons.* World Bank Technical Paper 271. Washington, D.C.

*Alaerts, G. J. 1994. "Water, Wastewater and Sanitation Projects: A Review of Environmental Assessment in the Asia Regions FY90–97" World Bank, Asia Technical Department, Washington, D.C.

Alberini, Anna, Maureen L. Cropper, Tsu-Tan Fu, Alan Krupnick, Lu Jin-Tan, Daigee Shaw, and Winston Harrington. 1995. "What Is the Value of Reduced Morbidity in Taiwan?" In Robert Mendelsohn and Daigee Shaw, eds., *The Economics of Pollution Control in the Asian Pacific.* London: Edward Elgar Publishers.

Anderson, Dennis, and Kulsum Ahmed. 1995. *The Case for Solar Energy Investments.* World Bank Technical Paper 279. Washington, D.C.

*Anderson, Robert J. Jr. 1995. "Joint Implementation of Climate Change Measures." Climate Change Series 5. World Bank, Environment Department, Washington, D.C.

*Antholt, Charles, and Willem Zijp. 1995. "Participation in Agricultural Extension." Environment Department Dissemination Note 24. World Bank, Environment Department, Washington, D.C.

*Aronson, Dan. 1995. "Participation in Country Economic and Sector Work." Environment Department Dissemination Note 18. World Bank, ENVSP, Washington, D.C.

*Aronson, Dan, and Ellen Tynan. 1995. "Participation in Country Economic and Sector Work." Environment Department Participation Series Paper 6. World Bank, ENVSP, Washington, D.C.

Aruna Bagchee. 1990. *Agricultural Extension in Africa.* World Bank Discussion Paper 231. Washington, D.C.

*Ayres, Wendy, and John A. Dixon. 1995. "Economic and Ecological Benefits of Reducing Emissions of Sulfur Oxides in the Sostanj Region of Slovenia." Environmental Economics Series 9. World Bank, Environment Department, Washington, D.C.

Banerjee, Ajit K. 1995. *Rehabilitation of Degraded Forests in Asia.* World Bank Technical Paper 270. Washington, D.C.

*Banerjee, Ajit K., Gabriel Campbell, Maria C. Cruz, Shelton Davis, and Augusta Molnar. 1995. "Participation in Forest and Conservation Management." Environment Department Dissemination Note 23. World Bank, Environment Department, Washington, D.C.

*Baranzini, Andrew, Marc Chesney, and Jacques Morisset. 1995. "Uncertainty and Global Warming: An Option-Pricing Approach to Policy." Policy Research Working Paper 1417. World Bank, Policy Research Department, Washington, D.C.

*Bates, Robin, S. Gupta, and Boguslaw Fiedor. 1994. "Economywide Policies and the Environment: A Case Study of Poland." Environment Paper 63. Washington, D.C.: World Bank.

Berkoff, Jeremy. 1994. *Strategy for Managing Water in the Middle East and North Africa.* Directions in Development Series. Washington, D.C.: World Bank.

Bernstein, Janis D. 1994. *Land Use Considerations in Urban Environmental Management.* Urban Management Programme Paper 12. Washington, D.C.: World Bank.

Bhadra, Dipasis, and Antônio Salazar P. Brandão. 1994. *Urbanization, Agricultural Development, and Land Allocation.* World Bank Discussion Paper 201. Washington, D.C.

Binswanger, Hans P., and Pierre Landell-Mills. 1995. *The World Bank's Strategy for Reducing Poverty and Hunger: A Report to the Development Community.* Environmentally Sustainable Development Studies and Monographs Series No. 4. Washington, D.C.: World Bank.

*Bojo, Jan, and David Cassells. 1995. "Land Degradation and Rehabilitation in Ethiopia: A Reassessment." World Bank, ENVLW and Africa Technical Department, Washington, D.C.

*Carroll, Thomas, Mary Schmidt, and Tony Bebbington. 1995. "Participation and Intermediary NGOs." Environment Department Dissemination Note 22. World Bank, Environment Department, Washington, D.C.

Cernea, Michael, John Dixon, Ernst Lutz, Mohan Munasinghe, Colin Rees, Ismail Serageldin, and Andrew Steer. 1994. *Making Development Sustainable: From Concepts to Action.* Environmentally Sustainable Development Occasional Paper 2. Washington, D.C.: World Bank.

*Chomitz, Kenneth, and David A. Gray. 1995. "Roads, Land, Markets, and Deforestation: A Spatial Model of Land Use in Belize." Policy Research Working Paper 1444. World Bank, Policy Research Department, Washington, D.C.

Cleaver, Kevin M., and Götz A. Schreiber. 1994a. *Reversing the Spiral: The Population, Agriculture, and Environment Nexus in Sub-Saharan Africa.* Directions in Development Series. Washington, D.C.: World Bank.

———. 1994b. *Supplement to Reversing the Spiral: The Population, Agriculture, and Environment Nexus in Sub-Saharan Africa.* Directions in Development Series. Washington, D.C.: World Bank.

*———. 1995. "The Downward Spiral in Sub-Saharan Africa: Population Growth, Agricultural Decline, and Destruction of the Environment." Environment Department Dissemination Note 12. World Bank, Environment Department, Washington, D.C.

Cointreau-Levine, Sandra. 1994. *Private Sector Participation in Municipal Solid Waste Services in Developing Countries.* Vol. 1, *The Formal Sector.* Urban Management Programme Series Paper 13. Washington, D.C.: World Bank.

*Colletta, Nat J., and Gillian Perkins. 1995. "Participation in Education." Environment Department Participation Series 1. World Bank, ENVSP, Washington, D.C. A summary is available as Environment Department Dissemination Note 14.

Convery, Frank J. 1995. *Applying Environmental Economics in Africa.* World Bank Technical Paper 277. Washington, D.C.

Cook, Cynthia, and Paula Donelly-Roark. 1994. "Public Participation in Environmental Assessment in Africa." In Robert Goodland and Valerie Edmundson, eds., *Environmental Assessment and Development.* World Bank: Washington, D.C.

Cropper, Maureen L. 1994. "Economic and Health Consequences of Pesticide Use in Developing Country Agriculture: Discussion." *American Journal of Agricultural Economics* 76: 605–07.

———. 1995. "Discussion: Valuing Food Safety, Which Approaches to Use?" In Julie Caswell, ed., *Valuing Food Safety and Nutrition.* Boulder, Colo.: Westview Press.

———. Forthcoming. "Comment on 'Estimating the Demand for Public Goods: The Collective Choice and Contingent Valuation Approaches.'" In David Bjornstad and James Kahn, eds., *Using Contingent*

Valuation to Measure Non-Market Values. London: Edward Elgar Publishers.

*Dasgupta, Susmita, Ashoka Mody, Subhendu Roy, and David Wheeler. 1995. "Environmental Regulation and Development." Policy Research Working Paper 1448. World Bank, Policy Research Department, Washington, D.C.

Davis, Shelton, and Katrinka Ebbe, eds. 1995. *Traditional Knowledge and Sustainable Development: Proceedings of a Conference*. Environmentally Sustainable Development Proceedings Series 4. Washington, D.C.: World Bank.

*Davis, Shelton, and Lars T. Soeftestad. 1995. "Participation and Indigenous Peoples." Environment Department Participation Series Paper 21. World Bank, ENVSP, Washington, D.C. A summary is available as Environment Department Dissemination Note 21.

Dixon, John, Louise Fallon-Scura, R. Carpenter, and P. B. Sherman. 1994. *Economic Analysis of Environmental Impacts*. 2d ed. London: Earthscan Publications.

*Eskeland, Gunnar S., and Tarhan N. Feyzioglu. 1994. "Is Demand for Polluting Goods Manageable? An Econometric Study of Car Ownership and Use in Mexico." Policy Research Working Paper 1309. World Bank, Policy Research Department, Washington, D.C.

*Eskeland, Gunnar S., Emmanuel Jimenez, and Lilu Liu. 1994. " Energy Pricing and Air Pollution: Econometric Evidence from Manufacturing in Chile and Indonesia." Policy Research Working Paper 1323. World Bank, Policy Research Department, Washington, D.C.

Farahn, Jumanah. 1994. *Pesticide Policies in Developing Countries: Do They Encourage Excessive Use?* World Bank Discussion Paper 238. Washington, D.C.

*Faruqee, Rashid. 1995. "Pakistan's Agriculture Sector: Is 3 to 4 Percent Annual Growth Sustainable?" Policy Research Working Paper 1407. World Bank, South Asia Country Department, Washington, D.C.

Fox, William F. 1994. *Strategic Options for Urban Infrastructure Management*. Urban Management Programme Paper 17. Washington, D.C.: World Bank.

Frederiksen, Harald D., Jeremy Berkoff, and William Barber. 1994. *Principles and Practices in Dealing with Water Resources Issues*. World Bank Technical Paper 233. Washington, D.C..

Goldenman, Gretta. Forthcoming. *Environmental Liabilities and Privatization in Central and Eastern Europe: A Report for the Environmental Action Programme for Central and Eastern Europe*. Washington, D.C.: World Bank.

Goodland, Robert, and Valerie Edmundson, eds. 1994. *Environment Assessment and Development. Selected Papers from the International Con-*

ference on Environmental Assessment, August 19–22, 1992, at the World Bank, Washington, D.C. Washington, D.C.: World Bank.

*Greve, Albert. 1995. "Institutional Structures for Environmentally Sustainable Development." Towards Environmentally Sustainable Development in Sub-Saharan Africa Paper 3. World Bank, Africa Technical Department, Washington, D.C.

Grut, Mikael, John A. Gray, and Nicolas Egli. 1993. *Politique de redevances et de concessions forestières: Gestion des futaies en Afrique occidentale et centrale.* World Bank Technical Paper 143. Washington, D.C.

Gupta, Shreekant, George L. Van Houtven, and Maureen L. Cropper. 1995. "Do Benefits and Costs Matter in Environmental Regulation? An Analysis of EPA Decisions under Superfund." In R. Revesz and R. Steward, eds., *Reauthorizing Superfund: Theoretical and Empirical Issues.* Baltimore: Johns Hopkins University Press for Resources for the Future.

*Haq, Bilal U. 1994. "Sea Level Rise and Coastal Subsidence: Rates and Threats." World Bank, ENVLW, Washington, D.C.

*Hartman, Raymond, David Wheeler, and Manjula Singh. 1995. "The Cost of Air Pollution Abatement." Policy Research Working Paper 1398. World Bank, Policy Research Department, Washington, D.C.

Hertzman, Clyde. 1995. *Environment and Health in Central and Eastern Europe: A Report for the Environmental Action Programme in Central and Eastern Europe.* Washington, D.C.: World Bank

*Hettige, Hemamala, Mainul Huq, Sheoli Pargal, and David Wheeler. 1995. "Determinant of Pollution Abatement in Developing Countries: Evidence from South and South-East Asia." Paper presented at the annual meetings of the AEA in Washington, D.C. World Bank, Policy Research Department, Washington, D.C.

*Hettige, Hemamala, Paul Martin, Manjula Singh, and David Wheeler. 1995. "The Industrial Pollution Projection System." Policy Research Working Paper 1448. World Bank, Policy Research Department, Washington, D.C.

Idelovitch, Emanuel, and Klas Ringskog. 1995. *Private Sector Participation in Water Supply and Sanitation in Latin America.* Directions in Development Series. Washington, D.C.: World Bank.

*Isham, Jonathan, Deepa Narayan, and Lant Pritchett. 1994. "Does Participation Improve Project Performance? Establishing Causality with Subjective Data." Policy Research Working Paper 1357. World Bank, Policy Research Department, Washington, D.C.

John, Joshua. 1994. *Managing Redundancy in Overexploited Fisheries.* World Bank Discussion Paper 240. Washington, D.C.

Khouri, Nadim, John M. Kalbermatten, and Carl R. Bartone. 1994. *Reuse of Wastewater in Agriculture: A Guide for Planners.* Water and Sanitation

Report 6. UNDP–World Bank Water and Sanitation Program. Washington, D.C.: World Bank.

Kirmani, Syed, and Robert Rangeley. 1994. *International Inland Waters: Concepts for a More Active World Bank Role.* World Bank Technical Paper 239. Washington, D.C.

Klavens, Jonathan, and Anthony Zamparutti. Forthcoming. *Foreign Direct Investment and Environment in Central and Eastern Europe: A Survey. A Report for the Environmental Action Programme for Central and Eastern Europe.* World Bank: Washington, D.C.

*Lantran, Jean Marie, Jacques Baillon, and Jean-Marc Pages. 1995. "L'entretien routier et l'environnement." World Bank, Technical Department and Environmentally Sustainable Development Department, Washington, D.C.

Laplante, Benoit. Forthcoming. "It's Not Being Green: The Politics of Canada's Green Plan: A Comment." *Canadian Public Policy.*

*Laplante, Benoit, and Peter Kennedy. Forthcoming. "Equilibrium Incentives for Cleaner Technology Adoption under Emissions Pricing." Policy Research Working Paper. World Bank, Policy Research Department, Washington, D.C.

Laplante, Benoit, and Martin Luckert. 1995a. "Impact of Newsprint Recycling Policies on Canadian Waste Production and Forests." *Canadian Public Policy* 20(2): 440–14.

———. 1995b. "The Wastepaper Dilemma: Can Newsprint Recycling Legislation Kill Two Birds with One Stone? A Reply." *Society and Natural Resources* 7(6): 601–03.

*Laplante, Benoit, and Paul Rilstone. 1995. "Environmental Inspections and Emissions of the Pulp and Paper Industry in Quebec." Policy Research Paper 1447. World Bank, Policy Research Department, Washington, D.C.. Forthcoming in *Journal of Environmental Economics and Management.*

Laplante, Benoit, Paul Lanoie, and Georges Tanguay. 1994. "La firme et l'environnement." *L'Actualité Économique* 70(2): 97–111.

*Larsen, Bjorn, and Anwar Shah. 1994. "Global Tradable Carbon Permits, Participation Incentives, and Transfers." Policy Research Working Paper 1315. World Bank, Policy Research Department, Washington, D.C.

*Ledec, George, Maria Clara Majia, and Juan David Quintero. 1995."Good and Bad Dams: Ranking Hydroelectric Projects in Latin America Using Environmental and Social Criteria." LATEN Dissemination Note. World Bank, Latin America Technical Department, Environment Division, Washington, D.C.

*Lee, Donna J., and Ariel Dinar. 1995. "Review of Integrated Approaches to River Basin Planning, Development, and Management." Policy Research Working Paper 1446. World Bank, Policy Research Department, Washington, D.C.

Leitmann, Josef. 1994. *Rapid Urban Environmental Assessment: Lessons from Cities in the Developing World*. Vol. 2, *Tools and Outputs*. Urban Management Programme Series 15. Washington, D.C.: World Bank.

LeMoigne, Guy, Ashok Subramanian, Mei Xie, and Sandra Giltner, eds. 1994. *A Guide to the Formulation of Water Resource Strategy*. World Bank Technical Paper 263. Washington, D.C.: World Bank.

Loayza, Eduardo A., ed. 1994. *Managing Fishery Resources*. World Bank Discussion Paper 217. Washington, D.C.

*Meinzen-Dick, Ruth, Richard Reidinger, and Andrew Manzardo. 1995. "Participation in Irrigation." Environment Department Participation Series Paper 3. World Bank, ENVSP, Washington, D.C. A summary is available as Environment Department Dissemination Note 16.

Menke, Christoph, and P. Gregory Fazzari. 1994. *Improving Electric Power Utility Efficiency: Issues and Recommendations*. World Bank Technical Paper 243. Washington, D.C.

*Metrick, Andrew, and Martin L. Weitzman. 1994. "Patterns of Behavior in Biodiversity Preservation." Policy Research Working Paper 1358. World Bank, Policy Research Department, Washington, D.C.

Millington, Andrew, C. Richard, W. Critchley, Terry D. Douglas, and Paul Ryan, eds. 1994. *Estimating Woody Biomass in Sub-Saharan Africa*. Washington, D.C.: World Bank.

*Mintzer, Irving, David von Hippel, and Stan Kolar. 1994. "Greenhouse Gas Assessment Methodology." ENVGC, Washington, D.C.

*Munasinghe, Mohan. 1995. "Sustainable Energy Development (SED): Issues and Policy." Environment Department Pollution Management Series Paper 16. World Bank, Environment Department, Pollution and Environment Economics Division, Washington, D.C.

Munasinghe, Mohan, and Wilfrido Cruz. 1995. *Economywide Policies and the Environment: Lessons from Experience*. World Bank Environment Paper 10. Washington, D.C.

Munasinghe, Mohan, and Jeffrey McNeely. 1994. *Protected Area Economics and Policy: Linking Conservation and Sustainable Development*. Washington, D.C.: World Bank.

Narayan, Deepa. 1995a. *The Contribution to People's Participation: Evidence from 121 Rural Water Supply Projects*. Environmentally Sustainable Development Occasional Paper Series 1. Washington, D.C.: World Bank.

*———. 1995b. "Designing Community-Based Development." Environment Department Participation Series Paper 7. World Bank, ENVSP, Washington, D.C. A summary is available as Environment Department Dissemination Note 17.

Narayan, Deepa, and Lyra Srinivasan. 1994. *Participatory Development Tool Kit: Materials to Facilitate Community Empowerment*. Washington, D.C.: World Bank.

*National Environmental Protection Agency of China, State Planning Commission of China, UNDP, and World Bank. 1994. " China: Issues and Options in Greenhouse Gas Emission Control." World Bank, East Asia and Pacific Region, China and Mongolia Department, Industry and Energy Division, Washington, D.C.

*Norton, Andrew, and Thomas Stephens. 1995. "Participation in Poverty Assessments." Environment Department Participation Series Paper 20. World Bank, ENVSP, Washington, D.C. A summary is available as Environment Department Dissemination Note 20.

*Ostro, Bart, José Miguel Sánchez, Carlos Aranda, and Gunnar S. Eskeland. 1995. "Air Pollution and Mortality: Results from Santiago, Chile." Policy Research Working Paper 1453. World Bank, Policy Research Department, Washington, D.C.

*Pagiola, Stefano. 1995. "Environmental and Natural Resource Degradation in Intensive Agriculture in Bangladesh." Environment Department Environmental Economics Series Paper 15. World Bank, Environment Department, Washington, D.C.

*Pargal, Sheoli, Hemamala Hettige, Manjula Singh, and David Wheeler. 1995. "Formal and Informal Regulation of Industrial Pollution: Comparative Evidence from Indonesia and the U.S." Paper presented at the annual meetings of the AEA in Washington, D.C. World Bank, Policy Research Department, Washington, D.C.

*Pargal, Sheoli, and David Wheeler. 1995. "Informal Regulation of Industrial Pollution in Developing Countries: Evidence from Indonesia." Policy Research Working Paper 1416. World Bank, Policy Research Department, Washington, D.C.

*Partridge, William L. 1994. "People's Participation in Environmental Assessment in Latin America: Best Practices." LATEN Dissemination Note 11. World Bank, Latin America Technical Department, Washington, D.C.

Pearce, David W., and Jeremy J. Warford. 1993. *World Without End: Economics, Environment, and Sustainable Development.* New York: Oxford University Press.

Rangeley, Robert, Bocar M. Thiam, Randolph A. Anderson, and Colin Lyle. 1994. *International River Basin Organizations in Sub-Saharan Africa.* World Bank Technical Paper 250. Washington, D.C.

*Rodenburg, Eric, Dan Runstall, and Frederik van Bolhuis. 1995. "Environmental Indicators for Global Cooperation." Global Environment Facility Working Paper 11. World Bank, GEF, Washington, D.C.

Scheirling, Susanne M. 1995. *Overcoming Agricultural Pollution of Water: The Challenge of Integrating Agricultural and Environmental Policies in the European Union.* World Bank Technical Paper 269. Washington, D.C.

*Schmidt, Mary, and Alexandre Marc. 1995. "Participation in Social Funds." Environment Department Participation Series Paper 3. World Bank, ENVSP, Washington, D.C. A summary is available as Environment Department Dissemination Note 19.

Serageldin, Ismail. 1994. *Water Supply, Sanitation, and Environmental Sustainability: The Financing Challenge*. Directions in Development Series. Washington, D.C.: World Bank.

———. 1995. *Toward Sustainable Management of Water Resources*. Directions in Development Series. Washington, D.C.: World Bank

Serageldin, Ismail, and Michael Cohen. 1995. *The Human Face of the Urban Environment: A Report to the Development Community*. Environmentally Sustainable Development Proceedings Series 5. Washington, D.C.: World Bank.

Serageldin, Ismail, and Pierre Landell-Mills (eds.). 1994. *Overcoming Global Hunger: Proceedings of a Conference on Actions to Reduce Hunger World Wide*. Environmentally Sustainable Development Proceedings Series 3. Washington, D.C.: World Bank.

Serageldin, Ismail, and Andrew Steer, eds. 1994. *Valuing the Environment: Proceedings of the First Annual International Conference on Environmentally Sustainable Development*. Environmentally Sustainable Development Proceedings Series 2. Washington, D.C.: World Bank.

Serageldin, Ismail, Richard Barrett, and Joan Martin-Brown, eds. 1995. *The Business of Sustainable Cities: Public-Private Partnerships for Creative Technical and Institutional Solutions*. Environmentally Sustainable Development Proceedings Series 7. Washington, D.C.: World Bank.

Serageldin, Ismail, Michael A. Cohen, and Josef Leitmann, eds. 1995. *Enabling Sustainable Community Development: An Associated Event of the Second Annual Conference on Environmentally Sustainable Development*. Environmentally Sustainable Development Proceedings Series 8. Washington, D.C.: World Bank.

Serageldin, Ismail, Michael A. Cohen, and K. C. Sivaramakrishnan, eds. 1995. *The Human Face of the Urban Environment: Proceedings of the Second Annual World Bank Conference on Environmentally Sustainable Development.*. Environmentally Sustainable Development Proceedings Series 6. Washington, D.C.: World Bank.

Sharma, Narendra P., Simon Rietbergen, Claude R. Heimo, and Jyoti Patel. 1995. *Stratégie pour le Secteur Forèstier en Afrique Subsaharienne*. World Bank Technical Paper 251. Washington, D.C.

Shihata, Ibrahim F. I. 1994. *The World Bank Inspection Panel*. Washington, D.C.: World Bank.

Sun, Peter. 1994. *Multipurpose River Basin Development in China*. World Bank EDI Seminar Report. Washington, D.C.

*Swait, Joffre, and Gunnar S. Eskeland. 1995. "Travel Mode Substitution in São Paulo: Estimates and Implications for Air Pollution Control." Policy Research Working Paper 1437. World Bank, Policy Research Department, Washington, D.C.

*Tlaiye, Laura, and Dan Biller. 1994. "Successful Environmental Institutions: Lessons from Colombia and Curitiba, Brazil." LATEN Dissemination Note 12. World Bank, Latin America Technical Department, Washington, D.C.

UNDP (United Nations Development Programme), UNEP (United Nations Environment Programme), and the World Bank. 1994. *Global Environment Facility: Independent Evaluation of the Pilot Phase*. Washington, D.C.: World Bank.

*Uquillas, Jorge, and Francisco Pichón. 1995. "Poverty Alleviation and Natural Resources Management through Participatory Technology Development in Latin America's Risk-Prone Areas." World Bank, Environment Division, Latin America Technical Department, Washington, D.C.

Van Tuijl, Willem. 1994. *Improving Water Use in Agriculture: Experiences in the Middle East and North Africa*. World Bank Technical Paper 201. Washington, D.C.

*Varangis, Panayotis N., Rachel Crossley, and Carlos A. Primo Braga. 1995. "Is There a Commercial Case for Tropical Timber Certification?" Policy Research Working Paper 1479. World Bank, Policy Research Department, Washington, D.C.

*Von Amsberg, Joachim. 1994. "Economic Parameters of Deforestation." Policy Research Working Paper 1351. World Bank, Policy Research Department, Washington, D.C.

*Watson, Gabrielle, and N. Vijay Jagannathan. 1995. "Participation in Water and Sanitation." Environment Department Participation Series Paper 2. World Bank, ENVSP, Washington, D.C.

Wijetilleke, Lakdasa, and Suhashini A. R. Karunaratne. 1995. *Air Quality Management: Considerations for Developing Countries*. World Bank Technical Paper 278. Washington, D.C.

World Bank. 1991a. *The Forest Sector*. A World Bank Policy Paper. Washington, D.C.

———. 1991b. *Urban Policy and Economic Development: An Agenda for the 1990s*. A World Bank Policy Paper. Washington, D.C.

———. 1992. *World Development Report 1992: Development and the Environment*. New York: Oxford University Press.

———. 1993a. *Energy Efficiency and Conservation in the Developing World*. A World Bank Policy Paper. Washington, D.C.

*———. 1993b. "Overview: Early Experience with Involuntary Resettlement." Operation Evaluation Department, Washington, D.C.

———. 1993c. *Water Resources Management*. A World Bank Policy Paper. Washington, D.C.

———. 1993d. *World Bank and the Environment, Fiscal 1993*. Washington, D.C.

———. 1993e. *The World Bank's Role in the Electric Power Sector: Policies for Effective Institutional, Regulatory, and Financial Reform*. A World Bank Policy Paper. Washington, D.C.

*———. 1994a. "China: Urban Environmental Service Management." China and Mongolia Department, Environment and Urban Development Division, Washington, D.C.

*———. 1994b. "Desertification: Implementing the Convention. A World Bank View." ENVLW, Washington, D.C.

*———. 1994c. "Environmental Assessment Sourcebook Updates." Environment Department, Washington, D.C.

———. 1994d. *Indonesia: Environment and Development*. A World Bank Country Study. Washington, D.C.

———. 1994e. *Jamaica: Economic Issues for Environmental Management*. A World Bank Country Study. Washington, D.C.

———. 1994f. *Making Development Sustainable: The World Group and the Environment. Fiscal 1994.* Washington, D.C.

———. 1994g. *Population and Development: Implications for the World Bank*. World Bank Development in Practice Series. Washington, D.C.

*———. 1994h. "Resettlement and Development: The Bankwide Review of Projects Involving Involuntary Resettlement 1986–1993." Environment Department, Washington, D.C.

*———. 1994i. "Review of Implementation of the Forest Sector Policy" ENVLW and Agriculture and Natural Resources Department, Washington, D.C.

*———. 1994j. "Survey of Funding for Biodiversity Conservation in Latin America and the Caribbean". ENVLW, Washington, D.C.

*———. 1994k. "The World Bank and Participation." Operations Policy Department, Washington, D.C.

*———. 1995a. "Environmental Assessment: Challenges and Good Practice." Environment Department Environmental Management Series Paper 18. World Bank, ENVLW, Washington, D.C.

*———. 1995b. "Environmental Assessments for Asian Forestry Projects: A Review of Recent World Bank Experience." Asia Technical Department, Environment and Natural Resources Division, Washington, D.C.

*———. 1995c. "Final Report: Regional Remedial Action Planning for Involuntary Resettlement." Internal report to the Board of Directors, Washington, D.C.

*———. 1995d. "Africa: A Framework for Integrated Coastal Zone Management." Towards Environmentally Sustainable Development

in Sub-Saharan Africa Paper 4. Africa Technical Department, Environmentally Sustainable Environment Division, Washington, D.C.

*———. 1995e. "Implementing the Convention on Biological Diversity: Toward a Strategy for World Bank Assistance." Environment Department Biodiversity Series Paper 14. Environment Department, Global Environment Coordination Division, Washington, D.C.

*———. 1995f. "Implementing Geographic Information Systems in Environmental Assessment: Environmental Assessment Sourcebook Update." ENVLW, Washington, D.C.

*———. 1995g. "Industrial Pollution Prevention and Abatement Handbook." Draft. Environment Department, Washington, D.C.

*———. 1995h. "Middle East Department—Environmental Business Plan, FY95–98." Middle East Department, Washington, D.C.

———. 1995i. *Monitoring Environmental Progress: A Report on Work in Progress.* Washington, D.C.

*———. 1995j. " National Environmental Strategies: Learning from Experience." ENVLW, Washington, D.C.

*———. 1995k. "A Progress Report on World Bank Global Environment Operations, March–May 1995." ENVGC, Washington, D.C.

*———. 1995l. "Toward Environmentally Sustainable Development in Sub-Saharan Africa. A World Bank Perspective." Africa Technical Department, Washington, D.C.

*———. 1995m. "Working with NGOs: A Practical Guide to Operational Collaboration Between the World Bank and NGOs." Operations Policy Department, Washington, D.C.

*———. 1995n. "World Bank Participation Sourcebook." ENVSP, Washington, D.C.

*———. 1995o. "The World Bank and the U.N. Framework Convention on Climate Change." Environment Department Working Paper Series 12. ENVGC, Washington, D.C.

*———. Forthcoming a. "Handbook on Greenhouse Gas Assessment Methodologies" ENVGC, Washington, D.C.

*———. Forthcoming b. "Second Review of Environmental Assessment." ENVLW, Washington, D.C.

*World Bank and GEF (Global Environment Facility). Forthcoming. "Greenhouse Gas Abatement Investment Project Monitoring and Evaluation Guidelines." ENVGC, Washington, D.C.

*World Bank and IFC (International Finance Corporation). 1994. "Power and Energy Efficiency: Status Report on the Bank's Policy and IFC's Activities." Joint World Bank and IFC seminar presented to the Executive Directors. July 7. World Bank, Industry and Energy Department and IFC, Infrastructure Department, Washington, D.C.

World Bank, IUCN (World Conservation Union), and Great Barrier Reef Marine Park Authority. 1995. *A Global Representative System of Marine Protected Areas*, 4 vols. Washington, D.C.

World Bank, Latin America Technical Department, and World Wildlife Fund. 1995. *A Conservation Assessment of the Terrestrial Ecoregions of Latin America and the Caribbean.* World Bank Handbook Series. Washington, D.C.

World Bank and OECD (Organisation for Economic Co-operation and Development). Forthcoming. *Environmental Action Programme for Central and Eastern Europe.* Report endosed by the Ministerial Conference, Lucerne, Switzerland, April 1993. Washington, D.C.: World Bank and OECD.

*World Bank and SETRA (Service d'Etudes Techniques des Routes et Autoroutes). 1994. "Roads and the Environment: A Handbook." Report TWU 13. World Bank, Transport, Water, and Urban Development, Washington, D.C., and SETRA, Ministry of Equipment, Transport and Tourism, France.

*World Bank, TWU (Transport, Water, and Urban Development Department). 1995. "Sustainable Transport: A Sector Policy Review." Draft. Washington, D.C.

Xie, Mei, Ulrich Küffner, and Guy LeMoigne. 1994. *Using Water Efficiently: Technological Options.* World Bank Technical Paper 205. Washington, D.C.